Transforming Financial Services with Generative AI

From Strategy and Design to Practical Applications

Srinath Godavarthi
Ravi Nagvekar

Apress®

Transforming Financial Services with Generative AI: From Strategy and Design to Practical Applications

Srinath Godavarthi
Aldie, VA, USA

Ravi Nagvekar
Metuchen, NJ, USA

ISBN-13 (pbk): 979-8-8688-2052-6
ISBN-13 (electronic): 979-8-8688-2053-3
https://doi.org/10.1007/979-8-8688-2053-3

Managing Director, Apress Media LLC: Welmoed Spahr
Acquisitions Editor: Celestin Suresh John
Desk Editor: Laura Berendson
Editorial Project Manager: Gryffin Winkler

Cover image designed by freepik

Distributed to the book trade worldwide by Springer Science+Business Media New York, 1 New York Plaza, New York, NY 10004. Phone 1-800-SPRINGER, fax (201) 348-4505, e-mail orders-ny@springer-sbm.com, or visit www.springeronline.com. Apress Media, LLC is a Delaware LLC and the sole member (owner) is Springer Science + Business Media Finance Inc (SSBM Finance Inc). SSBM Finance Inc is a **Delaware** corporation.

For information on translations, please e-mail booktranslations@springernature.com; for reprint, paperback, or audio rights, please e-mail bookpermissions@springernature.com.

Apress titles may be purchased in bulk for academic, corporate, or promotional use. eBook versions and licenses are also available for most titles. For more information, reference our Print and eBook Bulk Sales web page at http://www.apress.com/bulk-sales.

Any source code or other supplementary material referenced by the author in this book is available to readers on GitHub. For more detailed information, please visit https://www.apress.com/gp/services/source-code.

If disposing of this product, please recycle the paper

Table of Contents

About the Authors

Srinath Godavarthi has over 20 years of experience in the IT industry serving both public sector and commercial customers. He held leadership positions with global technology and consulting companies, including Amazon and Accenture. In his previous roles, Srinath led digital transformation for a number of customers across multiple industry verticals, including financial services, healthcare, and telecommunications. Srinath is an accomplished author, specializes in GenAI and AI/ML technologies, and has published over a dozen white papers and blogs. He has been a speaker at various industry conferences, including Generative AI summits, AWS Public Sector summit, AWS re:Invent, and The American Public Human Services Association among others. He holds a master's degree in Computer Science from Temple University and has completed a Chief Technology Officer program from the University of California, Berkeley. Srinath is deeply passionate about causes that impact veterans and kids. In his spare time, he volunteers to help veterans and enables the next generation by teaching AI/ML technologies to high-school students and assisting them with research projects.

Ravi Nagvekar brings over two decades of expertise at the intersection of information technology and financial services. He has worked with leading institutions, including Amazon Web Services, JPMorgan Chase, Capital One, ABN Amro, and Bank of Baroda, where he has led initiatives in Generative AI strategy, bank modernization, and large-scale cloud migration. A respected voice in the industry, Dr. Nagvekar is a frequent speaker at international conferences such as FinTech Devcon, the Latin American AI for HR Seminar, and various AWS events. He also serves as a Professor with the Academy of Leadership Sciences Switzerland (ALSS), further contributing to academic and executive education in digital transformation and leadership. His academic credentials include a doctorate in business administration, with research focused on the impact of Generative AI on North American financial institutions, along with dual master's degrees in Computer Science from the University of Arizona and the University of Pune. He is also the lead inventor of a patented multi-cloud data mesh implementation pattern.

About the Technical Editor

Mandy Kinne is a technical writer and editor with a passion for language and technology. She loves connecting with people from diverse backgrounds and working with people across cultures, which taught her the power of sharing knowledge through words and illustrations. Mandy has been working with AI and its precursors, in some form, since 1994, when she was employed by the Center for Machine Translation at Carnegie Mellon University. Mandy has been a technical writer in a variety of industries - health insurance, telecom, and computer networking and hardware - and before becoming a freelancer, she worked at a fintech company. She holds BAs in Rhetoric and French from Carnegie Mellon University and is active in the Write the Docs technical writing community. Mandy volunteers with the NOVA Roller Derby, serves as the Communications Chair for her fiber art guild, and is always knitting or spinning something.

Acknowledgments

This book wouldn't have been possible without the contributions from many people.

We are grateful to our colleagues at Amazon Web Services and other industry peers who engaged in ongoing discussions and shared their insights. These interactions were instrumental in shaping the core ideas presented throughout the book.

We extend our sincere thanks to Mike Harasimowicz, Director of AI innovation at Lockheed Martin, for taking the time to review our work and for outlining a thought-provoking foreword. We are indebted to our publisher for their patience and guidance throughout the entire process. Their expertise and support were essential in bringing this project to fruition.

Our deep appreciation goes to our families and loved ones for their unwavering love and support. To Sandya, Sriya, and Suchir from Srinath. To Jyostna, Riva, and Rita from Ravi. To Ky, Brandon, Ethan and Abbey, and Henry from Mandy.

Foreword

In every era of human progress, there are inflection points that redefine not only industries but also the way we think, work, and live. Today, Generative AI stands as one of those transformational forces. What you hold in your hands, *Transforming Financial Services with Generative AI*, is both a strategy and a roadmap for leaders, technologists, regulators, and everyday citizens to understand and harness this revolution.

Generative AI has moved beyond prototypes to actively reshape how organizations think and operate. Its power lies not just in speed and scale, but in its ability to reason, create, and adapt in human-like ways. In financial services, where trust and precision are paramount, it enables contextual data interpretation, adaptive risk anticipation, and personalized insights at scale. Regulatory and compliance teams once seen as barriers are now early adopters, using AI to monitor transactions, enforce adherence, and produce audit-ready reporting with unprecedented accuracy. Applied responsibly, Generative AI becomes a trusted partner, accelerating research, streamlining compliance, and revealing opportunities in complex markets.

This book is not about abstract promises or passing trends. The authors, Srinath Godavarthi and Dr. Ravi Nagvekar, deliver a grounded perspective, combining architecture rigor, engineering discipline, and ethical design with clear, practical guidance. What makes this work especially valuable is its comprehensive coverage of real-world use cases across retail banking, investment banking, asset and wealth management, and risk and compliance, each explored with detailed technical implementations using both Generative AI and the emerging paradigm of Agentic AI.

From investment research automation and compliance monitoring to personalized client engagement and advanced trade surveillance, the book demonstrates how financial institutions can move beyond experimentation and scale these innovations responsibly. It is designed to serve as a reference for the entire financial industry from senior leaders shaping strategy to risk officers ensuring transparency, to engineers implementing AI-driven systems. By blending strategy, use cases, architectures, and governance considerations, this book establishes Generative AI not just as a technology, but as a strategic enabler for the next era of financial services.

As someone who has served both in the crucible of military operations and in the high-stakes world of financial services, I recognize the common challenges: data overload, decision ambiguity, integration complexity, and the constant race against adversarial threats. The authors do not shy away from these realities; instead, they offer frameworks, architectures, and case studies that can equip leaders to navigate them. Their message is clear: Generative AI is not a magic wand. It is a powerful instrument, one that demands discipline, resilience, and foresight to wield effectively. What excites me most about this work is its accessibility. Whether you are a senior executive charting strategy, a technologist designing platforms, or a curious reader seeking to understand how finance intersects with AI, you will find insights and language that make this frontier tangible. Like any good guide, this book points beyond itself: to a future where financial services are not only more efficient and profitable but also more transparent, inclusive, and resilient. Generative AI will not solve every problem. But it will change how we approach them. This book provides the compass to ensure that change leads us toward a better horizon.

—Colonel Michael "Rabbi" Harasimowicz, USAF (ret.), WS98B, SAASS13
Managing Director, JPMorgan Intelligent Solutions
Managing Director, Lockheed Martin AI Center

Introduction

Generative Artificial Intelligence (GenAI) is rapidly reshaping the landscape of the global financial services sector (FSS). Until a few years back, GenAI was a science fiction, but it now stands at the forefront of innovation, promising to revolutionize how financial services organizations (FSOs) operate, serve customers, manage risk, and drive economic growth. As the financial world becomes increasingly complex and interconnected, the need for intelligent, adaptive, compliant, and secure solutions has never been greater.

This book is your comprehensive guide to understanding and harnessing the transformative power of GenAI within the FSS. Whether you are a banking executive, technology leader, regulator, fintech entrepreneur, or simply curious about the future of finance, this book will equip you with the foundational knowledge, strategic frameworks, and practical insights needed to navigate the GenAI revolution.

We begin with **Chapter 1** by demystifying the fundamentals of AI and GenAI, laying the groundwork for readers of all backgrounds. This chapter sets the stage for the rest of the book, ensuring that everyone, regardless of prior experience, can follow the journey from core concepts to advanced applications.

Chapter 2 explores the unique characteristics and mission objectives of the financial services sector, from facilitating global trade and managing risk to supporting economic growth and addressing societal challenges. Here, we introduce a fictitious organization, Global Fiscal Group (GFG), that will serve as our guide through real-world scenarios and use cases. We examine the sector's competing priorities, including customer experience, productivity, compliance, security, and cost optimization, and highlight how GenAI is poised to address these challenges.

In **Chapter 3**, we present a high-level GenAI strategy and blueprint for successful adoption within financial organizations. Through the lens of Maria, a Chief Information Officer navigating the GenAI journey, we address the critical questions: Where should you start? What are the risks and best practices? How can you build a resilient, future-ready GenAI practice and a roadmap?

Chapter 4 delves into the practicalities of building GenAI applications. We cover the anatomy of prompts, the art of prompt engineering, the role of agents, and advanced techniques such as Retrieval Augmented Generation (RAG), Agentic AI, and model fine-tuning. By the end of this chapter, you'll have a clear understanding of the core building blocks required to develop GenAI solutions tailored to the financial sector.

Chapter 5 turns to one of the most vital aspects of finance: risk and compliance management. Drawing lessons from the 2008 financial crisis, we explore how GenAI can empower organizations to detect early warning signals, predict emerging risks, and automate compliance processes – ultimately safeguarding assets and ensuring market stability.

From **Chapter 6** onward, we dive into domain-specific applications. **Chapter 6** examines how GenAI is transforming retail banking, enabling hyper-personalized experiences, streamlining operations, and redefining customer engagement. We follow GFG's journey as it leverages GenAI to modernize its retail banking operations and deliver intelligent, predictive, and personalized services at scale.

Chapter 7 focuses on investment banking, where GenAI is revolutionizing capital markets, M&A advisory, and institutional trading. We discuss how intelligent agents and advanced language models are automating data aggregation, enhancing compliance, and delivering client-specific insights in a high-stakes, data-rich environment.

In **Chapter 8**, we explore the wealth and asset management, which faces mounting pressure to deliver superior returns and personalized experiences. Here, GenAI emerges as a pivotal technology, enabling hyper-personalized investment strategies, automating portfolio management, and enhancing client engagement.

Chapter 9 addresses the operational realities of implementing and maintaining GenAI applications in financial services. We cover the evolution from MLOps to FMOps/LLMOps, security and privacy considerations, performance management, and cost optimization – equipping you with the technical and organizational know-how to deploy GenAI responsibly and at scale.

Finally, **Chapter 10** provides a comprehensive summary, highlights emerging industry trends, and outlines actionable next steps for organizations seeking to lead in the age of GenAI. We revisit the key themes, recap the transformative potential of GenAI, and offer guidance for charting your own path forward.

While the book is structured to build knowledge sequentially, each chapter is designed to stand alone, allowing you to focus on the topics most relevant to your interests or organizational needs. The use cases, frameworks, and architectures presented throughout are illustrative, intended to spark your imagination and inspire your own GenAI initiatives.

Our ultimate goal is to empower you to navigate the world of GenAI with confidence, transforming financial services for the better - making them more intelligent, secure, and resilient for the challenges and opportunities that lie ahead.

CHAPTER 1

Introduction to Generative AI

In 2008, the global markets experienced a catastrophic collapse. Financial institutions failed, investors lost billions, and economies plunged into recession. The crisis was triggered largely by the collapse of the subprime mortgage market; risky loans were bundled into complex financial products that even experts struggled to understand.

If you were like us and invested in the stock market or owned a house during this time, you definitely remember the impact this crisis has had on all of us.

Despite the availability of data, traditional financial methods and models couldn't foresee the intricate web of risks. Human analysts relied on historical trends and limited predictive modeling, often failing to account for

- Complex interdependencies across global markets
- Rapidly changing conditions in real time
- The deceptive stability of financial institutions, particularly mortgage-backed securities

In essence, most banks confidently invested in mortgage-backed securities, relied on human analysis, and trusted that the real estate prices would continue rising. But both the banks and the homeowners paid a big price while common investors lost money in the stock market.

Now in 2025, the golden age of Artificial Intelligence (AI) and Generative AI (GenAI), that crisis may have resulted in a totally different outcome. With GenAI, we can simulate multiple economic scenarios with AI models, including a potential downturn. In most scenarios, a drop in home prices leads to cascading defaults. The bank would receive an AI-generated warning, prompting a strategic pivot. This would potentially reduce the risk and impact of a downturn and may even prevent a crisis similar to that of 2008.

S. Godavarthi, R. Nagvekar, *Transforming Financial Services with Generative AI*,
https://doi.org/10.1007/979-8-8688-2053-3_1

We'll dive deep into this discussion in this book, but first, let's quickly understand the significance of AI and ML. In this chapter, we introduce the basic terminology and concepts behind AI, ML, and GenAI.

AI and ML have impacted our lives and virtually every industry in a meaningful way over the last decade. In fact, it is hard to imagine our lives without AI or ML, from Google Maps to self-driving cars, to Netflix recommendations, and Amazon's excellence in delivering packages! The explosion of data, access to compute power, and advancements in ML algorithms have resulted in AI and ML transforming from aspirational technologies to become integral parts of our lives and day-to-day business operations. AI and ML are revolutionizing enterprises by enhancing user experience, improving productivity, reducing costs, helping innovation, and improving operational efficiencies.

GenAI goes one step ahead. We can now generate new content, such as contracting, marketing, and financial documents; art, music, and videos; architecture, design, and code, all with natural language instructions. According to McKinsey, the potential total annual value of AI and analytics across various industry verticals is estimated at $9.5 trillion to $15.4 trillion[1] and GenAI could add the equivalent of $2.6 trillion to $4.4 trillion annually, increasing the impact of AI by 15–40%.

So what exactly is GenAI? To understand it, we first need a conceptual grasp of what AI is; let's start by answering the question "What is AI?"

1.1 What Is AI?

AI has captured the human imagination for a long time. Movies such as Star Wars and sci-fi books, such as those by Isaac Asimov, talk about AI as a self-governing intelligence that has the ability to think independently and act like a human. But from a practical standpoint, we use AI in our daily lives in a number of ways.

Google Maps speaks to us in a similar way a human would, providing us with directions from one place to another, probably more patiently than a human when we take a wrong turn. Amazon Alexa is a personal assistant that listens, performs actions, comprehends, and speaks naturally. Alexa answers verbal questions in a natural human speaking voice and can accomplish tasks such as recommending the right flight for you and completing the flight reservation. Finally, there's Tesla: this AI powered car

[1] `https://www.mckinsey.com/capabilities/mckinsey-digital/our-insights/the-economic-potential-of-generative-ai-the-next-productivity-frontier`

can sense the surrounding environment - including traffic signals, other vehicles, pedestrians, and adjust its actions accordingly. For example, a Tesla brakes automatically to avoid collisions.

To be more formal: in modern terms, AI is the ability of computer systems (also known as machines) to listen, comprehend, sense, and act like humans do. In other words, AI is the ability of machines to mimic human intelligence and cognitive functions.

If we continue to enhance and improve this technology and push AI concepts further to their natural conclusion, the result is a completely autonomous capability. An AI with autonomous capabilities is known as an Artificial General Intelligence (AGI). At this point in time, we haven't quite achieved AGI but we're getting closer by the day.

Beyond AGI lies Artificial Superintelligence (ASI). ASI refers to a hypothetical AI that would not only possess intelligence equal to or surpassing human intelligence across virtually all cognitive tasks but would also be vastly superior to the best human brains in practically every field, including scientific creativity, general wisdom, and social skills. An ASI would be capable of self-improvement and recursive self-enhancement, potentially leading to an intelligence explosion and an intelligence far beyond human comprehension.

1.2 AI and Estimating Home Prices

Machines use AI to complete tasks without receiving explicit instructions in the form of programming logic. How can we use this capability in a practical way? With a nod to the financial crisis of 2008, let's see if we can predict trends in the housing market, more specifically say, estimate the future price of houses given various characteristics and market conditions. These include square footage, number of bedrooms, number of bathrooms, whether there was a default on mortgage and so on. We refer to these characteristics as features. Taking the features of a property into account, how can you calculate the price?

One way to estimate the price is to use a computer program with business logic, business rules, and calculations. You create a rules-based program to sum up the square footage of the house and multiply that with the estimated price per square foot based on the location. You also need to account for other features that typically influence the price of a house, for example, the age, the number of floors, the type of residence, neighboring amenities, and so on.

But how do you know how much each of these contribute to the overall price? How do you account for seasonal factors? What about flood zones? Or current economic conditions, including loan defaults? Explicitly listing the value of each feature and factoring it into the actual house value is too complex to do accurately using a computer program with business logic and is better solved using other techniques.

You can apply rules of thumb or heuristic methods to estimate the price, such as decrease $x amount for each year the house ages, increase $y amount for a brick front, decrease $z amount if there was a loan default. These heuristics are the contribution or weight that each of the features adds to the home price. Using this rules-based or heuristic technique, your computer can calculate the price of the house given the various feature weight inputs described previously. This method is shown in Figure 1-1.

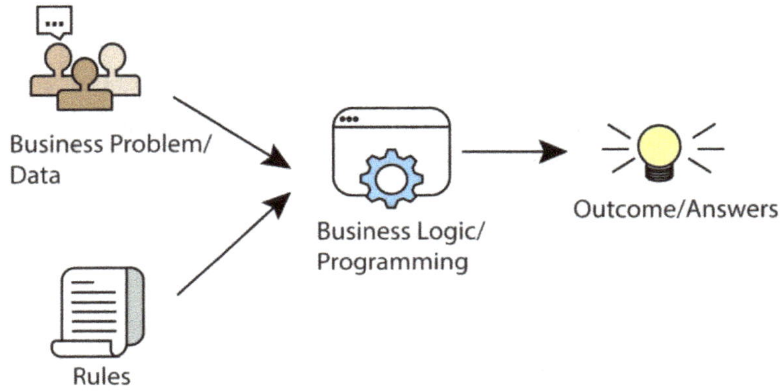

Figure 1-1. *Rules-Based Computer Programming*

However, using rules-based or heuristic programming to solve the problem raises several issues. One issue is generalization; for example, there's a chance that you haven't captured all the features that ultimately impact the final market value. There's also a high chance that the heuristics you use aren't accurate enough. Lastly, conditions may have changed and the rules that you use may not apply anymore; think here about the sudden change in market conditions say in 2000, 2008, or during the COVID pandemic in 2020 and how these factors might render heuristics too inaccurate to use.

Another method we can use to more accurately measure home price is a technique called machine learning (ML). This technique is in the realm of modern AI.

1.2.1 Machine Learning (ML)

In ML, using the historical data and other patterns that you provide, the computer or machine comes up with a formula that can estimate the price of a house. ML is a two-step process, as shown in Figure 1-2: the first step is training, the second is prediction, which is also sometimes called inference.

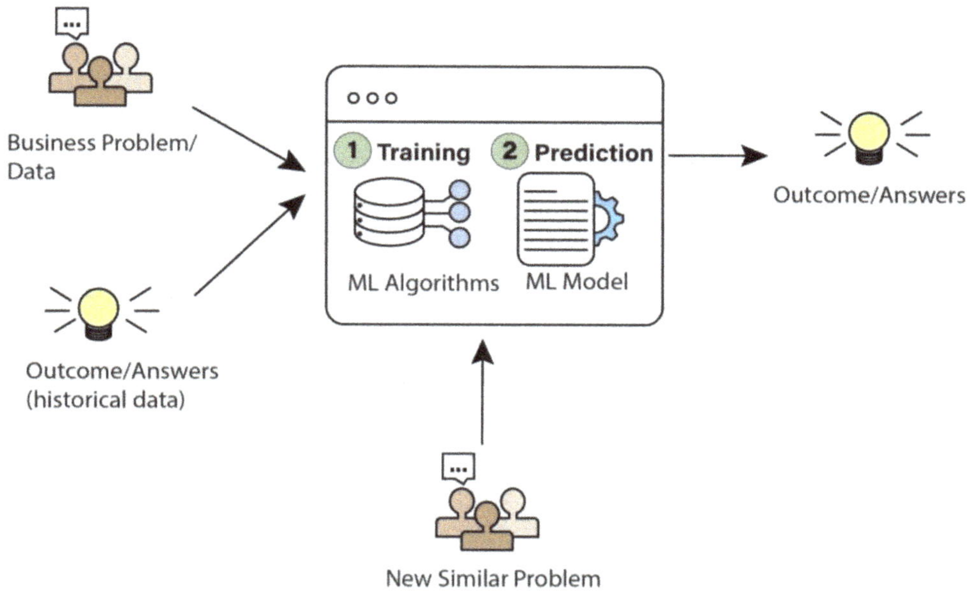

Figure 1-2. *Machine Learning*

In Step 1, training, you provide the computer with historical data about various types of houses, let's say the last twenty years of data. At a minimum, this data includes the price as well as various features of the house we previously used as an example. You also need to include other relevant features for which you may not have an accurate heuristic. For example, you may need to include an indicator that tells the computer the current interest rates that may impact the house price. The more data you provide under different conditions (such as economy, unemployment, interest rates), the better and easier it is for the computer to understand the pattern of the features. In addition to these features, you also provide the computer with the historical sale price for each of the houses; data that has the feature combined with the outcome or the label is referred to as labeled data.

> **Note** This is called supervised machine learning; the computer or machine learns the patterns and characteristics that impact the value of the house.

In this case, using the historical data and other patterns that you provide, the computer creates a formula that can estimate the price of a house. You're not providing the business rules and calculations; the machine uses the historical data to come up with the formula and then optimizes the weights of each feature to get the overall value of the house. This equation, with all the optimized weights used in the prediction, is called an ML model.

The method by which the computer creates a model is called an algorithm. The type of algorithm used in this example is a simplified version of Linear Regression; there are several other types of algorithms, including Logistic Regression, Support Vector Machines, Naive Bayes Algorithm, and Artificial Neural Networks (ANNs). Later in this chapter, we'll explore ANNs.

Once you have the ML model, you can use this model to predict or infer the value of any house; this step in ML is also called the inference.

In the second step of our ML-based approach to estimate the value of a house. You plug in all the features of the specific house you're trying to sell and the model provides an estimated price of that house. But how does this work? How does the algorithm create a model? Let's walk through it in more detail.

1.2.2 How Machine Learning Algorithms Work

First, the computer randomly assigns weights (the contribution amount) to each of the features you provided. So, for example, it randomly assigns 100 to the number of square feet in the house, assigns 10 to the number of floors, and so on for each feature; it is simply assigning a numeric decimal value to a feature. But what about those other indicators, such as whether there was a previous loan default on this house? In that case, you assign a value of 1 to the feature if there was a loan default and assign a value of 0 if there wasn't a loan default.

Let's translate this into an equation:

V = (w0 x land value) + (w1 (total square footage)) + (w2 (number of floors)) + (w3 (number of bedrooms)) + (w4 (number of bathrooms)) + (w5x1) where

V = the sale value

w(i) = the weight or contribution toward the sale value of each feature

(w5x1) = a previous loan default

Note that a bias term (w0) is added to manage the distributions of data. For example, in this case, the base land value (V) may be considered as the bias. We don't need to really worry about it for the scope of this book. As we mentioned earlier, the computer assigns random weights w1, w2, and so on to each feature and comes up with a value (V).

Note that the "bias term" in this case refers to a constant added to adjust the model's output independent of input features or a starting point/baseline adjustment for the house value prediction.

The computer then compares that estimated value with the actual value of the house or similar houses. Since the weights were initialized at random, the initial value of the house is probably wrong and there is a large difference (error) between the actual and estimated values. The algorithm then changes the weights to determine a new value for the house to reduce this error; this continues until it finds weights that provide reasonably correct answers based on the values of the houses.

The weights are changed using optimization techniques such as Gradient Descent. A full discussion of Gradient Descent and other specific optimization techniques is outside the scope of this book; however, you can think of Gradient Descent as a means of continuously and iteratively adjusting the weights by minimizing the error or the difference between the actual and estimated value. In other words, Gradient Descent is used to optimize the model, to increase accuracy by minimizing the difference between predicted value and actual value of the house.

Sometimes, illustrating the final equation visually helps us better understand how it works. In order to do that with this example, we need to simplify the equation either as if we were using one input - for example, number of square feet (Figure 1-3) - or as if we were using two inputs, number of square feet and number of floors (Figure 1-4). Any more than two inputs implies a diagram with more than three dimensions, which is impossible for us to visualize.

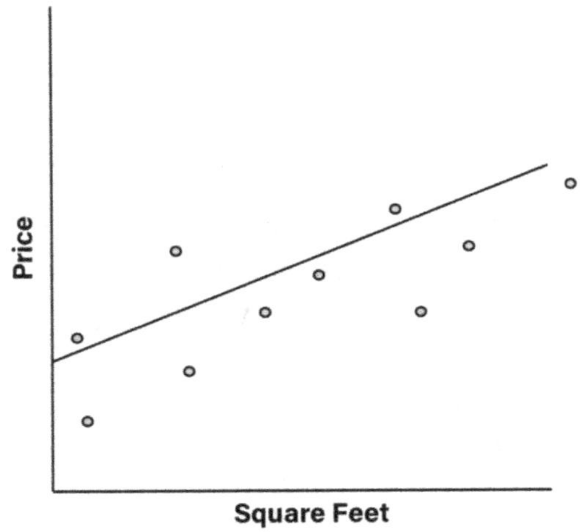

Figure 1-3. *Linear Regression with One Feature*

As Figure 1-3 shows, you can think of the equation or model as the straight line drawn on the graph. The straight line here provides the best approximation of the price of a house given the square feet. If we were to provide a new data point and add it to the graph, the square feet of another house, the model would determine the price by finding the corresponding value using the adjusted straight line.

The same concept extends for two inputs, as shown in Figure 1-4. However, here the equation or model is represented by the floating blue plane enclosed. You provide two inputs and the model then gives you the corresponding price.

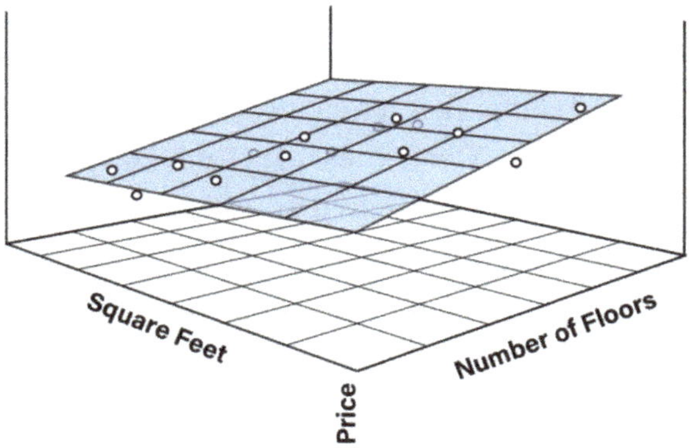

Figure 1-4. *Linear Regression in Two Dimensions*

We mentioned several types of algorithms, such as Logistic Regression, Support Vector Machines, Naive Bayes Algorithm, and Neural Networks. Each of these algorithms essentially do the same thing: they use an optimization technique to come up with an ML model that is then used to complete a task or make a prediction.

The task itself may vary; for example, the task was to estimate the price of a house. Another task is to look at a radiology image and determine whether or not there is a tumor or to take a conversation and determine whether the overall sentiment is positive, negative, or neutral.

You may be wondering how a machine is able to understand non-numeric inputs such as images and sentences. You might already know that computers only work with numbers, particularly with binary digits or bits – zeros and ones. Machines cannot directly understand non-numeric inputs, but we can translate these types of inputs into numbers using certain techniques, which we'll cover later in the book when we look at the case studies.

Of these algorithms, Artificial Neural Networks (ANNs) or neural networks have become one of the most researched and used algorithms in ML, so much so that an entire branch of ML called deep learning is used to describe tasks that use these algorithms. Let's take a look at neural networks and deep learning.

1.2.3 Artificial Neural Networks and Deep Learning

At its core, an artificial neural network is a machine learning algorithm modeled after the neurons in the human brain. The term comes from initial efforts by researchers to mimic the way the human brain works. However, in reality, the two work quite differently, where the human brain is more complex than an artificial neural network.

Let's take our same example problem to estimate or predict the house price. In a neural network, the features related to the property (such as the number of bedrooms, square footage, location, age, and so on) are fed into an abstract representation of an equation called a neuron. The equation works similarly to Linear Regression; each neuron receives multiple inputs related to each feature and creates an output.

Let's work through our property estimation example using one neuron, neuron 1. The equation for neuron 1 would be

$$\sum = w1^*x1 + w2^*x2 + w3^*x3 + w4^*x4 + \text{Bias}$$

where

x1 = square feet

x2 = number of floors

x3 = presence near a school

x4 = presence near a grocery store

$\sum$ = output

One difference between a neural network and Linear Regression is that we then convert this linear equation into a nonlinear equation using something called an *activation function* to make the model more flexible. The activation function is similar to using a dimmer switch for a light on the output of the equation. It also transforms the neuron into a decision-making system that can adjust responses to the data, helping the neural network learn and make better decisions.

To get an answer or *output* for our question – "*What is the predicted sale price for a house?*" We need another equation:

$$O = \sum (f)$$

where

O = output

$\sum$ = the results of the equation for neuron 1

f = the activation function

This equation is shown in Figure 1-5.

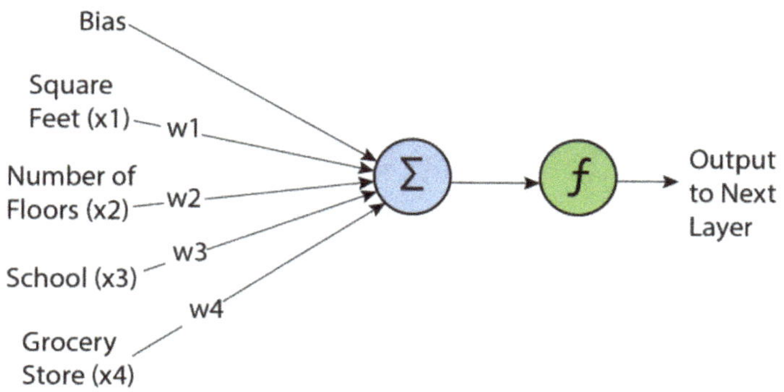

Figure 1-5. *Single Neuron for Predicting House Prices*

The actual activation function used varies depending on the type of learning task. Some examples include ReLU and Sigmoid, which takes a value and converts it to a value between 0 and 1.

Another difference between non-linear and linear regression techniques is that each of the inputs is passed to a number of neurons, not just one. In other words, it is passed to a network of neurons stacked in multiple layers, hence the name *neural network*.

A neural network stacked in multiple layers is also called a Multi Layer Perceptron (MLP). The MLP is a neural network divided into layers, with one layer as an input layer, another as an output layer, and one or many hidden layers in between, as shown in Figure 1-6. Every neuron in the network acts in the exact same way except for the type of activation function used for each layer. The type of activation function varies depending on the type of data and the type of output being generated.

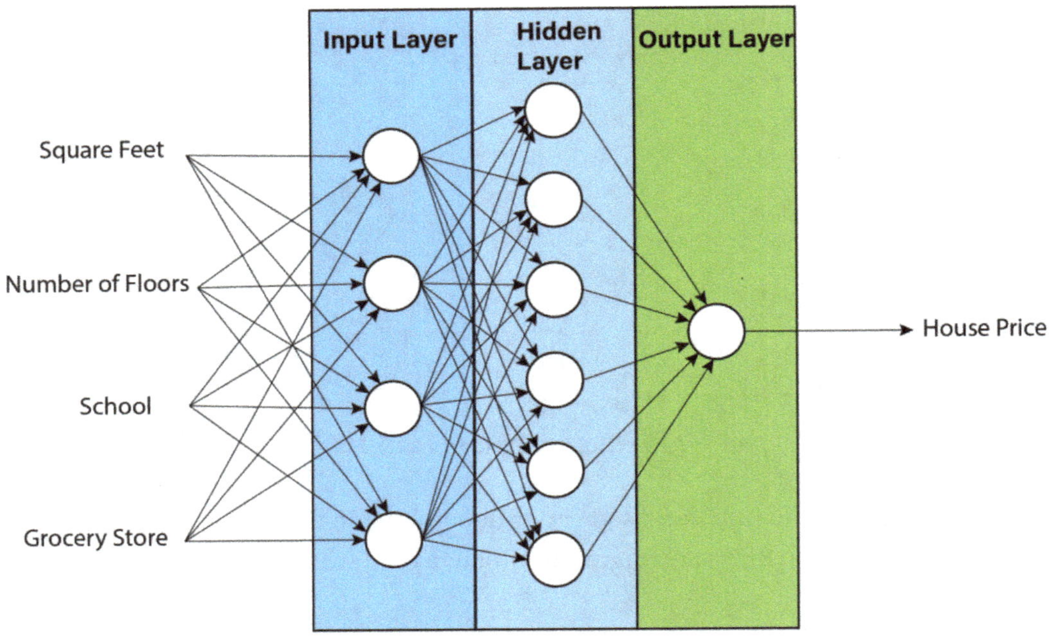

Figure 1-6. *Multi Layer Perceptron (MLP) for Predicting House Prices*

The greater the number of layers are, the more complex the MLP is. In general, accomplishing tasks using a large number of layers is referred to as *deep learning*. The weights (values of `W`, a matrix of weights `W1`, `W2`, and so on) are adjusted or optimized in a way similar to the technique described for the linear regression. This ultimately results in a model that can be used on new data. The major difference is that the error from the output layer is used to derive the errors for each neuron using *back propagation*, a mathematics formula that uses calculus.

You may be wondering why neural networks are necessary to understand GenAI. Neural networks and deep learning are some of the fundamental forces driving the rise of AI. Self-driving cars, voice recognition devices such as Alexa, and many current AI-based technologies all use neural networks. Through the last decade, hardware and chips such as Graphical Processing Units (GPUs) have been invented to accelerate the processing of data for deep learning tasks. These developments have further propelled the use of deep learning into the realms of fields such as GenAI. The immense computational demands of training GenAI models, particularly those with billions of parameters, necessitate highly efficient processing.

So far, we've focused on estimating the sale price of a house. This is just one type of machine learning or deep learning *task*. There are several different types of learning tasks that are important to understand as well. Let's take a closer look.

1.3 Different Types of Learning Tasks

Machine learning or deep learning tasks fall into several broad categories. The task we've covered so far, estimating or predicting the price of a house, falls under something called *supervised learning*. Other types of tasks include unsupervised learning, reinforcement learning, and self-supervised learning. Let's review the concepts behind each of these.

1.3.1 Supervised Learning

As mentioned earlier, predicting house prices is a type of supervised learning task. In this ML type, the algorithm learns the mappings from input data to output predictions using a given dataset in the *training* phase. This type of input data is called "labeled" data where a label column (the actual value of the house) is provided together with all the other features. "Supervised" refers to the fact that the algorithm is guided by the labeled data to make predictions or decisions. The primary objective of supervised learning is to generalize from the training data, build an ML model, and then use that model to make accurate predictions on unseen, new data (*inference*).

Supervised learning can be further divided into two main categories:

1. **Classification**: In classification tasks, the goal is to assign input data points to predefined categories or classes. For example, for financial applications, you provide historical data with labels for mortgage loan defaults, build a model and ask the model to detect whether a new loan is at risk of default or not. Other common applications include whether a given card transaction is fraudulent or not, and predicting customer churn and so on.

2. **Regression**: In regression tasks, the algorithm predicts a continuous numerical value. The house price-based examples are in this category. Other applications could include forecasting stock prices, credit scores and portfolio valuations.

1.3.2 Unsupervised Learning

Unsupervised learning differs from supervised learning in that it doesn't rely on labeled data for training. Instead, it focuses on uncovering patterns, structures, or relationships within the data without predefined target labels - unlabeled data.

One type of unsupervised learning task is clustering, in which, for example, the customers are divided into clusters with similar credit characteristics. Another type of unsupervised learning is dimensionality reduction. Let's say you have a data set with a large number of features. Some of these features might be dependent on each other. In this case, adding these features to your model may not provide the best results. In dimensionality reduction, you use unsupervised learning to determine the features that are most representative or relevant to the data set.

1.3.3 Reinforcement Learning

Reinforcement learning (RL) is a type of machine learning where a machine interacts with an environment and learns to make a sequence of decisions to maximize a reward signal. This machine is often called the "agent." The vacuum robots that clean your house are a classic example that use this method; RL relies on trial-and-error learning. For example, the robot vacuum initially learns your house layout by bumping into objects and taking note of each bump. Over time, the robot learns to take actions that minimize bumping.

RL is often used in scenarios where an agent needs to make a sequence of decisions over time, such as game playing, robotics, and autonomous navigation. Both the Mars Rover and Tesla are trained using RL for navigation. However, RL can also be used to fine-tune the performance of a machine learning model developed using other methods such as supervised or unsupervised learning.

1.3.4 Self-Supervised Learning

Self-supervised learning falls into the broader category of unsupervised learning. Both approaches aim to train a model from unlabeled data. In traditional unsupervised learning, the model doesn't have any specific task or labels to guide its learning; it typically focuses on clustering, dimensionality reduction, or density estimation. Self-supervised learning, on the other hand, involves creating supervised-like tasks within the unlabeled data itself. These tasks are specifically designed to capture meaningful information and relationships present in the data. One example of this is the Masked Language Model (MLM). In an MLM, random words in a sentence are replaced with a mask and a neural network tries to predict the original word from the context provided by the other non-masked words in the sentence. For example, for the sentence "I want to apply for [MASK]," the model might try to predict the word "loan" or "credit card" for the masked word.

1.4 What Is GenAI and Where Does It Fit?

Now that you have a basic understanding of neural networks and types of AI tasks, let's delve into what GenAI really is. At its core, GenAI is a branch of deep learning that focuses on creating or generating new content using an input or a context. As such, it uses some of the same concepts we've already defined and described. The *task* for a GenAI model is to predict or generate content based on a given input. The content could be a word, an image, document, code, and so on, depending on what the task is. Figure 1-7 illustrates the evolution of AI and GenAI since 1950.

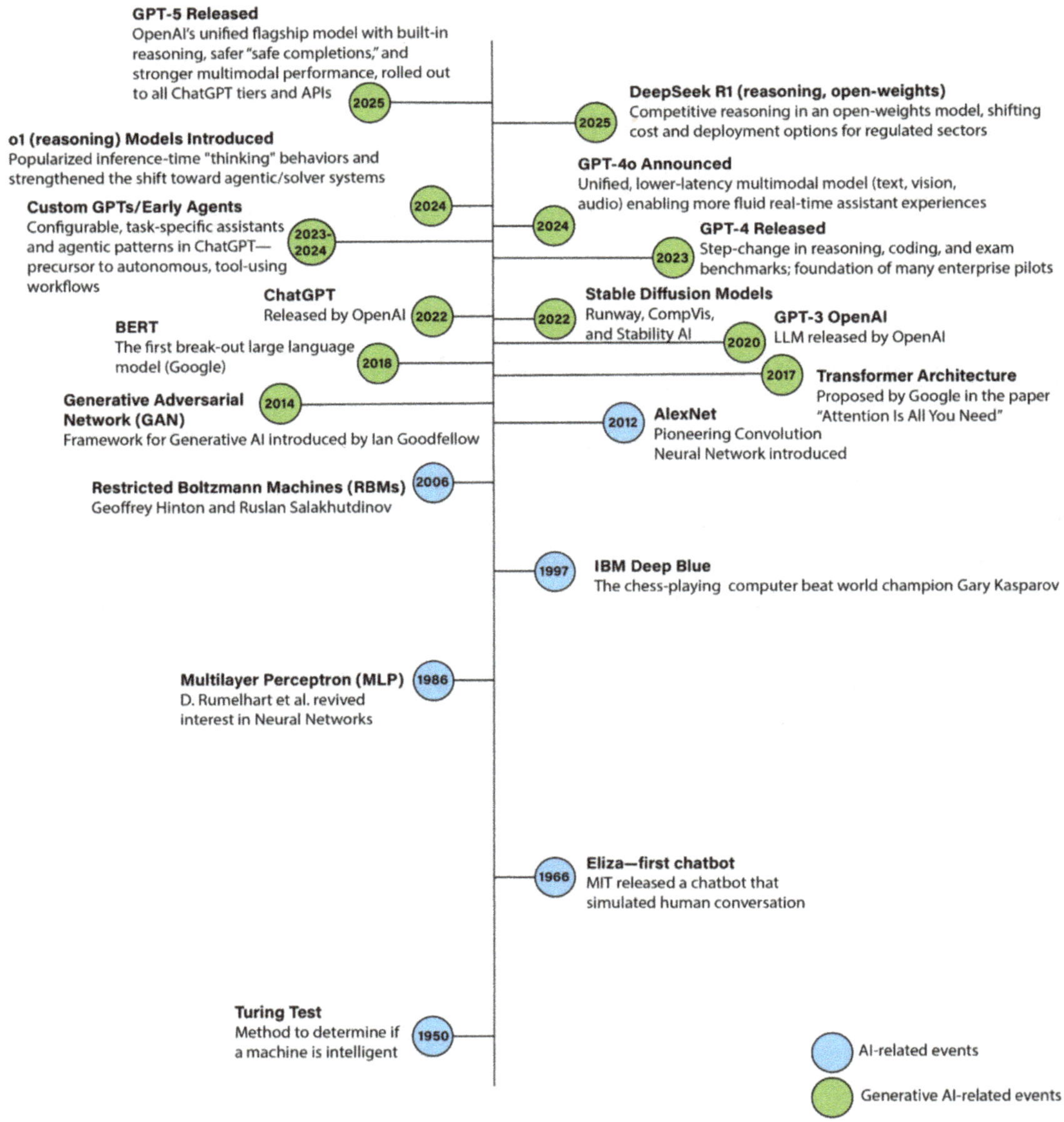

***Figure 1-7.** AI and GenAI Evolution Timeline*

We discussed the Multi Layer Perceptron (MLP) earlier. MLPs were useful for pattern recognition or classification but they struggled with any task that involved the generation of new content. To solve this issue, additional variations of deep neural networks such as Autoencoders, Variational Autoencoders (VAEs), and Restricted Boltzmann Machines (RBMs) were introduced.

Generative Adversarial Networks (GANs), introduced by Ian Goodfellow and his colleagues in 2014, marked a significant breakthrough in GenAI. GANs introduced a game-theoretic approach to training generative models.

In 2017, a new type of neural network called transformers[2] revolutionized natural language processing and generative modeling, and ultimately led to the explosion in the scale and size of generative models such as BERT (Bidirectional Encoder Representations from Transformers) and GPT (Generative Pre-trained Transformer).

Transformers are complex neural networks especially attuned to processing large sets of input sequences of words in parallel. They use self-supervised learning during a pre-training phase to learn representations of language and context from unlabeled text data and, subsequently, need to be fine-tuned for specific supervised tasks.

Using transformers and hardware specifically developed for neural networks such as Graphical Processing Units (GPUs), we can train models on Internet-scale data. This is typically extremely large: think of the entire public datasets available on the Internet, for example, Wikipedia. The number of weights or parameters we mentioned earlier range on the order of millions, billions, and even trillions. This model is called a *Foundation Model (FM)*. An FM that takes words as inputs and generates words as outputs is called a *Large Language Model (LLM)* or a text-to-text generation model.

Once you have a pre-trained model, you can use it on a wide range of tasks. For example, an FM can be used to generate content on any given subject that can be found on the Internet. You can also use it in other ways, such as to summarize content for an executive briefing. We'll go deeper into the specifics on how an FM is trained later in this chapter.

An input to an FM is called a *prompt*, an instruction or a question, and the quality and type of output generated by an FM is largely dependent on the prompt. An entire field of creating these prompts has developed; we cover *prompt engineering* in more detail in Chapter 4.

1.5 Examples of Foundation Models

There is no hiding the fact that the introduction of ChatGPT has led to a tremendous interest in GenAI. ChatGPT is a web application built to interact with an underlying

[2] `https://proceedings.neurips.cc/paper_files/paper/2017/file/3f5ee243547dee91fbd053c1c4a845aa-Paper.pdf`

LLM for natural language processing tasks. It was developed by OpenAI and launched in November 2022. The exact model used varies between different versions. For example, at the time of writing, we can use GPT 3.5, GPT 4, or GPT 5.0, the latest version. GPT stands for generative pre-trained transformers, which is a variation of the original transformer model.

We can also have FMs that can take in words as inputs and generate images as outputs. These are called *text-to-image generation models*. Stable Diffusion, introduced in August 2022, is an example of a text-to-image generation model.

In addition to text-to-text and text-to-image models, we can also have models that use multiple types of inputs such as images, text, audio, and video and can create multiple types of outputs! These are called *multi-modal large language models* (MLLM). Multi-modal stands for different modes, or different methods, by which information can be processed. Initial GPT models were text-to-text models but the models have been evolving to include multi-modal capability. We provide a more exhaustive list of FMs.

Detailed understanding about how FMs/LLMs work is useful in building and implementing GenAI applications. First, let's take a look at these concepts and then we'll examine an image generation model such as Stable Diffusion.

1.6 How an LLM Works

At the core, an LLM is an FM that performs language-related tasks using a mix of unsupervised, self-supervised, and reinforcement learning techniques. These tasks might include predicting randomly masked words, helping understand context, or determining sentence sequence, teaching coherence and flow, or reconstructing the original text from a compressed version focused on information preservation.

Similar to those in any other model, there are two steps in how the FM is able to do this: the first step is training and the second is inference. However, for an FM, we label the first step as *pre-training*. The reason is that the model is first trained on a very large dataset of text and code, including books, articles, poems, and even code repositories. Later, it is optionally trained again for a specific data set; this is called fine-tuning, which we discuss in Chapter 4.

Now, let's take a deeper look at pre-training and inference.

1.6.1 Pre-training

To make it easier to understand what happens during pre-training, let's concentrate on the steps for one type of task: predicting randomly masked words.

1. **Data Preparation**: First step is to clean and process a massive dataset of text and code (books, articles, code repositories), breaking sentences down into tokens. A *token* is a word, subword, or character. To be computed, the LLM has to turn each token into a numerical representation called an *embedding*, which captures meaning and relationships.
2. **Process Embeddings**: The next step is to process the sequence of embeddings using Transformer layers. Each embedding examines all the other words in the input and calculates its relevance or how different words affect other word's meanings. This process is called *self-attention*, which enables the LLM to capture long-range dependencies and complex grammatical structures. The information flows through multiple layers that refine the LLM's understanding of word relationships.
3. **Output and Fine-Tuning**: Finally, after processing the embeddings, the LLM's main task is Masked Language Modeling (MLM), in which the LLM masks or replaces random words in the sentence with a special token. The LLM predicts the masked word based on the context of the remaining words. By predicting correct words repeatedly, the LLM learns associations between words and their contexts.
4. The task of selecting the best choice for the masked word isn't as simple as selecting the word with the most probable score; using this method, known as *greedy search*, tends to generate unimportant words, ignoring words that have the most contextual relevance. Instead, most models use some or all of the following techniques:
    - **Beam Search**: This expands on greedy search by maintaining several promising word candidates (the beam size or beam width) at each step. It explores multiple paths and improves diversity and fluency compared to greedy search at the expense of increased computational cost.

- **Top-K Sampling**: Instead of directly picking the highest probability word, this method samples from a smaller set of the top K most probable words. This method introduces randomness and can lead to more surprising and creative outputs at the expense of generating occasional nonsensical sentences.
- **Temperature**: This hyperparameter controls the randomness knob. A low temperature prioritizes high-probability words, leading to safer, more conservative outputs. A high temperature increases the influence of less likely words, encouraging exploration and potentially more novel, interesting results.
- **Top-p Sampling or Nucleus Sampling**: Instead of focusing on individual word probabilities, top-p sampling sums the probabilities of all the words. We set a threshold value, p, representing the desired proportion of the total probability mass we want to consider, then sort words by their individual probabilities in descending order. In this method, we keep adding words to the candidate pool until their cumulative probability reaches or exceeds p. Finally, we randomly choose the next word from this smaller pool of top-p candidates.

5. **Repeat**: Step 3, output- and fine-tuning, is repeated for every masked word in the dataset, iteratively improving the model's ability to predict the next word based on context.
6. **Feedback**: Some models incorporate this step; humans provide feedback to indicate the quality of the response (also known as Reinforcement Learning from Human Feedback or RLHF). This typically happens in a completely separate phase after the model has been through several rounds of Steps 1–4. The model can then adjust its internal representations and probabilities to generate refined outputs that better align with user preferences or address identified issues.

1.6.2 Inference

Once the LLM has been pre-trained, it can now be used to generate words with a given input. To understand how this works, let's look at an example.

You may have heard this quote from Abraham Lincoln, who was a pivotal figure in US history: "...that government of the people, by the people, for the people, shall not perish from the earth."

Let's say, you forgot that quote and you need GenAI to reproduce it to see how the LLM would work. Note that this is a very simple example used for illustrative purposes; we really don't need GenAI for this when a simple Internet search would give us a correct answer.

Here is the sequence of steps that the LLM follows to generate the output for this task:

1. **Understand the Prompt**: You provide an instruction to the model "Complete the quote – that government of the people, by the people..." This instruction is called a *prompt*. The model breaks it down into individual tokens and their embeddings, capturing their meaning and potential connections.

2. **Generate the Next Word**: Since the LLM has already been trained to predict a word given a set of words, it simply generates the next word. This involves using techniques such as beam search or top-k sampling to explore various possibilities of the word as described in the pre-training phase earlier in this chapter. In this case, it would be the word "For."

3. **Repeat**: The next word is added to the input sentence and the rest of the words are again processed through the model. This iterative approach builds the entire quotation.

That's pretty much it; it is hard to imagine, but this is how an entire book can be written by the LLM, one word after the next. Of course, there is a lot more complexity and sophistication in the actual FMs that are beyond the scope of this book and not necessary for a basic understanding of GenAI.

We discussed how LLMs work; next, let's take a look at how image generation FMs work.

1.7 How Image Generation FMs Work

In LLMs, a model is pre-trained to estimate the next word given a sentence. As with LLMs, text-to-image models are pre-trained to generate images from text or a combination of text and images. Let's focus on one type of model called Stable Diffusion. The main architectural components of Stable Diffusion models are a variational autoencoder (VAE), forward and reverse diffusion, a noise predictor, and conditioning. Some components are used during pre-training while others are used during inference (to generate an image from your prompt). Similar to our approach for an LLM, let's peel back the layers to examine what happens in each stage from a conceptual standpoint.

1.7.1 Pre-training

1. The encoding component of the variational autoencoder compresses an image into a smaller dimensional space called a *latent representation*. This reduces the amount of computational power required.
2. The model selects a random image and slowly transforms it into a noisy version in a series of steps called *forward diffusion*. Adding noise is equivalent to making an image blurry.
3. A U-Net, a specific type of neural network, learns to predict the noise of an image in each step. However, this process runs progressively backwards, starting from the most noisy image to the cleanest image, and is called *reverse diffusion*. Research has shown that predicting noise in small incremental steps allows the model to learn the probabilities of data distribution much faster.
4. The model runs steps 1–3 iteratively for billions of images until the U-Net learns to accurately predict noise in any image.
5. We train the model to generate images from text once the initial pre-training is done in steps 1–4. During this step, the model begins with random noise for the image. Then a prompt, in the form of text or text and image, is converted into a vector and injected into the U-Net as noise. The conversion of a prompt to a vector is handled by another model, such as Contrastive

Language-Image Pre-training (CLIP), which is a neural network model based on the transformer architecture that can represent the relationship between text and images as vectors.
The U-Net model then starts denoising the random vector using this noise as reference. The result after denoising is the latent representation of the desired image corresponding to the prompt entered. You can think of this whole process as starting with a chunk of clay (random noise), slowly molding it into an artifact (the latent image).

6. Step 5 is repeated for billions of prompts until the U-net learns to accurately remove the noise generated by prompts.
The actual process of training is much more complicated than this simplified version; there are many variations and options possible for training the U-net. In addition, different types of loss functions as well as different parameters and equations are used for optimizing the model.

1.7.2 Inference

Now that we've pre-trained the model, typically using billions of images and prompts, we can use it to generate images. When you provide a prompt, the U-net model constructs an image using the denoising process. Remember that this is the *latent image* or the representation of the image in a lower dimensional space.

During inference, the decoding component of the variational autoencoder recreates the final image in a higher dimensional space. The prompt was text or text and an image; if an image is provided, it influences the outcome of the final image.

The architecture of Stable Diffusion has been evolving and the latest versions, such as Stable Diffusion 3.0, use transformers instead of the U-net mentioned previously. These models are beyond the scope of this book and are not really necessary for a basic understanding of GenAI.

1.8 Key Takeaways

In this section, we talked about how LLMs (text to text) and Image Generation (text to image) FMs work. If you found the concepts confusing, don't worry, as these are advanced concepts in ML; there are only a few main takeaways to keep in mind, the rest are there to provide you with additional context and background information.

Let's examine the key takeaways from the previous section:

- A *Foundation Model (FM)* is a machine learning model that has been trained with a very large set of data.
- A FM takes an input known as a prompt to create an output. Every model has a limit on the size of the prompt (number of tokens).
- There are different types of FMs: text-to-text, text-to-image, and multimodal. Text-to-text models are also known as Large Language Models (LLMs). Multimodal models are often represented as Multimodal Large Language Models (MLLMs).
- An FM simply *generates* the next word or an image using an input sequence of words. Some people may think that the model is finding and using data from the Internet (as in an Internet search); that's not the case here. However, keep in mind that a front-end application, such as ChatGPT, that interfaces with an FM, such as GPT 3.5, may add features to incorporate Internet search results and then pass these search results to the FM as context. We'll talk about this in more detail in Chapter 4.
- Since the next word or image is generated purely based on probability, there is a chance that the model generates incorrect information. For example, in the previous scenario, the model could have generated "Of the people, by the people and for the Citizens." This is especially true if you modify the randomness or number of words available for selection using temperature, top K, or top p.
- The FM outputs can be modified by changing some parameters, such as temperature. In general, a higher temperature increases randomness, and a higher top K or top p increases the number of choices for words; both can increase the chance of incorrect words

in the output. Therefore, it is important to carefully select the right values to give you the best results for your particular use case. For example, if you want the model to be creative for use cases such as poetry, you try increasing the temperature. Model cards, short documents that provide key information about the model, generally provide details on how you should set these values for the most desired results.

You should now understand some of the basic concepts behind GenAI. This groundwork will help you understand the use cases and applications discussed in the remainder of this book. As you read those chapters, you may often come back to this chapter to refresh your memory and get more insight into GenAI concepts.

1.9 Chapter Summary

In this chapter, we explored the fundamental concepts behind GenAI and its underlying technologies, such as machine learning, deep learning, and neural networks. We explored the inner workings of LLMs and text-to-image models, provided a conceptual overview of how to pre-train and use these models for inference tasks.

While some of the concepts may seem complex on your first read-through, the key takeaways are that FMs, similar to LLMs and text-to-image models, generate content based on prompts, using probability distributions learned from vast amounts of training data. GenAI has already made significant strides forward with models such as GPT, Claude, Gemini, and Stable Diffusion that enable us to generate new content, from text to images and beyond.

In the next chapter, we'll delve into the relevance of GenAI specifically in the financial services sector, exploring how this technology can be leveraged to address challenges and create value for customers, employees, and other stakeholders within the industry.

CHAPTER 2

GenAI and the Financial Services Sector

In Chapter 1, we discussed the fundamentals of GenAI and provided examples on how it can be used in our day-to-day lives. This book, however, is primarily about the application of GenAI to the financial services sector (FSS). At its core, financial services are critical for global economic growth and development. The FSS encompasses a wide range of segments, from banks and insurance firms to investment companies and fintech startups. This chapter explores the FSS landscape and how GenAI can serve as a powerful mechanism to help the Financial Services Organizations (FSOs) overcome challenges and to fulfill their objectives

Some of the primary mission objectives are common across the FSS. These objectives often revolve around

- **Facilitating Financial Transactions:** This includes providing secure and efficient methods for individuals and businesses to manage their money, such as deposit accounts, loans, and payment processing.
- **Managing Risk and Uncertainty:** This involves offering products and services that help individuals and businesses mitigate financial risks, such as insurance, investment products, and risk management advice.
- **Supporting Economic Growth:** Financial institutions play a crucial role in supporting economic growth by providing capital to businesses, facilitating trade, and investing in infrastructure projects.
- **Facilitating Global Trade and Investment:** This involves providing cross-border financial services such as international payments, foreign exchange, and trade finance, which are crucial for the smooth functioning of the global economy.

S. Godavarthi, R. Nagvekar, *Transforming Financial Services with Generative AI*,
https://doi.org/10.1007/979-8-8688-2053-3_2

- **Addressing Global Challenges:** This includes addressing global challenges such as poverty and inequality through sustainable finance initiatives, impact investing, and other socially responsible practices.

Organizations within the FSS deal with a number of competing priorities, including providing seamless customer experiences, improving the productivity of the workforce, dealing with regulatory compliance, safeguarding against fraud and cyber threats, while optimizing operational costs and providing value to shareholders.

GenAI tasks spanning content generation, conversational interfaces, data analytics, summarization, and more can drive efficiencies in customer experience, employee productivity, corporate decision-making, regulatory compliance, and operational excellence.

Before we dive deeper into understanding how GenAI can help the FSOs, we first need to understand the domain, opportunities and the challenges that the organizations face.

2.1 Overview of the Domain

As discussed earlier, the financial services domain encompasses a broad range of businesses and institutions that provide financial products and services to individuals and organizations. The financial services sector is the largest in the world in terms of earnings, comprising a wide range of businesses, including merchant banks, credit card companies, stock brokerages, and insurance companies, among others.[1] According to a McKinsey global banking annual review, in 2023, the global financial system intermediated US$410 trillion generating about US$7 trillion.[2] The breakdown of this revenue is depicted in Figure 2-1.

[1] https://www.hks.harvard.edu/sites/default/files/centers/mrcbg/programs/cri/files/report_19_EO%2BFinance%2BFinal.pdf

[2] https://www.mckinsey.com/industries/financial-services/our-insights/global-banking-annual-review

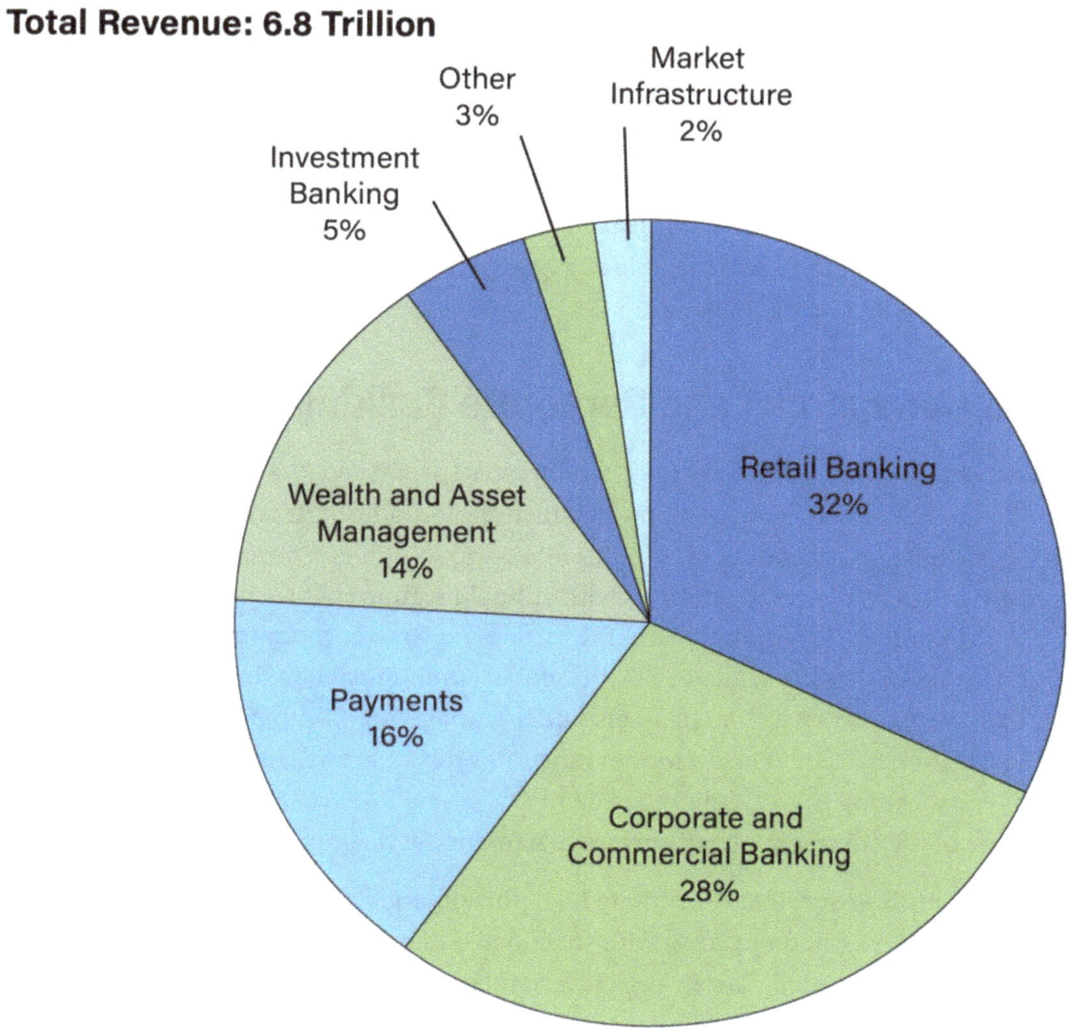

Figure 2-1. *Share of Total Annual Revenue from Global Financial Intermediation*

2.2 Key Segments

The following sections outline the key segments within the FSS domain.

2.2.1 Retail Banking

Retail banking is a crucial segment of the financial services industry that caters to individual consumers, offering a variety of products and services tailored to personal financial needs. In 2023, retail banking accounted for 33% of the total annual revenue from global financial intermediation, which amounted to US$6.8 trillion.[3] Retail banking core offerings include basic accounts for everyday transactions, savings accounts for cost-effective money management, and specialized loan products such as mortgages for home purchases and home equity-based credit lines for home improvement or debt consolidation. Retail banking also supports consumer finance by providing short-term credit options with flexible repayment terms, making it a cornerstone of personal financial management.

2.2.2 Commercial and Corporate Banking

Commercial and corporate banking encompasses specialized financial services provided to businesses, corporations, and institutions, offering a range of products, from basic business accounts to complex financing solutions. Commercial banking typically serves mid-sized businesses with annual revenues between US$10 million to US$500 million, while corporate banking focuses on large corporations with revenues exceeding US$500 million. As of 2023, the global commercial banking market reached approximately US$49.9 trillion in assets under management, with projected growth to US$56.8 trillion by 2027. The sector demonstrates robust growth, with corporate banking revenues exceeding US$1.2 trillion in 2023.[4]

Some of the commercial and corporate banking services and market trends include

Lending Services: Corporate loan portfolios globally reached US$12.4 trillion in 2023, with sustainable finance and Environmental, Social, and Governance (ESG)-linked loans representing 23% of total lending.

Transaction Banking: Generated US$375 billion in revenue (2023), with cash management services contributing 58% of the revenue stream.

Trade Finance: Working capital solutions grew to US$8.7 trillion globally, showing 15% year-over-year growth.

[3] https://www.mckinsey.com/industries/financial-services/our-insights/global-banking-annual-review

[4] https://www.mckinsey.com/industries/financial-services/our-insights/global-banking-annual-review

Digital Banking Solutions: Technology investments reached US$118.3 billion in 2023, projected to hit US$180.2 billion by 2025.

Emerging markets show the fastest growth rate at 12% annually.

2.2.3 Investment Banking

Investment banking is a specialized financial service that helps organizations raise capital and execute complex transactions through strategic advisory services. It facilitates businesses in issuing debt securities and provides guidance on mergers, acquisitions, and spin-offs based on strategic objectives.

The global investment banking sector commanded a significant market share within financial services, with revenues reaching approximately US$172.5 billion in 2023.[5] Bloomberg Intelligence's 2023 Global Investment Banking Outlook suggests continued expansion in emerging markets, particularly in Asia, with projected industry revenues expected to reach US$190 billion by 2025.[6]

2.2.4 Asset and Wealth Management

Wealth management is a comprehensive approach to managing the financial life of individuals, especially high-net-worth individuals and ultra-high-net-worth individuals. It helps to develop a customized financial plan that addresses long-term goals such as retirement, education, and major life events. Wealth and asset management plays a significant role in shaping the financial landscape and influencing capital market and investment strategies. The financial industry encompasses the management of investment on behalf of individuals and corporations, focusing on strategies that grow and protect wealth over the long term.

According to sources, wealth and asset management firms have spurred the development of a wide range of investment products designed to meet the diverse needs of clients. These products range from mutual funds and exchange-traded funds to more bespoke solutions such as private equity funds and venture capital. The global wealth and asset management industry has experienced significant growth in recent years, reflecting its pivotal role in the financial sector. As of 2023, the global asset management

[5] www.statista.com/statistics/271008/global-investment-banking-fees/

[6] www.bloomberg.com/professional/investment-banking-outlook-2023

market was valued at approximately US$458.02 billion and is projected to expand at a compound annual growth rate (CAGR) of 36.4% from 2024 to 2030, reaching an estimated US$3,677.39 billion by 2030.[7]

2.2.5 Payments and Transactions

The payments and transactions market is a critical segment within financial services, serving as the backbone of global commerce and enabling seamless financial interactions. From retail transactions to cross-border payments, this segment facilitates the flow of money across economies, driving business operations and consumer engagement. With the global digital payments market projected to exceed US$12 trillion by 2025,[8] its rapid growth underscores its importance in fostering financial inclusion and accelerating the shift toward cashless societies. Real-time payment systems, mobile wallets, and innovations including blockchain are revolutionizing how individuals and businesses transact, offering greater speed, security, and convenience.

However, this dynamic segment faces significant challenges. Cybersecurity threats, including fraud and data breaches all pose risks to customer trust and system integrity. Money laundering with disguised transactions is another challenge. Regulatory complexities and uneven digital infrastructure adoption exacerbate operational hurdles, particularly in emerging markets. Meanwhile, competition from fintech disruptors and big tech players intensifies the pressure on traditional institutions to innovate. Despite these challenges, trends such as real-time payments, the rise of Central Bank Digital Currencies (CBDCs), and AI-driven fraud detection present immense opportunities for growth and transformation, positioning this segment as the foundation in the evolving financial ecosystem.

2.2.6 Financial Markets and Trading

Financial markets represent the cornerstone of the global economy, serving as sophisticated platforms where securities, currencies, commodities, and derivatives are traded, with the global financial markets reaching a total value of approximately US$274.7 trillion in 2023. These markets encompass various segments, including equities, bond markets, foreign exchange, and derivatives markets. The advent of electronic trading platforms and AI have revolutionized market operations, with

[7] https://www.reuters.com/breakingviews/global-markets-breakingviews-2024-11-20

[8] https://www.statista.com/outlook/dmo/fintech/digital-payments/worldwide

algorithmic trading now accounting for over 60% of US equity trading volume and approximately 50% of European equity markets.

The rise of retail trading platforms has democratized market access, with daily active retail traders increasing by 275% since 2019, executing approximately 25% of all US equity trading volume. Emerging trends include the growth of ESG-focused trading, which manages over US$35 trillion in assets globally, and the integration of blockchain technology in traditional markets, with major exchanges investing heavily in digital asset infrastructure. The global equity market share is depicted in Figure 2-2.

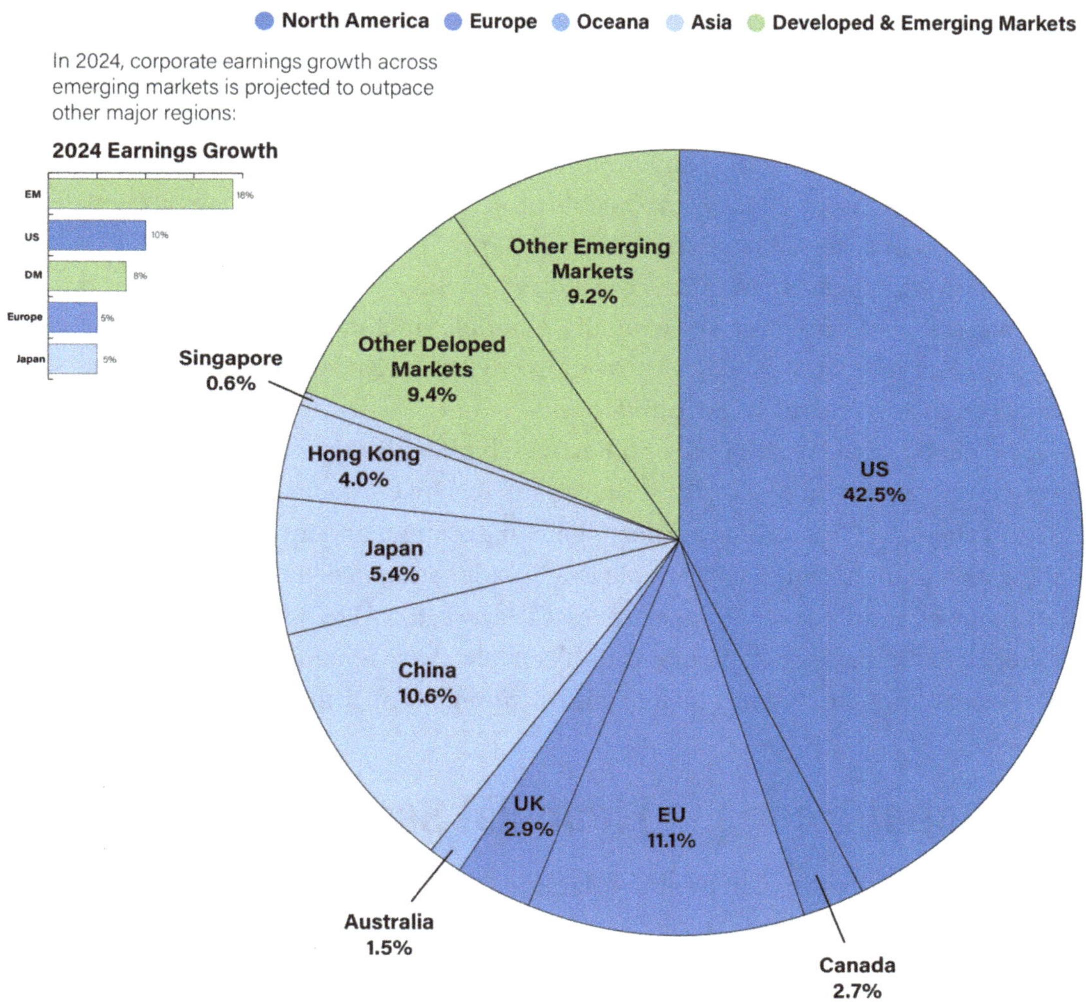

***Figure 2-2.** Global Equity Market Share as of 2024*

2.2.7 Emerging sectors

The financial services domain is undergoing rapid evolution, driven by technological innovation, changing customer expectations, and global economic trends. The following are some of the emerging segments within the FSS.

Fintech and Insurtech have gained significant momentum. Fintech companies are disrupting traditional banking and payment systems with innovative solutions such as peer-to-peer lending, digital wallets, and decentralized finance (DeFi) platforms. Insurtech focuses on leveraging data analytics, AI, and Internet of Things (IoT) to create personalized insurance products and improve operational efficiencies. These subdomains are democratizing financial access and reshaping customer engagement across the globe.

Another notable segment is **Sustainable Finance**, which emphasizes investments in environmentally and socially responsible projects. This trend is driven by regulatory mandates and investor demand for ESG compliance.

Similarly, the **Embedded Finance** sector, which integrates financial services into non-financial platforms, is growing rapidly. Examples include ride-hailing apps, offering in-app wallets, and retail platforms providing Buy Now, Pay Later (BNPL) options, enhancing customer convenience and loyalty.

Lastly, the rise of **WealthTech** and **RegTech** highlights the financial sector's pivot toward automation and personalization. WealthTech uses AI and machine learning to provide robo-advisors, automated portfolio management, and investment analytics, making wealth management accessible to a broader audience. RegTech solutions, on the other hand, streamline compliance processes, leveraging AI to detect fraud and ensure adherence to regulatory requirements. Collectively, these emerging segments signal a shift toward a more inclusive, efficient, and customer-centric financial ecosystem.

2.3 Global Trends in Financial Services

We discuss some of the global trends within the FSS below to highlight how GenAI is at the forefront of some of these trends.

2.3.1 Digital Transformation and Fintech Disruption

The financial services industry is undergoing a profound transformation, driven by digital innovation and fintech disruption primarily to improve customer experience and employee productivity. GenAI, with its ability to create, analyze, and optimize data-driven solutions, is at the forefront of this evolution. By redefining traditional processes and enabling unprecedented levels of personalization, efficiency, and intelligence, GenAI is shaping the future of financial services.

Digital transformation in financial services encompasses the integration of advanced technologies to modernize legacy systems, streamline operations, and enhance customer experiences. Traditional institutions are under pressure to adopt these technologies to remain competitive in an era of heightened consumer expectations and agile fintech disruptors.

GenAI is playing a pivotal role in this shift by offering solutions that

- **Enhance Customer Experience:** Through AI-driven chatbots, virtual assistants, and personalized product recommendations, financial institutions can provide hyper-personalized services tailored to individual needs. GenAI-powered chatbots and virtual assistants provide instant, personalized customer support. AI analyzes customer behavior to offer tailored financial products and services, improving satisfaction and retention.

- **Optimize Operational Efficiency:** AI-generated insights streamline workflows, automate routine tasks, and reduce errors, leading to cost savings and improved accuracy.

- **Enable Predictive Decision-Making and Business Intelligence:** GenAI analyzes vast datasets to provide predictive insights, allowing institutions to anticipate market trends, customer behaviors, and potential risks.

Fintech companies, known for their agility and innovative approaches, are disrupting the traditional financial services model. These companies leverage GenAI to

- **Accelerate Innovation:** By utilizing AI to rapidly prototype and test new products, fintechs can bring solutions to market faster than traditional institutions.

- **Democratize Financial Services:** GenAI enables fintechs to offer low-cost, accessible services such as robo-advisors and microloans, reaching underserved populations and fostering financial inclusion.
- **Enhance Risk Management:** GenAI powered tools assess credit-worthiness, detect fraudulent activities, and ensure compliance with regulatory requirements in real time.

2.3.2 Shift Toward Personalization

The shift toward personalization in financial services is driven by advancements in data analytics, AI, and customer-centric strategies. It mainly aims to provide tailored experiences that align with individual needs, preferences, and financial goals.

- **Drivers of Personalization**: The modern consumer demands services that feel tailored and intuitive, similar to those provided by tech giants such as Amazon and Netflix. Considering the technological advances, big data, AI, and machine learning enable financial institutions to analyze vast amounts of customer data and derive actionable insights. However, the fintech companies' prioritization of personalization as a differentiator is pushing traditional institutions to adapt.
- **Key Areas of Personalization**: Financial institutions are leveraging algorithms to suggest financial products such as loans, credit cards, or investment portfolios to customers based on their transaction history and life stage. For instance, Robo-advisor provides tailored investment strategies aligned with risk tolerance and goals, personalized messages, and advice through preferred communication channels. As a result, banks send reminders based on due dates for bills or suggest savings tips based on spending habits.

Additionally, the tools help the customer plan for future goals such as retirement, education, or homeownership, with recommendations on saving and investment. The major areas of personalization provide customers with immediate feedback or spending patterns and financial decisions. One example of this is banking apps that categorize expenses and offer real-time advice to improve saving habits.

GenAI enables personalization by analyzing vast amounts of customer data, including transaction history, browsing behavior, and interaction patterns to create hyper-personalized financial products.

2.3.3 Regulatory Evolution

The FSS has always been at the forefront of regulatory scrutiny, given its critical role in the global economy. Over time, regulatory frameworks have evolved to address emerging challenges, from globalization and digital transformation to the rise of advanced technologies such as GenAI. This evolution reflects a continuous effort to balance innovation, consumer protection, and economic stability. As an example, the global financial crisis in 2008 underscored systemic vulnerabilities, leading to the implementation of Dodd-Frank and similar regulations aimed at strengthening risk management and enhancing transparency. Additionally, the recent surge in AI adoption by the FSS, particularly GenAI, has introduced unprecedented challenges related to accountability, fairness, and data privacy, requiring a significant regulatory shift. Overall, FSS organizations have to deal with regulatory compliance and risk management. GenAI can help the organizations deal with regulatory compliance by

- Enabling automated compliance checks, streamlining processes such as anti-money laundering (AML), know-your-customer (KYC) protocols, and fraud detection
- Generating detailed reports and identifying risks in real time, ensuring institutions stay ahead of regulatory requirements

2.3.4 Integration of Blockchain and Cryptocurrency

In 2008, the launch of Bitcoin revolutionized distributed digital currency. Cryptocurrency, a digital or virtual currency, relies on cryptography for security and a blockchain, a decentralized ledger that documents transactions across various computers in a network.

The integration of blockchain and cryptocurrency in traditional finance has evolved from experimental projects to mainstream adoption, with major financial institutions increasingly embracing digital assets and distributed ledger technology. According to Deloitte's Global Blockchain Survey, over 76% of financial institutions believe they will lose their competitive advantage without blockchain adoption. The market capitalization of the entire cryptocurrency ecosystem reached approximately US$3 trillion at its peak in 2021, demonstrating the significant scale of digital assets.[9]

Traditional banks and financial institutions have invested heavily in blockchain infrastructure, with JPMorgan's Onyx platform processing over US$300 billion in short-term loan transactions using its blockchain network. The integration of traditional finance and blockchain technology is predicted to rapidly increase, potentially representing up to 10% of global GDP stored and transacted on blockchain by 2027.

Major banks use AI to automate smart contract development and risk assessment, reducing implementation time by 65% while improving security validation accuracy to 95%. In cryptocurrency operations, AI systems process over 100,000 transactions per second for AML compliance, reducing false positives by 43% and enabling real-time market surveillance across 200+ exchanges. Traditional banks leverage AI for developing personalized digital asset strategies, with machine learning algorithms analyzing market trends and portfolio composition to optimize cryptocurrency allocations while maintaining regulatory compliance. The technology has also enhanced blockchain-based payment systems, improving transaction throughput by 35% while reducing energy consumption by 28%.

2.3.5 Increased Focus on ESG and Sustainability

ESG considerations have become fundamental drivers in the financial industry, transforming how institutions evaluate investments, manage risks, and operate their businesses. ESG criteria are a set of standards for a company's operations that socially conscious investors use to screen potential investments. These criteria help assess how a company performs as a steward of nature, manages relationships with employees, suppliers, customers, and the communities where it operates, and upholds leadership, executive pay, audits, internal controls, and shareholder rights. ESG investing has experienced unprecedented growth, with global sustainable investment assets reaching US$35.3 trillion in 2023,[10] representing 36% of total assets under management

[9] https://www2.deloitte.com/content/dam/insights/articles/US144337_Blockchain-survey/DI_Blockchain-survey.pdf

[10] https://www.gsi-alliance.org/global-sustainable-investment-review-finds-us30-trillion-invested-in-sustainable-assets/

worldwide. Financial institutions are increasingly integrating ESG metrics into their core business strategies, with sustainable finance commitments from global banks surpassing US$4.5 trillion in 2023.

Sustainability, in a corporate context, refers to business strategies and practices that meet the needs of the enterprise and its stakeholders today while protecting, sustaining, and enhancing the human and natural resources that will be needed in the future. Green bonds and sustainability-linked loans have emerged as major financial instruments, with issuance reaching US$1.1 trillion in 2023, demonstrating a 128% year-over-year growth. Major financial institutions have pledged to achieve net-zero emissions in their lending and investment portfolios by 2050, with interim targets requiring a 50% reduction in financed emissions by 2030. Additionally, regulatory requirements for ESG disclosure and reporting have driven investments in sustainable finance infrastructure, with financial institutions spending approximately US$8.7 billion on ESG data, analytics, and reporting systems in 2023.

2.4 Major Challenges Within FSS

In this section, we outline the major challenges within the FSS and describe how GenAI can help address these challenges. In the subsequent chapters, we will dive deeper into each of the use cases and scenarios described here.

2.4.1 Customer Experience and Churn

In the FSS, customer experience (CX) is no longer a competitive advantage but a critical necessity. With the rise of digital platforms, consumers expect seamless, personalized, and intuitive interactions. A superior CX fosters trust, an essential currency in finance drives customer retention, loyalty, and advocacy. Studies consistently show that customers are more likely to remain with a financial institution that provides excellent service even when competitors offer better rates or lower fees. However, financial services companies have long suffered from a reputation for poor understanding of customer experience and, in 2020, had average NPS scores of 44 with a median churn rate of 19%.[11] FSS can use GenAI to improve CX and reduce churn.

[11] https://customergauge.com/blog/average-churn-rate-by-industry

2.4.1.1 How GenAI Can Help Improve CX and Reduce Churn

Streamlined Onboarding and Loan Processing

GenAI automates document analysis, application processing, and compliance checks, drastically reducing the time and effort required for onboarding and loan approvals. A faster, hassle-free process improves the initial customer experience, setting the tone for a long-term relationship.

Proactive Customer Support

Through AI-powered chatbots and virtual assistants, GenAI delivers instant, 24/7 support. These systems can handle complex queries, predict customer needs based on historical interactions, and provide real-time solutions, significantly reducing frustration and enhancing satisfaction.

Personalized Financial Advice

GenAI can analyze vast amounts of customer data to provide tailored financial insights, investment recommendations, and savings strategies. By understanding individual preferences and goals, it creates highly relevant and actionable advice, enhancing engagement and loyalty.

Enhanced Fraud Detection and Security Alerts

GenAI can identify anomalies in transactions and predict potential fraud scenarios. By notifying customers proactively and offering immediate resolutions, it builds trust and reassures customers about the safety of their financial assets.

2.4.2 Operational Inefficiencies and Employee Productivity

Despite a total of approximately US$600 billion spent globally by banks on technology that should be boosting productivity, labor productivity in some major markets (for example, the United States) is declining.[12] Despite advancements, many processes

[12] https://www.mckinsey.com/industries/financial-services/our-insights/unlocking-value-from-technology-in-banking-an-investor-lens

such as loan approvals, risk assessments, and fraud investigations remain manual to a large extent. Further, these processes are time-consuming and susceptible to human errors. Increasing technical debt is a major challenge[13] as well within the FSS and many institutions rely on outdated legacy systems that lack the agility to adapt to modern demands.

These factors lead to poor employee experience and productivity where employees are spending their time on dealing with manual processes and technical debt instead of focusing on the more important customer tasks. GenAI can help address some of these challenges.

2.4.2.1 How GenAI Can Address Operational Inefficiencies

According to McKinsey, the emergence of GenAI could be a game changer: GenAI can potentially improve productivity by 3 to 5% and enable a reduction in operating expenditures of between US$200 billion and US$300 billion.[14] GenAI can help in all of the following areas:

- **Improving Overall Productivity**: GenAI assists employees by automating repetitive tasks, freeing them to focus on higher-value work. These tasks include document verification and underwriting, significantly reducing turnaround times. AI-driven tools provide real-time insights and recommendations, enabling employees to make data-driven decisions quickly. AI-generated summaries and templates streamline document-intensive processes, including loan approvals and financial reporting.
- **Real-Time Assistance for Customer Interactions**: GenAI can act as a co-pilot for employees during customer interactions, offering real-time recommendations, scripting responses, and even analyzing sentiment. This enhances employee efficiency and ensures a consistent, high-quality customer experience.

[13] https://www.mckinsey.com/capabilities/mckinsey-digital/our-insights/breaking-technical-debts-vicious-cycle-to-modernize-your-business

[14] https://www.mckinsey.com/industries/financial-services/our-insights/global-banking-annual-review-2023

- **Enhanced Decision Support**: By generating detailed insights from financial data, market trends, and customer behavior, GenAI equips business leaders and employees with actionable intelligence. GenAI simplifies data visualization, enabling stakeholders to interpret trends and patterns effectively. This enables faster, data-driven decisions in areas such as investment management, credit underwriting, and risk assessment.

We will explore these efficiency gains further in the subsequent chapters when we delve into the use cases.

2.4.3 Regulatory and Compliance Pressure

The FSS is one of the most heavily regulated industries in the world. As institutions navigate an increasingly complex regulatory landscape, they face mounting challenges that demand significant resources, robust processes, and innovative solutions. GenAI is emerging as a powerful tool to address these pressures, enabling institutions to streamline compliance, reduce costs, and enhance transparency. Let's discuss some of these challenges further.

- **Increasing Complexity of Regulations**: The dynamic nature of regulations across jurisdictions requires institutions to keep up with evolving requirements, such as AML laws, KYC mandates, and data privacy regulations such as the GDPR and CCPA.
- **High Costs of Compliance:** Compliance processes often involve a significant manual effort, requiring teams to review documentation, analyze transactions, and produce reports. According to a 2022 study by LexisNexis,[15] the cost of compliance in the United States alone is currently estimated at US$274 billion. Further, non-compliance penalties can result in substantial fines, reputational damage, and loss of customer trust. According to an analysis by Zigram, in 2023 alone, a total of 1,450 organizations across the globe paid fines totaling US$44 billion.[16]

---

[15] https://risk.lexisnexis.com/insights-resources/article/entity-resolution-redefining-false-positive-problem

[16] https://www.zigram.tech/articles/regtech-in-kyc-and-aml-compliance/

- **Data Management and Integration**: Institutions must manage and integrate vast amounts of structured and unstructured data from disparate systems to ensure compliance. Ensuring data accuracy, consistency, and security is an ongoing challenge.
- **Fraud Detection and Risk Management**: Detecting fraudulent activities and assessing risks in real time are critical yet resource-intensive tasks. Identifying patterns indicative of fraud or anomalies often requires advanced analytical capabilities.

2.4.3.1 How GenAI Can Address Compliance Challenges

GenAI offers transformative solutions to help financial institutions overcome these challenges effectively.

- **Automation of Compliance Processes**: GenAI can automate time-consuming tasks such as document review, regulatory reporting, and KYC verification. By using AI-generated templates and summaries, institutions can ensure consistency and accuracy in compliance documentation.
- **Real-Time Monitoring and Fraud Detection**: Advanced AI models analyze transactional data in real time, flagging anomalies and suspicious activities for further investigation. GenAI's predictive capabilities enable institutions to identify potential risks before they escalate.
- **Enhanced Regulatory Reporting**: GenAI automates the generation of detailed, accurate reports tailored to regulatory requirements, reducing the risk of errors and ensuring timely submissions. Institutions can use AI to simulate various regulatory scenarios, preparing proactive responses to new mandates.

We will dive deeper into these aspects in Chapter 5.

2.4.4 Data Privacy, Security, and Management

Data privacy, security, and management have emerged as critical pillars of modern financial institution operations and digital governance, with global cybersecurity spending reaching US$219.7 billion in 2023[17] and is projected to exceed US$345.4 billion by 2026. In the financial sector, data privacy and security management encompass comprehensive frameworks protecting customer financial data, transaction records, and institutional assets from cyber threats, with banks investing approximately US$18.5 billion annually in cybersecurity infrastructure. Financial institutions leverage ML algorithms for fraud detection, processing over 1,000 data points per transaction in real time, achieving a 95% accuracy rate in identifying suspicious activities. The data management software market has expanded to US$83.6 billion, with financial institutions accounting for 32% of this spending. Banks particularly employ ML-powered systems for KYC processes, reducing verification time by 70% while increasing accuracy to 99%, and for AML screening, which processes over one million transactions daily per large institution. Advanced AI systems in major banks now prevent approximately US$2 billion in potential fraud annually, analyzing customer behavior patterns and flagging anomalies in milliseconds.

2.4.4.1 How GenAI Can Address Data Challenges

Financial institutions are leveraging GenAI to bolster data privacy and security, with banks allocating US$18.5 billion toward AI-driven security solutions in 2023. The GenAI enables advanced anomaly detection systems that process over 100,000 transactions per second, identifying potential fraud patterns with 95% accuracy while maintaining customer privacy through sophisticated anonymization techniques. Financial institutions use GenAI for synthetic data generation, creating realistic but non-sensitive datasets for testing and development that reduce privacy risks by 78%. In cybersecurity, AI systems analyze network behavior patterns across multiple layers, detecting and responding to threats in real time with 99.7% accuracy while simultaneously ensuring GDPR and financial regulatory compliance. Major banks report that AI-powered data management systems have reduced security incidents by 65% while improving data classification accuracy to 92%, enabling better protection of sensitive financial information through automated data governance and access control mechanisms.

[17] https://www.mckinsey.com/capabilities/risk-and-resilience/our-insights/cybersecurity/new-survey-reveals-2-trillion-dollar-market-opportunity-for-cybersecurity-technology-and-service-providers

2.4.5 Cybersecurity Threats

Cybersecurity threats in the financial industry represent malicious attempts to breach digital security systems, compromise sensitive financial data, or disrupt critical banking operations. These threats manifest through various attack vectors, including Advanced Persistent Threats (APTs), where sophisticated actors maintain long-term unauthorized access to systems, and ransomware attacks that encrypt critical data for extortion. The financial sector experienced a 238% increase in cyberattacks during 2023, with global damages reaching US$5.87 million per breach, significantly higher than the cross-industry average of US$4.45 million. The most prevalent attack types include social engineering attacks (accounting for 43% of breaches), where attackers manipulate employees to gain access, distributed denial of service (DDoS) attacks disrupting financial services, and credential stuffing attacks attempting to compromise customer accounts. Financial institutions invest approximately US$75.2 billion annually in cybersecurity measures, with large banks allocating 15% of their IT budgets to security operations. The rise of cloud-based banking services has expanded the attack surface, with cloud-specific security incidents costing financial institutions an average of US$4.1 million per breach.

2.4.5.1 Common Types of Cyber Attacks in the Financial Industry

- **Social Engineering and Phishing**: Sophisticated impersonation attacks targeting financial employees and customers, causing losses of US$12.5 billion in 2024[18]
- **Ransomware**: Targeted attacks encrypting financial data with demands averaging US$1.85 million per incident[19]
- **Supply Chain Attacks**: Compromising third-party vendors to access financial networks, increasing 149% year-over-year[20]

[18] https://www.thesslstore.com/blog/social-engineering-statistics/

[19] https://invenioit.com/continuity/ransomware-attacks-finance/

[20] https://www.insurancebusinessmag.com/us/news/cyber/supply-chain-cyber-attacks-surge-over-400-expected-to-continue-rising--cowbell-report-525369.aspx

- **API-Based Attacks**: Exploiting financial service APIs, with attacks rising 168% in 2023
- **Cloud Infrastructure Attacks**: Targeting cloud-based banking services, costing an average of $4.1 million per breach

2.4.5.2 How Can GenAI Help Address Cybersecurity Threats?

Cybersecurity in the financial and banking sectors is being reshaped by GenAI. It helps detect and mitigate threats, including social engineering, phishing, ransomware attacks targeting APIs, and cloud infrastructure weaknesses. It analyzes vast datasets to identify patterns of malicious behavior, predict potential attacks, and automate response mechanisms. For social engineering and phishing, GenAI powers advanced email filtering and user behavior analysis to detect anomalies. Against ransomware, it identifies unusual encryption activities and blocks threats proactively. In API-based and cloud attacks, GenAI enhances monitoring, ensuring secure configurations and detecting suspicious activities. Leveraging AI for real-time threat intelligence significantly fortifies cybersecurity.

2.5 Introduction: The Global Fiscal Group, a fictitious FSO

We provide the profile for a fictitious FSO called the Global Fiscal Group (GFG) that we use throughout this book to provide use cases, challenges, and in describing how GenAI can be used to address these challenges. Note that GFG is for illustrative purposes only and it does not represent an existing FSO; however, it does represent the various financial services that an FSO or a FinTech company provides.

2.5.1 Company Overview

Global Fiscal Group (GFG) is a leading, diversified financial services conglomerate with a presence in over 60 countries and a client base spanning individuals, corporations, and institutional investors. Headquartered in London, with major regional hubs in New York, Singapore, Frankfurt, and Dubai, GFG is recognized for its innovative approach, robust risk management, and commitment to sustainable finance. The Group's mission is to empower economic growth, facilitate global trade, and drive financial inclusion through cutting-edge technology and customer-centric solutions.

Founded in 1872 as a merchant bank, GFG has evolved into a multi-segment powerhouse, offering a comprehensive suite of services across retail banking, commercial and corporate banking, investment banking, asset and wealth management, payments and transactions, and financial markets. With over $2.1 trillion in assets under management and annual revenues exceeding $65 billion, GFG is consistently ranked among the world's top financial institutions.

2.5.2 Core Segments and Services

2.5.2.1 Retail Banking

GFG's retail banking division serves over 80 million customers worldwide, providing a full spectrum of products, including current and savings accounts, mortgages, personal loans, credit cards, and digital banking solutions. The division is lauded for its seamless omnichannel experience, AI-powered financial planning tools, and commitment to financial literacy and inclusion. In 2024, GFG launched "SmartBank," an AI-driven mobile platform that personalizes financial advice, automates savings, and offers real-time fraud alerts, resulting in a 40% increase in customer engagement and a 25% reduction in churn.

2.5.2.2 Commercial and Corporate Banking

GFG's commercial and corporate banking arm partners with over 500,000 businesses, from SMEs to Fortune 500 companies. Services include working capital solutions, trade finance, cash management, ESG-linked lending, and digital treasury platforms. GFG is a pioneer in sustainable finance, with $120 billion in green loans and sustainability-linked credit facilities issued in 2023 alone. The Group's "Trade360" platform leverages blockchain and GenAI to streamline cross-border transactions, reducing settlement times by 60% and enhancing transparency.

2.5.2.3 Investment Banking

GFG's investment banking division is a trusted advisor to governments, corporations, and institutional investors, specializing in capital markets, M&A, structured finance, and strategic advisory. In 2023, GFG advised on $350 billion in M&A transactions and underwrote $200 billion in debt and equity offerings.

2.5.2.4 Asset and Wealth Management

With $1.2 trillion in assets under management, GFG's asset and wealth management business offers tailored investment solutions, private banking, and fiduciary services to high-net-worth and institutional clients.

2.5.2.5 Payments and Transactions

GFG operates one of the world's largest payments networks, processing over $5 trillion in annual transaction volume. The Group's "PayX" platform supports real-time payments, cross-border remittances, and digital wallets, serving both retail and corporate clients. GFG is at the forefront of digital currency innovation, piloting Central Bank Digital Currency (CBDC) solutions and integrating blockchain for secure, transparent settlements.

2.5.2.6 Financial Markets and Trading

GFG's global markets division provides trading, market-making, and risk management services across equities, fixed income, currencies, commodities, and derivatives. The division's AI-driven trading algorithms account for 70% of its equity trading volume, delivering superior execution and liquidity. GFG is a leader in ESG-focused trading and digital asset infrastructure, with dedicated teams for sustainable finance and blockchain integration.

2.5.2.7 Emerging Sectors

GFG invests heavily in fintech, insurtech, and regtech, fostering innovation through its "GFG Labs" incubator. The Group partners with startups to develop solutions in embedded finance, decentralized finance (DeFi), and Wealth Tech, expanding access to underserved markets and enhancing customer experience.

2.5.3 Strategic Priorities and Challenges

2.5.3.1 Customer Experience and Personalization

GFG's strategy centers on delivering seamless, personalized experiences across all channels. The Group uses GenAI to analyze customer data, anticipate needs, and offer tailored products and advice. AI-powered chatbots and virtual assistants handle over 80% of routine inquiries, freeing staff to focus on complex client needs. GFG's Net Promoter Score (NPS) rose to 68 in 2024, reflecting its commitment to customer-centricity.

2.5.3.2 Operational Excellence and Productivity

Despite significant investment in technology, GFG faces challenges with legacy systems and operational silos. The Group's "Digital First" initiative aims to automate 60% of back-office processes by 2026, leveraging GenAI for document processing, compliance checks, and real-time decision support. Early pilots have reduced loan approval times by 70% and cut operational costs by $500 million annually.

2.5.3.3 Regulatory Compliance and Risk Management

Operating in multiple jurisdictions, GFG navigates a complex regulatory landscape. The Group employs GenAI for automated compliance monitoring, anti-money laundering (AML), and know-your-customer (KYC) processes, reducing false positives by 45% and ensuring real-time regulatory reporting. GFG's regtech solutions have cut compliance costs by 30% and improved audit readiness.

2.5.3.4 Data Privacy, Security, and Cyber Resilience

With cyber threats on the rise, GFG invests over $2 billion annually in cybersecurity and data governance. The Group's AI-driven security operations center monitors 100,000+ transactions per second, detecting anomalies and preventing fraud with 98% accuracy. GFG's synthetic data generation tools enable secure innovation while maintaining GDPR and global privacy compliance.

2.5.3.5 Sustainability and ESG Leadership

GFG is committed to achieving net-zero emissions in its lending and investment portfolios by 2050, with interim targets for 2030. The Group integrates ESG metrics into all business lines, offers green bonds and sustainability-linked loans, and publishes transparent ESG disclosures. GFG's "Impact Finance" division supports projects in renewable energy, affordable housing, and financial inclusion, aligning profitability with purpose.

2.5.3.6 Innovation and Digital Transformation

GFG's culture of innovation is driven by its "GFG Labs" and strategic partnerships with fintechs, universities, and technology providers. The Group invests $1.5 billion annually in research and development, focusing on GenAI, blockchain, and cloud-native platforms. GFG's open banking APIs and developer ecosystem foster collaboration and accelerate time-to-market for new solutions.

2.5.4 Vision and Values

GFG's vision is to be the world's most trusted financial partner, enabling prosperity for clients, communities, and shareholders. The Group's core values – integrity, innovation, inclusion, and sustainability – guide its strategy and operations. GFG is committed to ethical conduct, diversity and inclusion, and responsible stewardship of resources.

2.5.4.1 Looking Ahead

As the financial services sector undergoes rapid transformation, GFG is poised to lead through its commitment to digital innovation, operational excellence, and sustainable growth. By harnessing the power of GenAI and emerging technologies, GFG aims to redefine the future of finance; making it more accessible, secure, and impactful for all.

2.6 Chapter Summary

The FSS plays a pivotal role in the global economy, encompassing a diverse array of institutions that provide essential services such as retail and corporate banking, investment management, insurance, and more. Despite its critical contributions, the sector faces a myriad of challenges, including regulatory complexities, fraud prevention, operational inefficiencies, and the increasing need for personalized customer experiences. These challenges are further compounded by the rapid digitalization of services and heightened expectations from customers. To remain competitive and efficient, FSS organizations must embrace innovation and transform their operations.

GenAI emerges as a transformative force, offering solutions that address these industry-wide challenges. By leveraging advanced capabilities in content generation, conversational AI, data analysis, and summarization, GenAI enables financial institutions to enhance customer experiences, improve decision-making, and streamline operations. In this chapter, we discussed how GenAI can be a strategic enabler for the FSS, driving innovation and unlocking new growth opportunities across its key segments. In the next chapter, we will dive deeper into the strategy for adopting GenAI within the FSS.

CHAPTER 3

GenAI Strategy: A Blueprint for Successful Adoption

In Chapter 2, we explored the Financial Services Sector (FSS) landscape and how GenAI can serve as a powerful mechanism to help the Financial Services Organizations (FSOs) overcome challenges and to fulfill their objectives.

In this chapter, we lay out a high-level GenAI strategy and blueprint, a methodology for implementation, and a framework to address various challenges that FSOs face during implementation. We explore these topics through the lens of Maria, the Chief Information Officer of an FSO. She is excited about the promise and potential of GenAI. Her organization is hyper-focused on improving customer experience and workforce productivity.

Maria has heard from various industry experts that her organization should consider using GenAI to achieve some of these objectives. However, Maria has some questions and concerns about GenAI, including

1. What should be my GenAI strategy and what does a blueprint look like?
2. Where should I start and how do I implement GenAI within my organization?
3. What are the major risks and pitfalls of GenAI?
4. How can I overcome these risks and pitfalls? What are the GenAI implementation best practices?

S. Godavarthi, R. Nagvekar, *Transforming Financial Services with Generative AI*,
https://doi.org/10.1007/979-8-8688-2053-3_3

3.1 GenAI Strategy and Blueprint

Let's first address Maria's question about strategy and blueprint. At a high level, a GenAI strategy ensures that GenAI implementations align with overall organization goals and objectives. Figure 3-1 provides a blueprint that FSOs can use to develop this strategy.

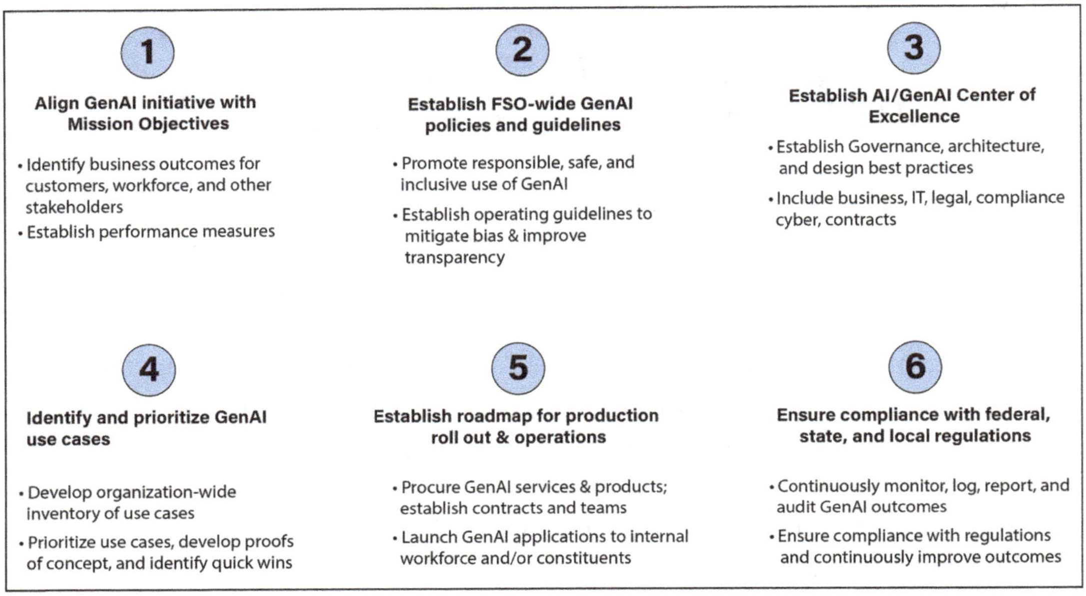

Figure 3-1. *GenAI Strategy Blueprint at the Organization Level for FSOs*

Let's review each of the major strategy areas of the blueprint illustrated in Figure 3-1.

3.1.1 Align GenAI with Organizational Initiatives

GenAI's transformative potential is immense but its success depends on how well it aligns with an organization's strategic goals. As a financial services leader, you're already navigating priorities, including enhancing customer satisfaction, improving operational efficiency, driving innovation, and meeting stringent compliance requirements. The key to success is to ensure that GenAI acts as an enabler for these initiatives rather than a stand-alone experiment.

Start the alignment process by asking yourself, *"What are our key initiatives, and where could GenAI make a difference?"* and begin mapping GenAI to your organizational goals. Let's say your focus is on elevating customer experience; AI can power hyper-ersonalized interactions through chatbots, tailored investment advice, or even dynamic product recommendations. If operational efficiency is your priority, consider deploying AI models to automate labor-intensive processes such as fraud detection or document verification. Aligning these applications to existing goals ensures GenAI contributes measurable value from day one.

3.1.2 Establish GenAI Policies and Operating Guidelines

As FSOs integrate GenAI into their operations, establishing robust policies and operating guidelines is essential. These frameworks not only ensure responsible AI adoption but also build trust with stakeholders by addressing risks and aligning AI usage with organizational goals and regulatory requirements. Policies and guidelines provide clarity on how GenAI should be deployed, governed, and monitored across the organization.

These policies should outline permissible use cases, explicitly addressing sensitive areas such as customer communications, decision-making, and data usage. For instance, AI-generated financial advice content must comply with regulatory standards to avoid misleading customers. These policies should also address data security and privacy, ensuring that GenAI applications adhere to frameworks such as GDPR, CCPA, and industry-specific mandates.

Operational guidelines translate these policies into actionable practices. For example, they might define protocols for training and deploying GenAI models, including requirements for regular audits to ensure ethical and unbiased behavior.

3.1.3 Establish AI/GenAI Center of Excellence (ACOE)

Creating an AI/GenAI Center of Excellence (CoE) is essential for FSOs seeking to maximize the potential of GenAI. The CoE acts as a central hub for driving innovation, ensuring governance, and aligning AI initiatives with strategic objectives. Its structure should bring together cross-functional expertise from technology, business, legal, compliance, and data science teams, fostering collaboration and ensuring a balanced approach to innovation and risk management.

One core responsibility of the CoE is to establish a repository of best practices, reusable assets, and standardized protocols for GenAI development and deployment. By creating templates and guidelines for GenAI use cases such as customer service bots or fraud detection tools, the CoE promotes consistency and compliance across implementations. It also ensures adherence to data privacy and security standards, mitigating risks, including bias and regulatory breaches, while maintaining the integrity of GenAI models.

Additionally, the CoE plays a pivotal role in cultivating a culture of AI literacy and innovation. Acting as a strategic advisor, the CoE identifies high-impact AI opportunities, monitors project performance, and ensures GenAI solutions deliver measurable business outcomes. With its centralized governance and expertise, the CoE enables the organization to unlock the transformative potential of GenAI while fostering responsible and scalable adoption.

3.1.4 Identify and Prioritize GenAI Use Cases

Identifying and prioritizing use cases is a critical step in developing an effective GenAI strategy for financial services. The process begins by aligning potential use cases with the organization's strategic objectives, such as improving customer experience, enhancing operational efficiency, or driving revenue growth. For instance, use cases such as personalized financial advice, automated customer support, and fraud detection directly address key industry pain points. A cross-functional team involving business, technology, and compliance stakeholders should collaborate to identify areas where GenAI can deliver the greatest impact.

Once potential use cases are identified, prioritization is crucial to maximize value while minimizing risks and resource constraints. A structured framework can help rank use cases based on factors such as business value, technical feasibility, regulatory complexity, and time-to-market. High-priority use cases might include automating routine processes, such as loan origination or claims processing, because these deliver measurable efficiency gains quickly. On the other hand, more complex initiatives, such as predictive risk modeling or regulatory reporting automation, may require additional investment but offer transformative potential over the long term. By systematically evaluating and prioritizing use cases, organizations can ensure that their GenAI initiatives align with strategic goals and deliver sustained business value.

3.1.5 Establish a Roadmap for Production Rollout and Operations

Establishing a well-defined roadmap for the production rollout and operations of GenAI initiatives is essential to ensure that they are successfully integrated into financial services. This roadmap should outline key phases, including pilot testing, scalability planning, and full-scale deployment, while addressing critical operational considerations such as monitoring, governance, and continuous improvement. By breaking up the rollout into manageable stages, organizations can minimize risks, address unforeseen challenges, and gather valuable feedback for refinement before expanding GenAI applications across the enterprise.

During the pilot phase, focus on testing the GenAI solution in a controlled environment (e.g., soft launch to internal users) with clearly defined success criteria. This includes assessing its accuracy, scalability, and alignment with regulatory requirements. Once validated, the roadmap should detail plans for scaling the solution, including infrastructure readiness, data integration, and training for operational teams. Post-deployment, operational success hinges on robust monitoring mechanisms to ensure the GenAI models perform reliably, remain unbiased, and comply with evolving regulations. Regular performance reviews, supported by observability tools, should be built into the roadmap to identify areas for optimization and maintain alignment with business objectives.

3.1.6 Ensure Compliance with Federal, State, and Other Industry Regulations

Compliance with federal, state, and industry regulations is a cornerstone of deploying GenAI in financial services. The highly regulated nature of the financial sector necessitates a rigorous approach to ensuring that AI systems operate within the bounds of legal and ethical standards. Non-compliance can result in hefty fines, reputation damage, and erosion of customer trust.

Note that there are a number of regulations that are evolving for AI governance – these include the *"AI bill of rights"*[1] in the United States, which outlines guidelines for building safe and effective AI systems, enabling data privacy and protection from

[1] `https://www.whitehouse.gov/ostp/ai-bill-of-rights/`

algorithmic discrimination. Additionally, the European Union AI Act, the world's first comprehensive legislation, came into force in 2024.[2] Specifically, within the FSS, the New York Department of Financial Services (NY DFS) has recently issued guidance regarding the use of AI in financial services, particularly focusing on cybersecurity risks associated with AI technologies.[3]

Based on these regulations, FSOs must proactively address key areas such as data privacy, fairness, transparency, and accountability. To achieve this, organizations should integrate compliance requirements into the GenAI development life cycle from the beginning. This involves conducting regular audits, maintaining detailed documentation of model decisions, and ensuring explainability in GenAI outputs to satisfy regulatory scrutiny.

Additionally, FSOs should establish AI governance structures to monitor adherence to compliance standards, incorporating legal, risk, and compliance teams into the governance framework. The use of automated compliance tools, powered by GenAI, can streamline regulatory reporting, detect anomalies, and flag potential non-compliance issues early, further safeguarding the organization.

3.2 GenAI Implementation

The blueprint described in this section assists an FSO in developing a strategic approach to adopt GenAI consistently, and align with your overall mission. However, Maria's question remains: "Where do I begin and how can I implement GenAI in my organization?" Addressing these questions requires more than just a strategy; it calls for a clear methodology to effectively manage GenAI implementation projects. Figure 3-2 illustrates this methodology.

[2] https://www.diligent.com/resources/blog/eu-artificial-intelligence-act

[3] https://www.dfs.ny.gov/industry-guidance/industry-letters/il20241016-cyber-risks-ai-and-strategies-combat-related-risks

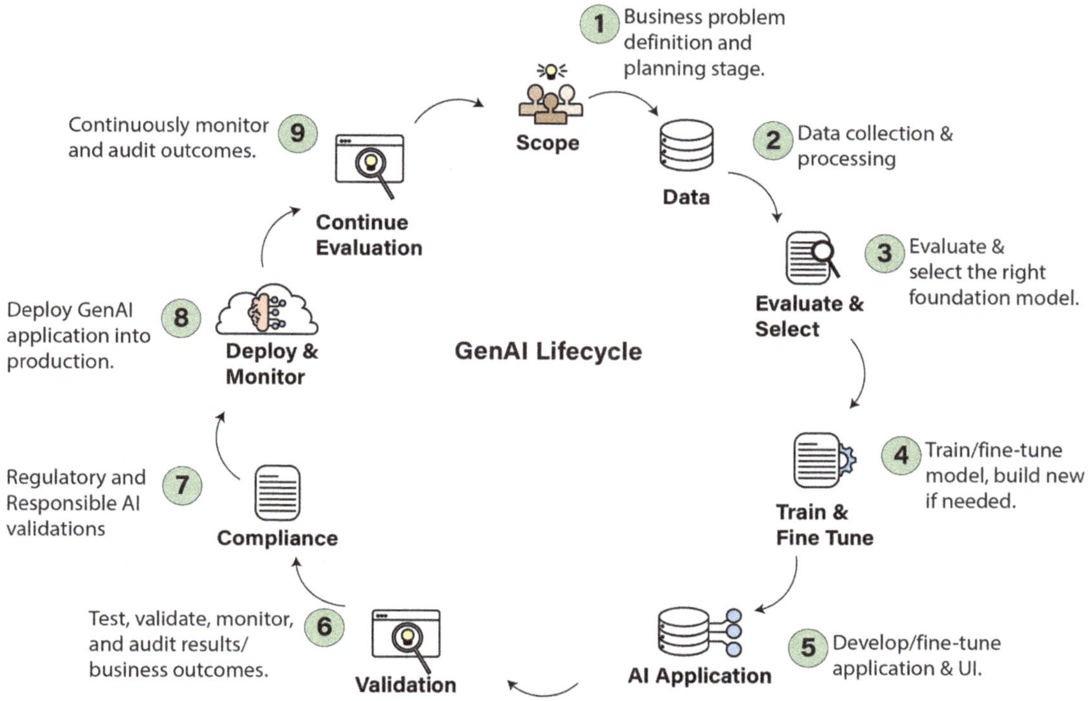

Figure 3-2. *GenAI Life Cycle*

As Figure 3-2 shows, the methodology consists of nine different phases that form the GenAI life cycle. Let's discuss each phase of the life cycle in detail.

3.2.1 Scope Definition for GenAI

Defining scope is a foundational step in the life cycle of a GenAI project. In this stage, focus on articulating a clear, high-impact use case that aligns with your strategic objectives. Proper scoping ensures that the project addresses the right problem by identifying your organization's business opportunities, evaluating feasibility, and setting clear outcomes. The scoping process involves several key considerations, including defining the problem, identifying and engaging stakeholders, establishing measurable success metrics, and understanding constraints related to data, resources, and timelines. Selecting manageable yet impactful use cases, such as developing a frequently asked questions (FAQ) chatbot, provides your teams with the opportunities for early success, building confidence and momentum before you progress to more complex applications.

Taking a structured approach, guided by Specific, Measurable, Achievable, Relevant, Time-bound (SMART) objectives, ensures your teams and the GenAI initiative itself will have clarity and focus. Writing a comprehensive scope document further solidifies this foundation, outlining goals, deliverables, and potential risks and challenges. When you follow best practices such as starting with simple, scalable projects, engaging stakeholders from the outset, and establishing clear success criteria - they help maintain alignment and avoid scope creep. Taking this disciplined approach is essential for you to deliver measurable value, ensure sustainable outcomes, and foster confidence in your organization's GenAI initiatives.

3.2.2 Data Collection and Preparation

Data is the pillar of GenAI outcomes and, as such, requires you to formulate a well-defined strategy to source, store, and manage data effectively based on your use case. In the data investigation phase, identify relevant data to supplement FMs through techniques such as Retrieval-Augmented Generation (RAG), enabling Large Language Models (LLMs) to leverage external, up-to-date information for enhanced accuracy and relevance. The data preparation phase ensures that the collected data is cleaned, formatted, and structured, often embedding it into vector store databases to optimize compatibility with the AI models you chose. This stage is critical for you to build a robust foundation for impactful AI solutions.

3.2.3 FM Evaluation and Selection

In this phase, FSOs decide how to procure and adapt FMs based on their business needs and budget. We discussed FMs in Chapter 1. In general, there are three options:

1. Use an existing model without any modifications.
2. Fine-tune the foundation model.
3. Develop a custom foundation model.

Pretrained models such as GPT-5 or Meta's LLaMA are cost-effective and efficient for general applications, such as chatbots or content generation, and require minimal customization. Custom models, however, are better suited to highly specialized use cases, such as financial analysis or legal document processing but they demand significant resources.

Key characteristics to consider when you select an FM include the level of customization, licensing agreements, inference performance, context window size, and latency. Your evaluation should also assess accuracy, scalability, cost, and ethics. Fine-tuning or transfer learning can further align models with your specific use cases. Conducting a feasibility analysis ensures the model aligns with your technical, timeline, and ethical requirements, paving the way for project success. We discuss these concepts in more detail later in this chapter.

3.2.4 FM Training and Fine-Tuning

In this phase, the focus shifts to building or fine-tuning the FM you selected based on the chosen approach. Developing a custom model is a complex and resource-intensive process, requiring you to carefully consider data, time, costs, and infrastructure. If you use a pretrained model without modification, you can skip this phase.

For cases requiring a custom model, use techniques such as prompt engineering, fine-tuning, and human feedback alignment to tailor the model to your specific use case. This process transforms a general-purpose model into a solution that understands the unique nuances of your data, context, and user expectations. The goal of this stage is to achieve accuracy, efficiency, and ethical alignment of the model within the defined parameters. This iterative phase often involves cycles of refinement and evaluation to ensure the model meets all criteria for success.

3.2.5 Testing, Validation, Monitoring, and Auditing

In this phase, you establish robust processes and metrics to test, validate, monitor, and audit FMs to ensure they align with business goals and ethical standards. Given the risk of hallucinations, where models generate false but seemingly accurate content, your continuous evaluation and updates are essential to enhance the accuracy of an FM and adapt to changing requirements.

The key evaluation metrics you'll use in this phase extend beyond traditional accuracy to include robustness (handling input variations), bias and fairness (avoiding demographic disadvantages), toxicity (minimizing harmful content), efficiency (response speed and computational resource use), and the Helpful, Honest, Harmless (HHH) metric for ethical AI use. Regular audits and refinements are vital to ensure that the GenAI application you build delivers reliable, safe, and business-aligned outcomes, fostering trust and sustaining performance. We cover some of the techniques to reduce hallucinations in Chapter 4.

3.2.6 Application and Orchestration Layer Development

After selecting the FM, the next step is building an application layer for interacting with user inputs, data, and the FM, along with an orchestration layer for integrating the model into existing systems. This involves creating APIs, connectors, or interfaces to enable seamless system interactions and user-friendly interfaces for end users and staff.

In this phase, you optimize the customized model for inference, integrate it into workflows, and prepare it for production deployment. Key objectives of this phase include ensuring scalability, reliability, and smooth operational embedding. Collaboration between data scientists, software engineers, and DevOps teams is essential for you to achieve a functional and efficient deployment that meets operational and user needs. We discuss all this in more detail in Chapter 4.

GenAI is constantly evolving, the new Agentic AI is an artificial intelligence (AI) in its current state that can perform tasks independently, learn, and adapt to new situations. AI agents work together to achieve goals without constant human intervention. Agentic AI, with its autonomous decision-making and adaptability, will revolutionize the financial industry by enhancing trading strategies, risk management, and personalized financial services.

3.2.7 Compliance

Compliance in the GenAI life cycle within financial services requires careful attention to regulatory requirements, risk management, and governance frameworks throughout the AI system's development and deployment. Financial institutions must ensure their AI models adhere to industry-specific regulations such as the GDPR, MiFID II, and Basel frameworks, while also maintaining data privacy, security, and fairness standards. Key compliance considerations include model validation, bias detection, data lineage tracking, and maintaining clear audit trails of model decisions. Organizations need to implement robust documentation practices, regular model monitoring, and validation processes to demonstrate regulatory compliance and responsible AI usage. This includes establishing clear roles and responsibilities for AI governance, implementing strong access controls, and ensuring transparency in how AI systems make decisions that impact financial operations and customer interactions.

3.2.8 Production Deployment

If the initial outcomes are satisfactory, plan for production deployment of the GenAI application. Note that you would have to consider a number of factors, including performance, scalability, availability, disaster recovery, and so on, as well as consider costs and trade-offs with these factors. Each of these factors have a great impact on the end user experience. We cover these in more detail in Chapter 9.

3.2.9 Continuous Monitoring, Auditing, and Fine-Tuning

Once the GenAI application is deployed into production, it's critical to continuously monitor and audit the application to ensure that it's meeting the mission outcomes. It's also important to ensure that the application is operating in compliance with federal regulations. If there is any deviation or drift, the application and/or the FMs will need to be adjusted.

The GenAI life cycle captures important steps in implementing GenAI solutions. However, it is critical to keep in mind that responsible AI practices should be adopted throughout the life cycle. Practicing *responsible AI* use includes minimizing bias, improving transparency, accountability, and fairness. Responsible AI also includes contemplating and mitigating the ethical concerns that are part of its development, deployment, and impact on the customers and society. We shall talk about this in more detail later in this chapter.

3.3 GenAI Risks and Challenges Within FSS

In this section we outline the specific risks and challenges with GenAI within the FSS. Note that in order for a successful GenAI implementation and rollout, these risks have to be proactively managed.

3.3.1 Data and Model Bias

Data bias is one of the most significant challenges when deploying GenAI in financial services. Bias arises when the datasets used to train AI models are unrepresentative, incomplete, or reflect historical prejudices. For FSOs, data bias can lead to unfair outcomes, damage customer trust, and expose the organization to regulatory and reputational risks. Left unaddressed, biased AI systems can perpetuate inequities in areas such as credit scoring, loan approvals, and customer service interactions.

Consider the case of an AI-driven loan approval system. If the training data reflects historical patterns of discrimination against certain demographics, the model may inadvertently replicate those biases, leading to unfair rejections of loan applications from minority groups. In 2019, a widely publicized example involved Apple's credit card algorithm, which was accused of offering women lower credit limits than men, even when their financial profiles were similar.[4] Such incidents underscore the need for rigorous bias detection and mitigation strategies.

Another example lies in AI-powered fraud detection systems. If the data used to train these models disproportionately flags certain geographic regions or ethnic groups, it could result in a higher rate of false positives for specific populations. This not only impacts customer experience but also raises ethical and regulatory concerns. Some FSOs, including Mastercard, have taken proactive steps to address data bias by adopting fairness toolkits and conducting regular audits of their AI systems to ensure equitable outcomes.[5]

To mitigate data bias, financial institutions must prioritize diverse and representative datasets, implement fairness audits, and leverage explainability tools to identify and address potential bias in AI models. These efforts are not just technical imperatives but also critical to ensuring that GenAI aligns with the organization's values and commitment to ethical practices.

3.3.2 Data Privacy and Security

Data privacy and security are critical concerns in the deployment of GenAI within FSS. Given the sector's reliance on sensitive customer and transactional data, any breach or misuse can lead to severe legal, financial, and reputational consequences. The top

[4] https://www.bbc.com/news/business-50365609

[5] https://www.mastercard.us/en-us/vision/corp-responsibility/data-responsibility.html

five data breaches of 2023 resulted in the exposure of tens of millions of customers and proved expensive for the FSOs.[6]

GenAI systems, which often require vast amounts of data for training and operations, introduce unique challenges in safeguarding privacy and ensuring robust security. These challenges include unauthorized data access, inadvertent exposure of personal information, and vulnerabilities in AI models that could be exploited by malicious actors.

A notable example of data privacy concerns emerged with OpenAI's ChatGPT. Early versions of the system raised alarms when users discovered that sensitive customer data entered into the system could potentially be stored or inadvertently used to improve future model iterations. In financial services, AI-based customer interaction tools must ensure that confidential financial data shared during conversations is not exposed or reused without consent.

To address these challenges, financial institutions must adopt privacy-by-design principles, embedding safeguards into every phase of GenAI development and deployment. Measures such as anonymization, differential privacy, and stringent access controls should be complemented by regular audits and compliance with global standards such as GDPR and CCPA. By prioritizing data privacy and security, organizations can harness the power of GenAI while maintaining trust and adhering to regulatory mandates.

3.3.3 Content Safety: Misinformation and Disinformation

GenAI's ability to produce realistic, high-quality content brings with it the significant challenge of misinformation and disinformation. For financial services, this risk is particularly acute, as false or manipulated content can erode trust, disrupt markets, and lead to regulatory scrutiny. Misinformation refers to false information shared without malicious intent, while disinformation involves deliberate efforts to mislead or deceive. Both pose substantial risks when GenAI models are misused to create fake reports, fabricated customer communications, or misleading market analysis.

One real-world example is the rise of deepfake technology, where AI-generated content convincingly mimics real individuals. In 2020, cybercriminals used deepfake audio to impersonate a bank executive, successfully directing a financial transaction

[6] https://www.metomic.io/resource-centre/the-biggest-financial-data-breaches-in-2023

worth millions.[7] To mitigate these risks, financial institutions must implement robust content safety mechanisms. This includes deploying AI models that detect and filter malicious content, monitoring for deep fake or misleading media, and educating stakeholders about emerging threats. Furthermore, FSOs should establish clear policies and collaborate with regulators to define ethical boundaries for AI usage. By addressing misinformation and disinformation proactively, financial services firms can protect their reputation, safeguard customers, and maintain the integrity of the financial ecosystem.

3.3.4 Lack of Transparency and Explainability

One of the most pressing challenges in deploying GenAI within FSS is the lack of transparency and explainability of models and decisions. Many GenAI models, particularly those built on deep learning architectures, operate as "black boxes," producing results without clear insight into how decisions are made. This poses significant risks for FSOs, where trust, regulatory compliance, and ethical accountability are paramount. If stakeholders cannot understand the rationale behind AI-generated outputs, it becomes difficult to justify decisions to regulators, customers, and internal teams.

A notable example is the use of AI in credit risk assessments. When a GenAI model denies a loan application, explaining the reasoning behind that decision is essential to comply with regulations such as the Equal Credit Opportunity Act (ECOA). In 2021, a fintech company faced criticism when it was unable to adequately explain discrepancies in credit decisions for customers with similar financial profiles. Another instance involves algorithmic trading systems. Lack of explainability in AI-driven trades has led to regulatory scrutiny, as seen in cases where market manipulations occurred without clear accountability for the underlying logic.

To address these challenges, financial institutions must prioritize building explainable AI systems. This includes integrating tools such as SHapley Additive exPlanations (SHAP) or Local Interpretable Model-Agnostic Explanations (LIME) to provide transparency into model behavior. Additionally, organizations should adopt AI governance frameworks that mandate periodic audits, clear documentation, and mechanisms for human oversight. By focusing on explainability, FSOs can ensure regulatory compliance, foster trust among stakeholders, and minimize risks associated with opaque decision-making.

---

[7] https://business.bofa.com/en-us/content/cyber-security-journal/deepfakes-business-risks.html

3.3.5 Social and Economic Impact

The deployment of GenAI in financial services carries significant social and economic implications. While the technology promises efficiency, personalization, and cost reduction, it also introduces risks such as job displacement, increased inequality, and unintended societal consequences. Financial institutions must navigate these challenges carefully to ensure that the benefits of GenAI do not come at the expense of broader social well-being.

A real-world example of this impact is the automation of customer service roles through AI-powered chatbots. While these tools enhance efficiency and reduce operational costs, they may lead to job losses in traditional customer support roles. Another example is the potential for GenAI to exacerbate financial exclusion. If AI models are trained on biased datasets or prioritize profitability over fairness, they may deny loans or financial services to underserved communities, deepening economic disparities.

To address these challenges, FSOs must adopt a responsible approach to AI implementation. This includes investing in workforce reskilling programs, fostering an inclusive AI design process, and conducting social impact assessments before deploying new technologies. Collaborating with regulators and community stakeholders can further help align AI initiatives with societal goals. By considering both the social and economic ramifications, FSOs can leverage GenAI as a force for positive transformation while minimizing potential harms.

3.3.6 Legal, Copyright, and Liability Challenges

The adoption of GenAI in FSS introduces a complex web of legal, copyright, and liability challenges. These issues stem from the innovative yet unpredictable nature of AI-generated content, as well as the ambiguity in current legal frameworks. FSOs must navigate these challenges to avoid regulatory penalties, lawsuits, and reputational damage while ensuring compliance and accountability.

One major concern is the potential for copyright infringement. GenAI models, trained on vast amounts of publicly available data, may inadvertently produce content that replicates copyrighted material. In the FSS, these risks could emerge if AI tools generate market analysis or marketing content that mirrors proprietary insights from competitors.

Liability is another critical area of concern. When a GenAI system makes an erroneous recommendation such as advising a high-risk investment to a client, determining who is responsible for the resulting financial loss can be challenging.

For example, an AI-powered wealth management platform faced scrutiny when its algorithmic predictions led to significant client losses during market volatility, raising questions about the accountability of developers, users, and the organization deploying the AI.

To mitigate these risks, financial institutions should establish clear legal frameworks for AI usage, including licensing agreements for training data and robust intellectual property checks. Additionally, implementing AI governance structures to define accountability, coupled with proactive engagement with regulators to align AI practices with evolving legal standards, can help organizations manage these challenges effectively. By addressing these legal, copyright, and liability concerns, financial firms can responsibly integrate GenAI into their operations while safeguarding their reputation and compliance.

3.3.7 Challenges with People, Process, Technology, and Data

The successful implementation of GenAI in FSS hinges on the seamless alignment of people, processes, technology, and data. However, each of these pillars presents its own set of challenges, making integration a complex endeavor. Without addressing these issues holistically, organizations risk encountering roadblocks that can bring their AI initiatives to a screeching halt.

From a people perspective, a lack of AI literacy and resistance to change can hinder adoption. Employees may feel threatened by automation or lack the necessary skills to work alongside AI systems. Process challenges often arise when traditional workflows are not optimized for AI integration. FSOs with siloed operations or rigid legacy systems may struggle to adapt their processes to leverage AI-generated insights effectively.

Technology and data challenges also loom large. Legacy IT infrastructure often lacks the flexibility and scalability required to support advanced AI models. Additionally, inconsistent or poor-quality data can compromise the accuracy of AI outputs.

To overcome these challenges, financial institutions must invest in upskilling employees, fostering an AI-ready culture, and redesigning processes for AI compatibility. Modernizing IT infrastructure and implementing robust data governance frameworks are equally critical. By addressing the interconnected challenges across people, process, technology, and data, organizations can lay a strong foundation for successful GenAI adoption.

3.4 High-Level GenAI Implementation Framework

GenAI's innovative advancements have generated excitement across various sectors, particularly finance, although the finance industry is proceeding cautiously with its adoption and implementation. Building upon our discussion in Chapter 2 regarding the significant advantages of GenAI, we advocate for its adoption contingent on a proactive and thorough assessment and mitigation of associated risks and challenges. This directly addresses Maria's critical inquiries: How can organizations effectively navigate the potential risks and drawbacks inherent in GenAI implementation? What best practices should be prioritized? To provide a comprehensive response, we introduce a high-level framework for GenAI adoption. This framework is grounded in the four interconnected perspectives outlined in the preceding section: People, Process, Technology, and Data.

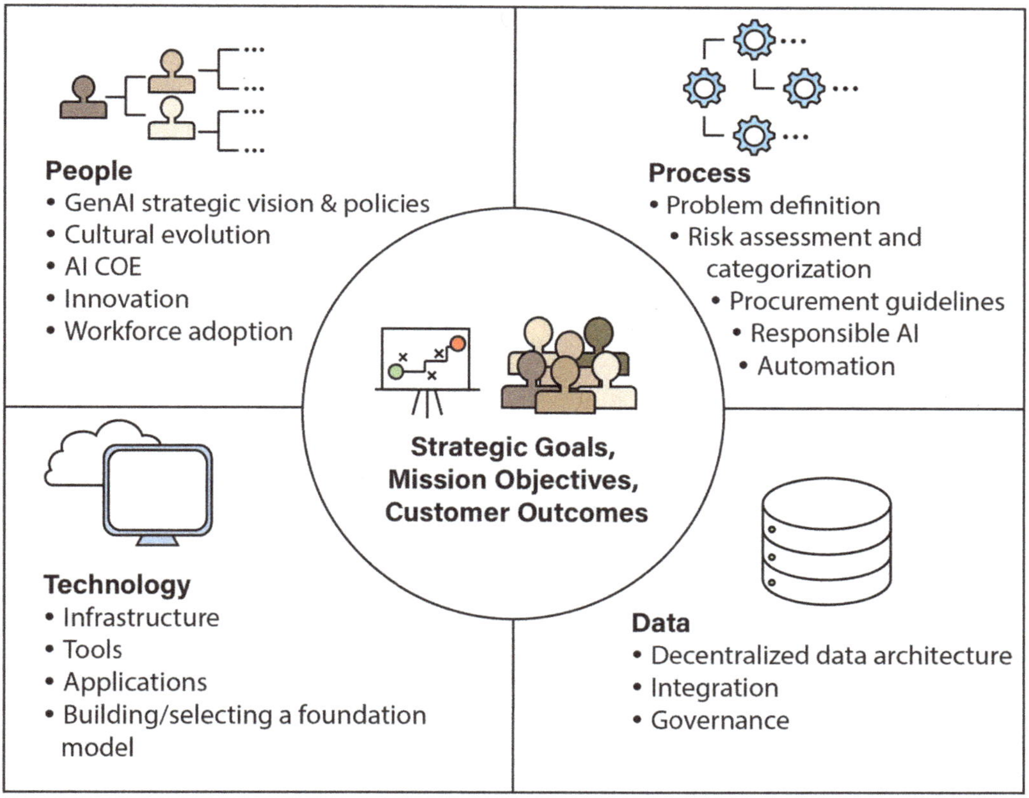

Figure 3-3. *Successful GenAI Adoption and Implementation: Four Perspectives*

As shown in Figure 3-3, the implementation of GenAI in FSOs requires a carefully orchestrated approach that balances innovation with risk management and regulatory compliance. At the core of our framework lie the strategic goals and objectives that drive desired outcomes for both the institution and its customers. Every perspective within this framework must align with these strategic imperatives while maintaining the highest standards of financial security and compliance.

3.4.1 Implementation from a People Perspective

Financial institutions need a strategic GenAI vision that explicitly addresses regulatory compliance and risk. For instance, a vision statement might read: "Enhance customer services and operational efficiency through GenAI while maintaining the highest standards of security, compliance, and risk management. Therefore, our framework outlines several actions to make the workforce more comfortable reacting to change within the FSO in adopting GenAI:

- Establish the strategic vision and policies for GenAI.
- Establish a path for gradual culture evolution toward GenAI.
- Establish AI Centers of Excellence (ACOEs).
- Establish a culture of innovation.
- Identify the right workforce.
- Enable the workforce to adopt GenAI.
- Data privacy and protection frameworks aligned with GDPR, CCPA, and other relevant regulations.
- Utilize the model risk management policies in alignment with Federal Reserve SR 11-7 guidelines.[8]
- Establish clear protocols for AI governance and model validation.

Now, we can clearly see how having an overall strategy helps with GenAI adoption. The blueprint we mentioned earlier will enable FSOs to address several of these points. Let's go into more detail about each of these.

[8] https://www.federalreserve.gov/supervisionreg/srletters/sr1107.htm

3.4.1.1 Establish the Strategic Vision and Policies for GenAI

Setting a strategic vision for GenAI and communicating that vision with key stakeholders in the organization will go a long way in setting up a successful GenAI journey. For example, let's say the FSO leadership settles on a vision that says "*Enhance customer support where feasible using GenAI in a risk-averse manner.*" This vision provides the overarching scope within which GenAI must operate and sets the tone for implementation.

The vision also guides the development of policies that help govern the measured rollout of GenAI. For example, a policy aligning with the above strategic vision could be "*GenAI solutions shall be implemented with clear human oversight and control to ensure responsible decision-making.*" Once the policies are laid out, each individual department or operating division can include goals and objectives that are outcome-driven. These outcomes are related to customer services and experience, staff efficiency and cost savings, and/or digital transformation. These goals align with the FSO's mission and have specific metrics or objective key results (OKRs) with a feedback loop to measure the success of GenAI initiatives.

3.4.1.2 Establish a Path for Gradual Culture Evolution Toward GenAI

How do you overcome the resistance to change when adopting new technologies, especially to mitigate the fear of job displacement or loss? The FSO leadership can create a culture of continuous evolution in which the workforce is comfortable with the transformational changes to improve the quality of customer services. The leadership can achieve adoption of this culture by clearly communicating the vision by leading with the value of this transformation to the mission. The leadership can help articulate the benefits of GenAI and that it is there to help improve productivity rather than replace the workforce.

3.4.1.3 Establish AI Centers of Excellence (AICOEs)

As mentioned earlier, buy-in from key stakeholders within the organization is essential to successfully adopt GenAI. One of the best ways to achieve this objective is to establish an AICOE. This entity should have stakeholders and senior leadership representation from various teams (business, technology, finance, risk, legal, contracts, HR, and so on) to drive GenAI adoption and implementation within the organization. The AICOE sets the roadmap for GenAI within the organization, including prioritizing use cases, establishing governance, model risk management, ensuring ethical AI implementation, and providing architecture best practices.

3.4.1.4 Establish a Culture of Innovation

FSOs often lag in adopting new technologies due to the industry's stringent regulatory and compliance requirements. However, leaders can cultivate a culture of innovation by prioritizing customer-centric solutions and by addressing critical challenges such as risk management, compliance complexities, and operational inefficiencies. Leveraging cutting-edge technologies, including GenAI, empowers organizations to tackle these issues effectively. True innovation lies in delivering tangible value to customers and stakeholders. A key strategy involves embracing a mindset of experimentation, where teams iterate rapidly and learn from failures. By using cloud-based services, FSOs can innovate flexibly and cost-effectively, avoiding substantial up-front investments while accelerating transformation.

3.4.1.5 Identify the Right Workforce

GenAI adoption and implementation requires a variety of teams and personas with wide-ranging skills. Depending on your adoption and implementation patterns, including build or buy and customize or fine-tune models, you need to consider the right team composition. The team includes personas to architect, design, develop, evaluate, and manage the GenAI applications. Table 3-1 shows the typical roles and responsibilities of these personas (Note: we do not include resources required for training FMs.)

Table 3-1. *GenAI Team Roles and Responsibilities*

Role	Responsibilities
Chief Information Officer (CIO)	Strategic leadership: identify public sector needs where GenAI can improve efficiency, personalize services, or automate tasks. Develop a strategy/roadmap for implementation and scaling GenAI within the organization.
IT Director	Technical implementation: oversee platform build for deploying and managing GenAI models. Responsible for platform security, scalability, and accessibility.
GenAI Architect	Design and optimize the overall architecture of the GenAI application, ensuring scalability, performance, and integration with existing systems.
Model Risk Officer	GenAI Model Risk Officer (MRO): responsible for ensuring that AI models are developed, implemented, and maintained in compliance with ethical, legal, and operational standards while mitigating risks related to accuracy, bias, security, and misuse.
Prompt Engineer	Design and optimize prompts that guide FMs toward desired outputs. Build a library of predefined prompts, collaborate on user interfaces for effective prompt input, and work alongside data scientists and engineers to continuously refine prompts to ensure the GenAI application delivers the best possible results.
Data Scientist	Data and model management: evaluate FMs based on the use case and organization. Ensure data quality and security for fine-tuning and running GenAI models. Establish data governance policies and ensure compliance with regulations.
ML Engineer	Model development: use advanced machine learning techniques to fine-tune GenAI models. Collaborate with cross-functional teams to prepare data for model fine-tuning. Research and implement cutting-edge algorithms and architectures.
Policy Analyst/ Ethics Specialist	Governance and oversight: mitigate potential risks associated with GenAI, such as bias, misinformation, and security vulnerabilities. Implement robust monitoring and control mechanisms. Address ethical considerations such as fairness, transparency, and accountability.

(*continued*)

Table 3-1. (*continued*)

Role	Responsibilities
Program/Project Manager	Collaboration and change management: facilitate collaboration between IT teams and other departments for successful adoption of GenAI solutions. Develop and implement training programs. Address workforce concerns and facilitate adaptation to new workflows.
Data engineer	Responsible for data engineering tasks, including building and managing data pipelines for GenAI training and inference.
Full stack developer	Responsible for developing the UI/UX, application orchestration, and database integration.
DevOps Engineers	Responsible for provisioning and managing deployments and operations of GenAI application, infrastructure, and related services.
Auditors	Independent assessment of GenAI models and audit of GenAI responses.
Security Specialist	Responsible for ensuring that the GenAI applications adhere to the federal, state, and local security policies and other relevant regulations.

3.4.1.6 Enable the Workforce to Adopt GenAI

Workforce enablement, education, and transformation are critical for the success of GenAI initiatives. These include training the workforce on GenAI technologies and tools, educating them on the strengths and weaknesses of GenAI, risks, and mitigation strategies, and encouraging the workforce to innovate to fulfill the mission requirements. As part of this effort, FSOs can develop comprehensive training programs by partnering up with cloud and/or GenAI service providers.

3.4.2 Implementation from a Process Perspective in Finance and Banking

Establishing standardized processes is essential for addressing the unique challenges and risks of implementing GenAI in the finance and banking sector. Next, we explore the critical considerations for success.

3.4.2.1 Problem Definition and Benefits

The foundational step in implementing GenAI is to clearly define the problem or opportunity at hand. In the finance industry, this could involve automating customer support, enhancing fraud detection, or optimizing risk assessments. It's crucial to scope out the opportunity in detail, identifying realistic goals, measurable benefits, and success metrics that align with organizational objectives. For example, improving loan application processing time or enhancing investment recommendations can be defined as specific, actionable goals. Allow for iterative development by focusing on defining the problem and solution space, enabling flexibility to refine approaches and adapt to evolving business needs.

3.4.2.2 Risk Assessment and Categorization

Financial institutions must assess and categorize risks associated with deploying GenAI. Start with lower-risk applications, such as internal tools for compliance reporting or customer segmentation, to demonstrate tangible benefits with minimal exposure. For instance, deploying an internal GenAI-powered chatbot for employee queries poses lower risks than an external chatbot handling sensitive customer data. Use insights from smaller-scale projects to refine risk frameworks and scale GenAI solutions responsibly to higher-impact areas such as credit scoring or anti-money laundering (AML) systems.

3.4.2.3 Procurement Guidelines

GenAI implementation in finance requires robust vendor evaluation and procurement strategies. Ensure potential vendors meet strict requirements for data security, regulatory compliance, and model interpretability. Vendors should articulate their commitment to responsible AI principles and provide continuous support for risk mitigation. Implement ongoing knowledge transfer processes to empower internal teams with the necessary skills to maintain and enhance AI systems, thereby reducing long-term vendor dependency.

3.4.2.4 Responsible AI in Finance

Responsible AI refers to the ethical and compliant use of AI technologies, a critical consideration in highly regulated industries, including banking. Implementing Responsible AI involves

- **Ethical and Regulatory Compliance**: Align AI use with industry regulations such as Basel guidelines, GDPR, and region-specific laws such as the Dodd-Frank Act. For example, consider the White House Executive Order on AI[9] released in October of 2023. This executive order required state agencies to develop plans for the responsible use of all AI, including GenAI. Develop clear policies to restrict AI use in areas where decisions could disproportionately impact customers' financial rights or data privacy.
- **Error Handling and Transparency**: Establish robust monitoring mechanisms to ensure AI models perform reliably. For instance, continuously monitor credit decision systems for bias and inaccuracies. Clearly communicate to users when GenAI is involved in decision-making, and provide mechanisms for feedback and error reporting.
- **Bias and Fairness Detection**: Address data and algorithmic biases to prevent discriminatory outcomes, such as unequal loan approvals. Use model cards to evaluate AI systems under diverse conditions and ensure fairness in decision-making processes.
- **Content Filtering and Guardrails**: Implement input and output guardrails to prevent misuse, such as financial fraud or manipulation of trading algorithms. Use encryption to secure interactions with GenAI systems and conduct red-teaming exercises to identify vulnerabilities proactively.

3.4.2.5 Process Automation

Automation plays a critical role in managing GenAI risks in finance. Deploy automated systems to flag anomalies in transaction data, detect potentially fraudulent activity, and ensure compliance with financial regulations. Automated validation can streamline tasks such as model performance checks and audit trail generation. While automation enhances efficiency, it must be paired with human oversight to handle complex cases requiring contextual understanding.

[9] https://www.whitehouse.gov/briefing-room/presidential-actions/2023/10/30/executive-order-on-the-safe-secure-and-trustworthy-development-and-use-of-artificial-intelligence/

By adopting these strategies, FSOs can responsibly harness the power of GenAI, driving innovation while maintaining trust, transparency, and regulatory compliance.

Developing standardized processes holds the key to solving many of the challenges and risks discussed earlier. Let's take a look at some important considerations.

3.4.3 Implementation from a Technology Perspective in Finance and Banking

In the financial and banking industries, implementing GenAI technologies necessitates a structured approach, balancing innovation with regulatory compliance, security, and efficiency. FSOs face unique considerations when evaluating and deploying FMs. This includes deciding whether to procure pretrained FMs, fine-tune them for specific use cases, or leverage out-of-the-box applications. Let's explore these considerations in detail.

3.4.3.1 Building an FM or Selecting a Pretrained FM

For FSOs, leveraging pretrained FMs such as Anthropic's Claude, Amazon's Titan, OpenAI's GPT models offers significant time and cost savings. Building an FM from scratch is typically reserved for cases requiring highly specialized, proprietary datasets not available publicly. However, fine-tuning pretrained FMs for specific financial applications such as fraud detection, credit scoring, or personalized customer recommendations can deliver high precision with lower resource investment.

When selecting a pretrained FM, FSOs should consider the following:

1. **Define Objectives Clearly**: Establish clear goals, such as enhancing customer service through AI-driven chatbots, optimizing risk assessment processes, or improving trading strategies with real-time analytics.

2. **Model Characteristics**: Evaluate attributes such as the context window size, number of parameters, and suitability for financial use cases. Larger context windows can help models process complex financial documents, ensuring accurate outputs.

3. **Performance Benchmarks**: Rely on benchmarks relevant to finance, such as the model's ability to analyze transaction data or generate financial reports accurately.

4. **Ethical Considerations and Bias**: Assess for biases in model training that might skew predictions, such as favoring certain demographics in credit scoring.
5. **Compliance and Security**: Ensure models adhere to stringent financial regulations, including GDPR, PCI DSS, or industry-specific mandates, including Basel III.
6. **Cost and Scalability**: Evaluate costs, including licensing, infrastructure, and maintenance, against potential ROI. Choose solutions that scale with growing data and user demands, particularly for real-time applications such as high-frequency trading.

3.4.3.2 Procuring a Pre-trained FM

FSOs can choose from the following options based on their business needs and technical expertise:

- **Open-Source Models**: Models such as Llama and Falcon offer transparency and control but require in-house expertise for deployment and fine-tuning. These models can be ideal for organizations prioritizing data security and customization.
- **Commercial Licenses**: Providers such as OpenAI or Anthropic offer robust pretrained models with licensing options and support, which can be valuable for FSOs with limited technical resources.
- **Cloud-Based Platforms**: Cloud providers such as AWS, Microsoft Azure, and Google Cloud offer subscription-based access to pretrained models, enabling rapid deployment and scalability. For FSOs, this reduces up-front infrastructure costs and allows access to cutting-edge technology.
- **Transparency and Data Security** are critical for FSOs. Open-source models allow for greater customization and audits, but commercial and cloud-based models often provide stronger guarantees for compliance with financial regulations.

3.4.3.3 Infrastructure Considerations

Deploying FMs for financial applications demands robust, scalable infrastructure optimized for machine learning workloads. FSOs must focus on

- **Low-Latency Processing**: Essential for real-time applications including fraud detection or trading algorithms.
- **Scalability**: Cloud-based platforms allow FSOs to scale infrastructure dynamically, accommodating growing transaction volumes or expanded AI capabilities.
- **Cost Optimization**: By leveraging cloud-native services, FSOs can avoid significant up-front investments in on-premises hardware while ensuring they stay updated with rapidly evolving GenAI technologies.

3.4.3.4 Tools for Building GenAI Applications

Developing financial GenAI applications often requires additional tools:

- **Vector Databases**: For managing embeddings and enhancing the RAG capabilities in financial queries.
- **Orchestrators**: To streamline workflows, enabling seamless integration of AI models into existing systems, including core banking platforms or customer relationship management (CRM) systems.

3.4.3.5 Financial Data Integration

Many cloud providers offer GenAI-ready integrations with databases tailored for financial analytics and reporting, ensuring compatibility with FMs.

3.4.3.6 Out-of-the-Box Applications

Pre-packaged GenAI solutions can provide FSOs with quick wins. For instance, Amazon Bedrock and AI-powered chatbots, including Amazon Lex or fraud detection systems built on cloud platforms, can significantly reduce time-to-market. However, these solutions must align with specific financial requirements and regulatory standards.

3.4.3.7 Conclusion

Implementing GenAI in finance and banking requires careful evaluation of technology options, infrastructure, and use cases. By leveraging pretrained FMs, cloud-based platforms, and specialized tools, FSOs can unlock transformative potential while adhering to the strict compliance and security demands of the industry.

3.4.4 Implementation from a Data Perspective in FSOs

In previous chapters, we examined implementation of best practices from the perspectives of people, process, and technology. However, one of the most critical and complex challenges in an FSO lies in implementation from a data perspective.

The concept of a "*data-driven organization*" has become indispensable in the finance and banking industry, where data is at the heart of every decision. As the adage goes, "*Data is the new oil.*" For FSOs, data fuels innovation, risk management, compliance, and customer-centric services. McKinsey estimates that data and analytics could unlock approximately $1 trillion annually across industries, including finance and banking.[10]

FSOs rely on data-driven decision-making for a wide range of critical activities, including

- Enhancing customer experience through personalized services
- Ensuring compliance with financial regulations such as Basel III, GDPR, and AML directives
- Conducting risk assessments for credit, market, and operational exposures
- Supporting fraud detection and prevention efforts
- Allocating resources and managing budgets effectively

[10] https://www.mckinsey.com/industries/public-sector/our-insights/accelerating-data-and-analytics-maturity-in-the-us-public-sector

3.4.4.1 Empowering Customers with Insights Through Data-Driven Platforms and Tools

Data is one of the most valuable assets for FSOs; losing decades-worth of customer, transactional, or risk data could have catastrophic consequences. Data also serves as the foundation for innovation, enabling transformative applications based on GenAI. However, leveraging GenAI effectively requires robust data management, as the saying "garbage in, garbage out" holds true. Whether deploying GenAI for customer service chatbots, summarizing financial reports, or generating investment insights, data must be accurate, complete, up-to-date, and accessible. For many FSOs, this represents a significant challenge due to the following complexities:

1. **Data Volumes and Types:** The financial sector generates vast quantities of structured and unstructured data. Transaction records, loan applications, risk models, compliance reports, and market data form just a fraction of the information managed daily. For instance, banks process petabytes of transactional and market data in real time to support trading and operational functions.

2. **Data Quality:** The diversity and volume of data make ensuring quality a major challenge. Issues such as duplicate entries, missing values, incorrect formats, and outdated records can hinder the effectiveness of GenAI models. Poor-quality data leads to biased or inaccurate outputs, impacting decision-making and customer trust.

3. **Data Security and Privacy:** Given the sensitivity of customer and financial data, FSOs must comply with stringent data security and privacy regulations. Balancing regulatory compliance with operational agility requires robust frameworks for data access, ownership, and accountability.

4. **Data Silos and Integration Challenges:** FSOs often operate with fragmented systems across departments, leading to data silos. These silos hinder seamless sharing and integration, limiting the ability to derive insights and deploy GenAI effectively. Traditional databases and inflexible data warehouses further compound the issue.

3.4.4.2 Preparing Data for GenAI Success

For FSOs to succeed with GenAI, focus on three key areas:

1. **Decentralized Data Architecture:** The traditional siloed approach to data management is incompatible with the agility required for GenAI. FSOs should adopt decentralized data architectures where data is treated as a product. Using frameworks, including data mesh, individual business units can own and share data across the organization while adhering to strict governance policies.

   In cases where data sharing is restricted by regulatory or privacy concerns, FSOs can leverage federated learning. This approach enables decentralized model training without moving sensitive data, maintaining compliance while fostering innovation.

2. **Data Integration:** A decentralized architecture requires seamless data integration. FSOs must invest in technologies that harmonize data from disparate sources and formats, such as real-time data connectors and Extract, Transform, Load (ETL) tools. These tools ensure data is accessible, consistent, and ready for GenAI applications such as fraud detection and customer sentiment analysis.

3. **Data Governance:** Effective data governance is essential to support GenAI initiatives in FSOs. A robust governance framework should define clear policies for data sourcing, usage, and protection. Key practices include

   - **Establishing Data Standards**: Define rules for data quality, consistency, and security.
   - **Ethical and Responsible Use**: Incorporate ethical principles to ensure data practices align with regulatory and societal expectations.

- **Technology Enablement:** Use AI-driven platforms to monitor data quality, detect anomalies, and enforce privacy compliance. Implement robust security measures, such as encryption and access control, to prevent unauthorized data usage.
- **Data Ownership**: Implement roles such as data steward and data custodian with responsibility of data ownership, quality, and security.

Beyond technology, cultivating a culture of data governance is critical. This involves educating employees, from executives to developers, about data privacy, ethical considerations, and their roles in maintaining data integrity. Open communication channels and regular audits help reinforce these principles, ensuring data governance evolves alongside the organization's needs.

By embracing these data strategies, FSOs can unlock the transformative potential of GenAI while safeguarding their operations and reputation. This approach ensures responsible, ethical, and sustainable innovation in an industry where data is both the greatest asset and the greatest responsibility.

3.5 Chapter Summary

Adopting GenAI within the financial services sector presents a distinct set of challenges and considerations spanning people, processes, technology, and data. However, by implementing a strategic and responsible approach, FSOs can unlock the transformative potential of GenAI to enhance customer experience, drive operational efficiencies, and strengthen risk management. A well-defined vision aligned with organizational objectives coupled with a culture of innovation and robust governance mechanisms is critical to ensuring ethical and effective AI adoption. Establishing strong data strategies, investing in the right talent and infrastructure, and adhering to regulatory and compliance requirements are essential components of a successful GenAI implementation.

By leveraging the structured methodology and framework outlined in this chapter, FSOs can proactively address potential risks while ensuring responsible AI deployment. Continuous monitoring, iterative fine-tuning, and adherence to responsible AI principles will be imperative as the technology evolves. Given the dynamic nature of GenAI and its regulatory landscape, organizations must remain agile and adaptable, continuously reassessing their strategies to maintain a competitive edge.

The next chapter delves into the technical foundations of building GenAI applications, exploring core concepts such as prompt engineering, model optimization, and best practices for developing reliable and effective AI-driven solutions. A deeper understanding of these fundamentals will enable FSOs to implement GenAI-driven use cases that deliver tangible business value while maintaining compliance and governance standards.

CHAPTER 4

Architecting and Building a GenAI Application

In Chapter 3, we outlined a high-level GenAI strategy and blueprint, a methodology for implementation, and a framework to address various challenges that Financial Services Organizations (FSOs) face for GenAI adoption. In this chapter, we explore the key concepts of GenAI applications. Some of the concepts you'll learn are

- The anatomy of a prompt, which acts as the primary interface for communicating with GenAI applications and models.
- The art of prompt engineering, techniques to construct clear and effective prompts that guide FMs toward desired outputs.
- The concept of agents and how they can facilitate complex reasoning and multistep problem-solving.
- Various techniques to handle domain-specific data such as Retrieval Augmented Generation (RAG) and model fine-tuning.
- A generic application architecture for a GenAI application.

By the end of this chapter, you'll understand all the core concepts necessary for building a GenAI application in the financial services sector (FSS).

4.1 Anatomy of a Prompt

GenAI models, such as Large Language Models (LLMs), rely on prompts as their primary input mechanism. Well-crafted prompts determine the quality, relevance, and coherence of the AI's response. Understanding the anatomy of a prompt is crucial for optimizing model performance and obtaining desired outputs.

S. Godavarthi, R. Nagvekar, *Transforming Financial Services with Generative AI*,
https://doi.org/10.1007/979-8-8688-2053-3_4

Figure 4-1 depicts the basic interaction of a user with a Foundation Model (FM).

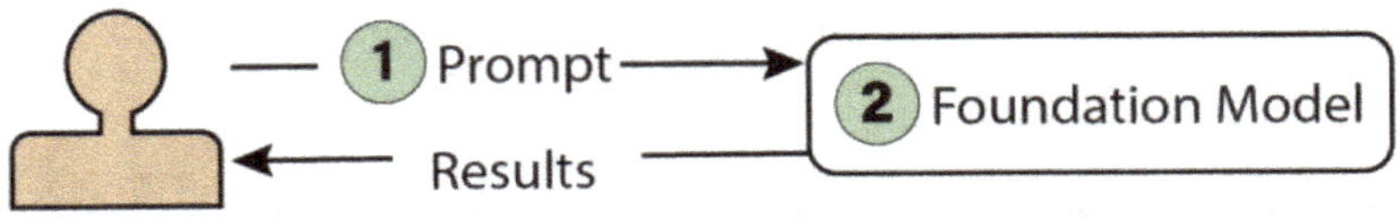

Figure 4-1. *Basic Request to a Foundation Model*

In Figure 4-1, the user makes a request to an FM and the FM provides a response. This request is the *prompt*. As in a conversation with a human, the clearer you are, the better the results you get back. For AI, the format of the prompt is crucial. We illustrate the general anatomy of a prompt in Figure 4-2.

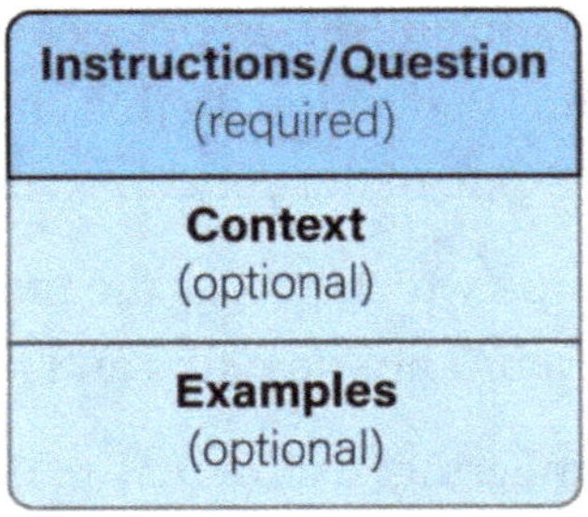

Figure 4-2. *The Anatomy of a Prompt*

You can break down a prompt into three broad sections as shown in Figure 4-2:

1. **Instructions or Question**: This is text that tells the model what you want to do.

2. **Context**: The *context* is additional information that helps guide the model toward a more comprehensive understanding of the task and its nuances. While not always required, *context* can significantly enhance the accuracy and relevance of the model's output.

Providing background information helps the model understand the request in the right frame of reference. Context can include relevant details, prior conversation history, or domain-specific knowledge.

Example context: *"In the context of financial services, explain how AI can improve fraud detection."*

3. **Examples**: Provide examples of similar tasks to get the model to answer a question with a better result. Again, this is not required but can be very helpful for complex scenarios.

The total length of the prompt, including instructions, context, and examples, can vary from model to model and even within a model. Some models may require additional mandatory components or words. For example, Anthropic Claude requires you to open the prompt by using the key word `Human`.

Note It is important to keep in mind that the format of a prompt is not fixed.

This format is simply a guideline; for example, you can add other things such as the role you want the FM to assume and the expected output format.

Let's say you are using the FM to write a contract. You can ask the FM to assume the role of a contract writer for developing a contract. If you are trying to use the FM to explain a complex concept, you might ask the FM to assume the role of a teacher to explain a concept to a student.

Given the wide range of possibilities in constructing a prompt and its critical nature in determining the output from a model, an entirely new field has emerged called Prompt Engineering.

4.2 Prompt Engineering

Prompt engineering is the process of writing instructions for AI models in order to produce your desired outputs. It's an iterative and creative process in which you choose words, phrases, and formats to the model to respond in a meaningful way.

There are several different types of prompt engineering techniques and formats that you can use to write prompts: zero-shot learning, few-shot learning, chain-of-thought prompting, prompt chaining, prompt templates, and reasoning and acting (ReAct). We'll dive into each of these techniques in this section.

4.2.1 Zero-Shot Learning

Zero-shot prompting, or zero-shot learning, is when a model performs a task without prior examples or specific preparation; it relies entirely on its language understanding to generate responses. This technique allows the model to handle tasks using general knowledge rather than needing task-specific training.

Prompt:

```
Instruction: Write a social media post summarizing a new cash reward
credit card.
Context: NA
Examples: NA
```

Output:

```
Earn unlimited cashback on every purchase, with bonus rewards on dining,
travel, and groceries! Plus, enjoy a welcome bonus when you sign up and
make your first purchase. No annual fees, flexible redemption options, and
24/7 fraud protection because your money should work for you!
Ready to maximize your rewards? Apply today!
```

Zero-shot learning is especially useful when you want the model to be creative and respond with new ideas.

4.2.2 Few-Shot Learning

This technique provides a small number of examples to the LLM, allowing it to learn from those examples and generalize to new instances. If you provide one example, it is called one-shot, two examples two-shot and so on. The example in the following prompt is two-shot.

Prompt:

```
Instruction: Create a concise reminder about credit card bill late pay.
Context: Focus on reminding people to avoid late fees and penalties.
Examples:
Input: Always pay credit card bills before the due date.
```

Output: `Reminder: Pay your credit card bill on time to avoid late fees and penalties! Set up autopay or reminders to stay on track.`
Input: `Check your credit card statement balance before every month due date.`
Output: `Reminder: Always check your credit card statement balance before the due date to avoid surprises and late fees! Stay on top of your finances.`

By giving specific examples, you help the model provide more accurate answers and reduce the likelihood for *hallucinations*, which are incorrect or misleading results. These results can be caused by a variety of things, including insufficient training data, incorrect assumptions made by the model, or biases in the data used to train the model.

4.2.3 Chain-of-Thought Prompting

Chain-of-thought prompting encourages the model to break a complex problem down into smaller steps and provide its thought process by giving it a few examples. Let's see how this works for a portfolio manager trying to manage a customer's investment:

Prompt:
Instruction: `Solve the following financial problem by breaking it down into steps and showing your work.`
Context: `A financial advisor is managing $100,000 in client funds. Each investment option requires a minimum of $20,000. How many different investments can the advisor make with the available funds?`

Examples:
Question: `"A portfolio manager has $60,000 and each stock purchase requires $15,000. How many different stocks can they buy with $60,000?"`

Answer:

```
We are given that the portfolio manager has $60,000.
Each stock purchase requires $15,000.
To find the number of stocks they can buy, we divide the total amount of
funds by the cost per stock: 60,000÷15,000=4.
Therefore, the portfolio manager can buy 4 different stocks with $60,000.
```

Output:

```
To solve this problem, we need to follow these steps:
```

- `The financial advisor is managing $100,000 in client funds.`
- `Each investment option requires a minimum of $20,000.`
- `To find the number of different investments the advisor can make, we divide the total amount of funds by the minimum required per investment: 100,000÷20,000=5`

  `Therefore, the advisor can make 5 different investments with $100,000.`

As you can see from the output, using this method allows you to provide clear guidance to the LLM and makes it easier for you to understand and verify the reasoning of the output.

4.2.4 Prompt Chaining

Prompt chaining involves breaking down a complex task into smaller subtasks and using the output of one subtask as the input for the next subtask, effectively chaining multiple prompts together.

Prompt 1:

```
Instruction: Identify the key details from a customer's complaint about a
fraudulent transaction.
Context: The customer reported an unauthorized charge on their credit card.
```

Output 1:

```
Unauthorized charge reported on credit card ending in [last four digits].
```

Prompt 2 (using Prompt 1 output):

```
Instruction: Draft a short message acknowledging the complaint and
outlining the next steps.
Context: The customer is concerned about security and wants a quick
resolution.
```

Output 2:

```
Thank you for reporting the unauthorized charge on your credit card ending
in [last four digits]. Your account's security is our top priority. We have
temporarily suspended the card to prevent further charges. Our fraud team
is investigating, and you will receive an update within 24 hours. If you
need immediate assistance, please contact our support team.
```

4.2.5 Prompt Templates

Prompt templates are a mechanism that allows you to standardize the prompt language while changing the inputs. This allows you to reduce the overhead of creating new prompts for each task especially if the task is repetitive only with a few changes that include different variables.

Let's say you want the LLM to generate biographies of a number of different innovators in financial services. You can create the following prompt template:

Prompt Template:

```
Instruction: Create a profile for the given financial services innovator.
Context:
```

- **Name:** `{Innovator}`
- **Lived:** `{Dates}`
- **Known for:** `{Major Contributions}`
- **Interesting Fact:** `{Key Information}`

You provide the model with the template and the name of the financial innovator, let's say **Amadeo Giannini**. The model recognizes the template as a structure to follow. It fills in the blanks with information about Amadeo Giannini as follows:

- **Name:** `Amadeo Giannini`
- **Lived:** `1870 - 1949`
- **Known for:** `Founding Bank of America and pioneering modern banking for the middle class.`

- **Interesting Fact:** `Provided loans to rebuild San Francisco immediately after the 1906 earthquake, carrying money on a wagon to help residents.`

Output:

```
Amadeo Giannini (1870 - 1949) was an American banker and founder of Bank of
America, which became one of the largest banks in the world. He is known
for revolutionizing the banking industry by making financial services
accessible to the middle class, breaking away from the norm of only serving
the wealthy
```

Notice that the details from the template are used to create a coherent and informative narrative. When you feed in the names of people, the model will create biographies that contain this information, ensuring consistency between outputs. Another benefit is that you don't need to create each prompt multiple times.

4.2.6 ReAct

The ReAct framework, described in the paper "ReAct: Synergizing Reasoning and Acting in Language Models" (Shunyu et al., 2022),[1] extends the chain-of-thought approach you learned about earlier. The core idea is to simulate human-like problem-solving by interspersing the reasoning steps with actions that gather additional information. Let's see how this works.

Similar to the chain-of-thought approach, you provide an LLM with a prompt that includes several examples. However, the format of the example is provided as follows:

Prompt:

```
Instruction: The instruction or question for the LLM
Context: relevant context if needed
Examples: Several examples of the task presented in the following manner:
Example1:
Instruction or Question: The instruction or question for the LLM
Action: A specific action the LLM can take to gather information (e.g.,
"Search the web for...").
```

[1] `https://arxiv.org/abs/2210.03629`

```
Observation: The expected outcome or information gained from the action.
Thought Process: Steps the LLM should consider while taking the action
(e.g., "Consider the context of the question...").
Example2:
Instruction or Question: The instruction or question for the LLM
Action: A specific action the LLM can take to gather information (e.g.,
"Search the web for...").
Observation: The expected outcome or information gained from the action.
Thought Process: Steps the LLM should consider while taking the action
(e.g., "Consider the context of the question...").
```

When this prompt is passed to the LLM, the LLM uses examples as the guide to accomplish the required task. This is especially useful when there are a number of different options that the LLM can consider to answer a question and to determine which option to choose. We explore this technique in the next section, agents.

4.3 Best Practices for Constructing Prompts

The methods discussed so far in this chapter are just a few examples of prompt engineering techniques for LLMs; there are many more variations and combinations that can be explored to improve the performance and capabilities of language models. Prompt engineering for text-to-image models is different from text-to-text and uses slightly different techniques, including negative prompts. We'll explore this in more detail in Chapter 5.

The goal of prompt engineering is always the same: guide the LLM to yield the desired results. The effectiveness of each technique greatly depends on the specific model and the task. You can also combine multiple techniques to achieve optimal results.

We discussed various techniques for creating prompts; however, in order to be effective, you also need to know how to construct each prompt, regardless of the technique used. Let's look at a few guidelines with examples.

4.3.1 Clarity and Specificity

Be precise and clearly specify what you need from the model. Vague prompts may lead to vague or irrelevant responses. For example:

Vague Prompt:

```
Analyze trends in customer satisfaction.
```

Clear Prompt:

```
Analyze trends in customer satisfaction ratings for retail banking
operations in the past five years, and identify areas for improvement.
```

While more information can be helpful, overly long prompts may confuse the model. Strive for a balance when providing context and details. This helps the FM understand the nuances of the request.

4.3.2 Structured and Logical Format

Present your request in a logical, structured manner. Bullet points or numbered lists can help in complex queries. If your prompt involves multiple steps or concepts, present them in a logical sequence. For example:

Complex Prompt:

```
Research and write a report on the economic impact of the new federal
interest rate.
```

Structured Prompt:

```
Gather data on mortgage interest rates before and after the program
implementation.
Analyze the data to identify any correlation between mortgage interest
rates and economic indicators.
Write a report summarizing the findings and potential economic impact.
```

4.3.3 Consider FM Capabilities and Limitations

Consider the FM's capabilities and limitations, including model parameters such as temperature and context window, the ability to work with multiple languages, or the ability to work with both text as well as images. Here are a few examples:

Prompt:

```
Generate a social media post in Spanish promoting the new childcare
program.
```

This considers the model's ability to handle multiple languages.

Prompt:

```
Design a new website for the city government using this large dataset.
```

This prompt might exceed the model's capability for complex tasks.

4.3.4 Iterative Approach

Begin with a broader query and then refine it based on the FM's responses to zero in on your exact need. Use the responses to tweak your prompts, learning how changes in your query affect the output. For example:

Initial Prompt:

```
Provide a summary of recent traffic accidents in the city.
```

Refined Prompt (based on initial response):

```
Based on the previous summary, identify high-accident zones and suggest
potential safety measures.
```

4.3.5 Use Examples

Use few-shot prompting with specific examples for more complex ideas or desired outcomes. Example:

Prompt:

```
Write a press release announcing the launch of a credit card for small
businesses. Here's an example of a press release from last year... Adapt it
to the new program details.
```

4.3.6 Avoid Biases and Assumptions

Use unbiased, neutral language to avoid leading the FM toward potentially biased or incorrect outputs. Ensure your prompt does not inadvertently contain assumptions that could skew the response. For Example:

Biased Prompt:

```
Identify the best neighborhoods for young families to live in.
```

Note that this prompt assumes a specific definition of "best."

Neutral Prompt:

```
Analyze factors that influence families' choices of neighborhoods,
considering aspects such as education, housing costs, and amenities.
```

4.3.7 Creative Use of Prompts

You can instruct the FM to assume a certain role (for example, a tutor, a specific expert) to shape its responses. Frame your query in the context of a hypothetical scenario for more focused responses. Here is an example:

Prompt:

```
Assume the role of a financial advisor and write a budget plan for a single
parent on a low income.
```

4.3.8 Ethical Considerations

Craft prompts that encourage ethical and responsible use of AI. Avoid prompts that could lead to harmful, biased, or unethical outputs.

Unethical Prompt:

```
Write a social media post encouraging people to use a new facial
recognition technology for crime prevention, highlighting its effectiveness
without mentioning potential privacy concerns.
```

Ethical Prompt:

```
Write a balanced social media post introducing the new facial recognition
technology for crime prevention. Briefly explain its benefits and potential
drawbacks, such as privacy concerns. Encourage customers to learn more and
participate in a public forum to discuss its implementation.
```

By mastering the art of constructing prompts, you can significantly enhance the effectiveness and accuracy of FM model interactions. Experimentation is the key! As LLMs continue to evolve, so too will the art of prompt engineering. Try different methods and evaluate responses to see which method works best for which model and task.

4.4 Model Parameters and Configurations

Beyond crafting the prompt itself, various model parameters also heavily influence the output generated by an LLM. These parameters can differ across different LLMs. We briefly explored some of them in Chapter 1, but let's dive deeper.

4.4.1 Temperature: the Creativity Knob

Imagine temperature as a dial controlling the creativity of the LLM's output. A lower temperature setting prioritizes factual accuracy, making it ideal for tasks including

- **Financial Risk Communication:** When issuing public advisories about market instability or economic downturns, a low temperature (around 0.0) ensures clear and accurate information delivery.
- **Legal Document Summarization**: Summarizing complex legal documents for customers requires factual accuracy. A low temperature setting minimizes creative embellishments.

Conversely, a higher temperature (around 1.0) injects more randomness, leading to creative and surprising outputs. This might be useful for brainstorming public engagement initiatives; for example, a high temperature setting can help generate diverse ideas for engaging consumers in community discussions.

4.4.2 Top-k Sampling: Focusing the Output

Top-k sampling restricts the LLM's vocabulary choices during text generation. Consider only the `top k` most probable words at each step. Here's how k values can impact the output:

- **Lower k Value (e.g., k=10)**: When generating grant application summaries for policymakers, a lower k value ensures a focused and concise output, highlighting key points.
- **Higher k Value (e.g., k=50)**: When generating different policy options for a complex social issue, a higher k value allows the LLM to explore a wider range of possibilities, providing policymakers with diverse perspectives.

4.4.3 Top-p Sampling: Balancing Control and Exploration

Similar to top-k sampling, top-p sampling focuses on a specific probability range for selecting the next word. This technique considers only words with a cumulative probability falling within a certain threshold (top_p). Choosing between top-k and top-p depends on your specific needs:

- **Lower top_p Value (Around 0.6)**: Imagine generating customer feedback summaries. A lower top_p value prioritizes the most common themes in the feedback while allowing for some exploration of less frequent, but potentially valuable, insights.
- **Higher top_p Value (Around 0.9)**: When writing a press release about a new environmental regulation, a higher top_p value allows for some creative phrasing while still prioritizing clear and accurate bias communication of the regulation's purpose.

Remember, these configurations significantly impact the output. Consulting the LLM provider's documentation is crucial for optimal parameter settings.

4.5 LLM Evaluation

Evaluating LLMs is a foundational step in building reliable, secure, and efficient GenAI applications for financial services. As FSOs increasingly adopt GenAI, evaluating the performance, reliability, and efficiency of LLMs becomes critical. Effective evaluation ensures that LLM-driven applications align with business objectives, meet compliance requirements, and deliver optimal user experiences.

In this section, we'll explore the need for LLM evaluation, present a structured evaluation framework, discuss key benchmarks, and examine third-party leaderboards and specific evaluation metrics relevant to financial services.

4.5.1 The Need for LLM Evaluation

LLMs power a range of applications, from customer service chatbots to fraud detection and risk assessment applications. However, their effectiveness depends on various factors, including accuracy, bias mitigation, interpretability, and scalability. FSOs must rigorously evaluate LLMs to ensure

- **Regulatory Compliance**: Ensure adherence to financial regulations such as GDPR and SEC guidelines.
- **Accuracy and Reliability**: Mitigate risks by avoiding hallucinations and misinformation in AI-generated insights.
- **Bias and Fairness**: Detect and mitigate biases that could lead to unethical or non-compliant outcomes.
- **Security and Privacy**: Evaluate how well the model protects sensitive financial data.
- **Performance and Efficiency**: Ensure optimal response times and cost-effectiveness in high-frequency trading, fraud detection, and customer service applications.

- **Benchmark and Optimize**: Measure model performance against industry standards to ensure that the models and applications are meeting specific standards. In addition, optimize models for cost and performance trade-offs.

4.5.2 Framework for LLM Evaluation

Incorporating a structured evaluation framework provides a repeatable approach to assessing LLMs across various FSO use cases. The framework is depicted in Figure 4-3.

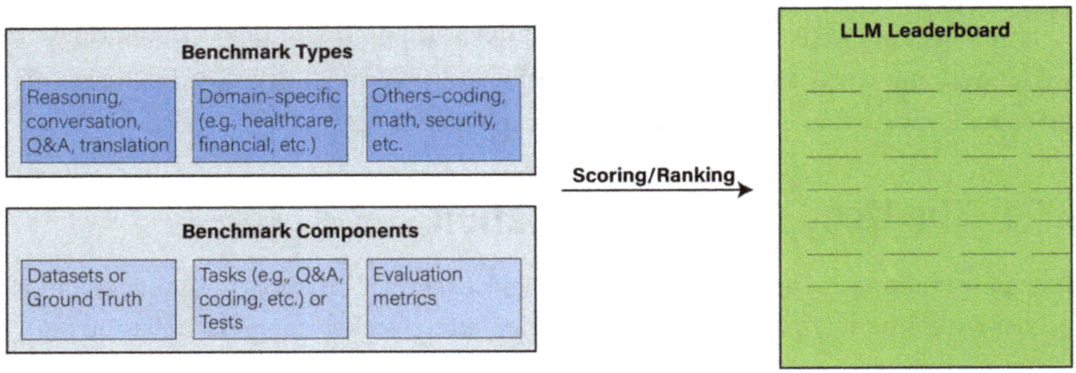

Figure 4-3. *LLM Evaluation Framework*

The framework consists of three key dimensions:

- **Benchmark Types**: There are benchmarks for a variety of tasks and domains, including Natural Language Processing (NLP) such as reasoning, conversation, Q&A, translation, chatbots, etc. In addition, these include domain-specific benchmarks for financial services, healthcare, and education, among others. Other types include coding, math problems, etc.
- **Benchmark Components**: The main constructs of these benchmarks include

  1) Data sets with ground truth. For example, if this is Q&A based, it includes a set of questions and the expected answer.

2) Tasks/Tests for each benchmark type.

3) Evaluation metrics for accuracy, bias, etc.

- **Leaderboards**: Using the evaluation metrics, the LLMs are evaluated on how the outputs or responses for certain tasks match against the ground truth provided in the datasets. For example, assessing how well a given model performs specific financial tasks such as risk assessment, portfolio optimization, or regulatory reporting. There could be a Human-in-the-Loop Validation as well in certain cases; for example, financial analysts and compliance experts charged with validating AI outputs. Other tests may include automated performance testing that measures latency, throughput, and efficiency in real-world conditions. Finally, the results are ranked or scored to publish the leaderboards.

4.5.3 Examples: LLM Evaluation Benchmarks

As we discussed earlier, standardized benchmarks provide quantitative insights into LLM performance. Some of the current industry benchmarks include

- **General Language Understanding Evaluation (GLUE)**: Tests NLP tasks such as sentiment analysis and text classification.
- **SuperGLUE**: An advanced benchmark for complex reasoning and natural language understanding.
- **Massive Multitask Language Understanding (MMLU)**: Evaluates knowledge across multiple domains, including finance.
- **Holistic Evaluation of Language Models (HELM)**: Assesses accuracy, bias, toxicity, and efficiency.
- **Financial NLP benchmarks**: Proprietary datasets focusing on financial text processing, such as Financial Question Answering (FiQA) and BloombergGPT's evaluation datasets. Other benchmarks derived from financial documents, risk reports, and regulatory filings.

4.5.4 Examples: Third-Party Leaderboards

Several organizations maintain leaderboards to track LLM performance across domains; some examples include

- **OpenAI Evals**: A platform for assessing the robustness and alignment of LLMs
- **Hugging Face Open LLM Leaderboard**: Ranks models based on multiple performance metrics
- **Stanford Center for Research on FMs (CRFM)**: Provides research-driven evaluations of LLMs
- **MLCommons**: Tracks efficiency and scaling of AI models

4.5.5 Key LLM Evaluation Metrics

FSOs should focus on domain-specific evaluation metrics, including

- **Perplexity**: Measures how well the model predicts a given sequence of words
- **Bilingual Evaluation Understudy (BLEU)**: Assesses the quality of text generation
- **Recall-Oriented Understudy for Gisting Evaluation (ROUGE)**: Evaluates summary accuracy
- **Factual Consistency**: Ensures generated content aligns with verifiable financial data
- **Toxicity and Bias Scores**: Identifies harmful or unfair model behaviors
- **Hallucination Rate**: Measures the frequency of incorrect or fabricated outputs

4.5.6 Challenges in LLM Evaluation

Despite advances in evaluation techniques, there are a number of challenges to evaluate LLMS; some of these include

- **Domain-Specific Adaptability**: General-purpose benchmarks may not fully capture financial services sector nuances.
- **Continuous Model Updates**: Frequent LLM updates necessitate continuous and ongoing evaluation.
- **Ethical Considerations**: Ensuring fair and unbiased AI-driven financial decision-making.
- **Operational Costs**: Balancing computational efficiency with performance requirements.

4.5.7 Best Practices for Financial Services Firms

To optimize LLM evaluation outcomes, FSOs should

- **Adopt a Hybrid Evaluation Approach**: Combine automated metrics with human assessments.
- **Leverage Industry-Specific Datasets**: Train and test models using financial services-related datasets.
- **Implement Continuous Monitoring**: Track model performance in production environments.
- **Ensure Regulatory Compliance**: Align AI evaluation with financial industry standards.

4.6 Techniques to Handle Domain-Specific Data

At this point, you should have a good understanding that FMs and LLMs are pre-trained with large sets of generally available data. But what if you want an FM to answer questions on domain-specific data within your organization, such as a regulatory requirement?

FSOs operate in a highly specialized domain where accuracy, compliance, and security are critical. Off-the-shelf LLMs, while powerful, often lack the contextual understanding to process intricate financial data, regulatory requirements, and industry-specific terminologies.

To bridge this gap, organizations must adopt advanced techniques to enhance LLM performance on domain-specific data. In this case, there are three options:

- You can find a way to pass your data as context to the model. One method to do this on a consistent basis is called Retrieval Augmented Generation (RAG).
- You can further train the model for your specific needs and data. This is called model fine-tuning.
- You can build your own custom FM.

Note that building your own custom FM is a very expensive, time-consuming, and a complex option; in most cases, we recommend using model fine-tuning and RAG. Each of these has their own benefits and disadvantages. This section explores these two methodologies, comparing their advantages and trade-offs.

4.6.1 Retrieval Augmented Generation (RAG)

RAG is a technique that enhances LLMs by retrieving relevant information from external data sources during inference rather than relying solely on the model's pre-trained knowledge. This is particularly useful in financial services, where real-time accuracy and up-to-date information are crucial for applications such as risk assessment, fraud detection, and regulatory compliance. Essentially, RAG is a technique used for passing domain data as context to an FM in a consistent and repeatable manner. Figure 4-4 illustrates how RAG works:

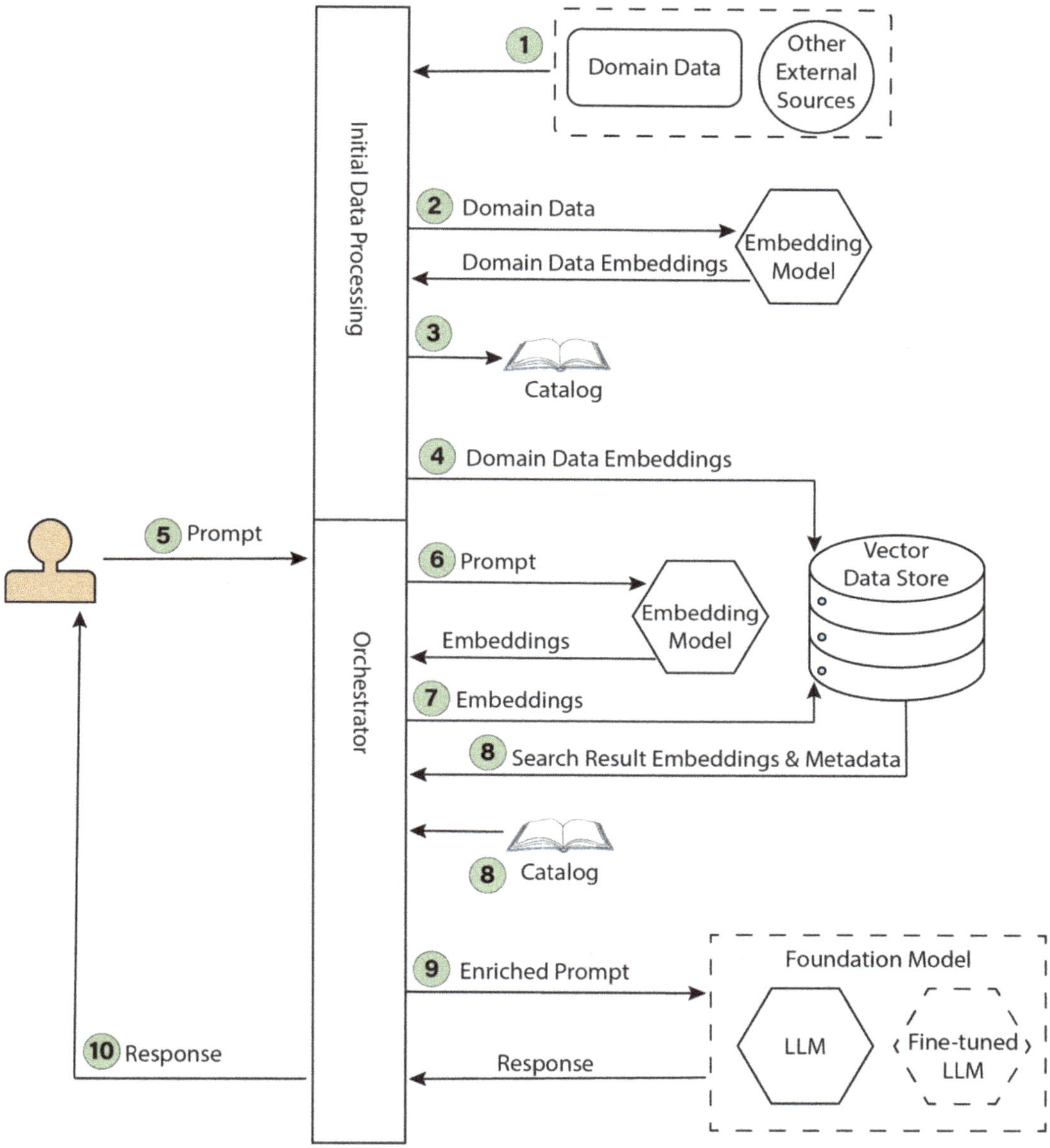

***Figure 4-4.** Retrieval Augmented Generation (RAG)*

Figure 4-4 shows each step in the RAG process from start to finish. The overall process has two phases:

Initial Data Processing Phase: In this phase, you convert the domain data into a format that is suitable for optimized retrieval of information. Whenever the source data changes, you need to repeat the ingestion phase to ensure that all data is updated. Let's take a look at each step in the process:

1. Domain data is retrieved from miscellaneous data sources such as document repositories, databases, or APIs.
2. The data is broken into smaller manageable chunks and sent to an embedding language model. The model converts the chunks of data into embeddings. *Embeddings* are numerical representations of the data within a vector space.
3. A catalog of the embeddings and corresponding chunks of text is maintained.
4. The embeddings are stored in a database, called a *vector database*, specifically designed to store such data. There are many vector databases, including one named Pinecone, available in the market. Cloud-based database services such as RDS from AWS and Azure Cosmos also offer this capability.

Execution Phase Using an Orchestrator: This phase is the interaction between a user and an LLM. When a user creates a request, the request is matched to the domain data and the most relevant pieces of information are retrieved. This data is then passed as context to the LLM along with the request. The LLM then provides a response to the request but most importantly uses the context as the basis of information.

In most cases, you would use an orchestrator to execute this workflow. An orchestrator is software that manages complex workflows and interacts with an FM using a prompt and an optional context. Let's walk through each step of this phase:

1. The orchestrator receives the prompt from the user. Let's call this the initial prompt.
2. The orchestrator sends the initial prompt to the embeddings model to convert the text into embeddings. Note that for MLLMs, images accompanying the text will also need to be embedded.
3. The embeddings of the query are compared with the embeddings in the vector database using a similarity search algorithm.

4. The search results are converted back into text by comparing the retrieved embeddings with the chunks of data in the catalog.

5. The orchestrator appends the initial prompt with the search results. Let's call this the "enriched prompt" to differentiate from the initial prompt. The enriched prompt is sent to the FM. The FM can be a pre-trained model or a fine-tuned one.

6. The response generated by the FM based on the enriched prompt is sent back to the user.

This technique opens up a vast number of possibilities and use cases within the corporate world.

A major benefit with RAG is the ability to increase accuracy and reduce hallucinations. However, in order to do so, your data should be accurate in the first place! And your prompts need to be engineered using some of the techniques discussed earlier in this chapter.

RAG is a complex technique and involves a number of steps. Because of this, it is important for you to evaluate the quality of RAG responses to ensure that the model is not hallucinating and is providing faithful, relevant, accurate responses. Next, we discuss some methods you can use to evaluate the responses.

4.6.1.1 Graph RAG

Graph RAG represents a significant evolution beyond traditional vector-based RAG systems by leveraging graph databases and knowledge graphs to capture complex relationships, hierarchical structures, and multi-hop reasoning paths within data. Unlike conventional RAG approaches that rely primarily on semantic similarity through vector embeddings, Graph RAG constructs explicit knowledge graphs where entities, relationships, and concepts are represented as nodes and edges, enabling more sophisticated query understanding and contextual retrieval. The system typically employs graph databases such as Neo4j or Amazon Neptune, combined with graph neural networks (GNNs) such as Graph Attention Networks (GAT) or GraphSAGE, to perform traversal-based retrieval that can follow relationship chains, identify connected concepts, and understand hierarchical dependencies. This architecture is particularly powerful for complex domains, including financial services, where understanding relationships between entities (customers, transactions, regulations, precedents) is crucial for accurate information retrieval and generation.

Advanced Graph RAG implementations incorporate dynamic graph updates through real-time entity linking and relationship extraction, multiscale graph reasoning that operates across different levels of abstraction (document-level, paragraph-level, sentence-level relationships), and explainable retrieval paths that provide transparency into the reasoning process by showing the specific graph traversal paths that led to retrieved information. Performance optimizations include graph partitioning strategies for distributed processing, caching mechanisms for frequently accessed subgraphs, and adaptive retrieval strategies that dynamically adjust the depth and breadth of graph exploration based on query complexity and confidence scores. The system can also implement temporal graph reasoning for time-sensitive domains, multimodal graph integration that connects textual, numerical, and categorical data types, and federated graph RAG architectures that enable secure querying across distributed knowledge graphs while maintaining data privacy and compliance requirements.

4.6.2 Evaluating RAG responses

The quality of RAG responses is crucial for its use in GenAI-related applications. Faithfulness, relevancy, and accuracy are three measures that can be used for this:

- **Faithfulness (Also Known As Groundedness)**: This refers to how closely the generated answer adheres to the factual information present in the retrieved context. A faithful answer accurately reflects the retrieved passages without fabricating or distorting the information. High faithfulness ensures that the answer is grounded in truth and reliable.

- **Relevancy**: This describes how pertinent the generated answer is to the specific question asked. A relevant answer directly addresses the query and provides information that is helpful for understanding it. While an answer can be faithful to the retrieved context, it might not be relevant if it doesn't answer the specific question effectively.

- **Accuracy**: This encompasses both faithfulness and relevancy, evaluating whether the generated answer is both correct and relevant to the question. An accurate answer provides true information that answers the query directly. It is the ideal outcome, combining factual grounding with the desired focus.

Note that these qualities can interplay; high faithfulness doesn't always guarantee high relevancy. An answer might accurately cite the retrieved context but not directly address the specific query, making it irrelevant. High relevance might involve slightly compromising faithfulness. To answer the question directly, the model might need to slightly adapt or summarize the retrieved information, impacting its strict faithfulness but still providing a useful response.

Understanding these dynamics helps us determine RAG's effectiveness in different scenarios. When accuracy is important, as it is in factual queries, both faithfulness and relevancy become crucial. However, for open-ended questions, relevancy might take precedence over strict faithfulness, as long as the answer provides insightful and helpful information.

In addition to purely metric driven measures, it can help to add human evaluation into the mix. This would mean creating benchmarked gold-standard responses for standard questions against which a human can compare and provide ratings.

By analyzing these qualities through appropriate metrics, you can evaluate the strengths and weaknesses of RAG models. This ultimately leads to improved effectiveness and more informative and impactful responses.

4.6.3 FM Fine-Tuning

Fine-tuning an FM is the process of adjusting a pre-trained model to perform better on specific tasks or with specific types of data. Fine-tuning involves retraining an existing LLM on domain-specific datasets (e.g., bank transactions or customer credit risk profiles) to adapt it to specialized use cases. This process modifies the model's internal parameters, allowing it to develop a deeper understanding of the domain. Overall, this process can significantly enhance the model's relevance and accuracy for your particular use case.

Fine-tuning can be divided into two broad areas:

1. **Domain Adaptation**: The objective here is to improve the FM's ability to understand domain-specific data, such as industry related terms, technical terms, or other specialized language.

2. **Instruction-Based**: The objective in this case is to improve the FM's ability to complete a specific task. Instruction-based fine-tuning uses labeled examples. The labeled examples are formatted as prompt, response pairs and phrased as instructions.

In both these cases, you can adjust the weights of an FM in such a way to provide better performance for your specific problems/objectives. Traditional methods for doing so include methods we have discussed before, such as supervised, unsupervised, or reinforcement learning with human feedback (RLHF). However, many organizations need to own the process of fine-tuning a model using their own data. Because FMs typically have billions of parameters (weights), adjusting these weights in the traditional method used for other models typically isn't feasible for end customers or organizations. Instead, a method called Parameter-Efficient Fine-Tuning (PEFT) has been gaining prominence. PEFT adjusts only a small subset of parameters, thereby significantly reducing the computational cost and memory requirements for fine-tuning. Popular PEFT techniques include Low-Rank Adapters (LoRA) and Quantized Low-Rank Adapters (QLoRA).

Fine-tuning does come with some additional work and overhead on your part; so, before embarking on fine-tuning, it is important to first thoroughly evaluate the performance of the base pre-trained model to determine if it can handle the task or recognize your data. We recommend using the RAG approach first using your corporate data. If you determine that the pre-trained model with RAG does not meet your requirements, then you may need to use fine-tuning. Here are some best practices to consider for fine-tuning:

1. **Understand the Pretrained Model**: Familiarize yourself with the capabilities and limitations of the base model. Understand what data the model was originally trained on to gauge its inherent biases and strengths.

2. **Define Clear Objectives**: Have a clear understanding of the outcome you want to achieve through fine-tuning. This will guide your data selection and fine-tuning strategy. For example, let's say a PSO wants to create a chatbot system to answer frequently asked questions (FAQs) about a new social welfare program. The PSO can fine-tune a pretrained LLM using a dataset specifically tailored to the new program. This dataset would include official program documents, FAQs and informational materials, and transcripts from past call center interactions about similar programs.

3. **Curate a High-Quality Dataset**: Ensure that the fine-tuned dataset closely aligns with your target domain or task. Use a diverse and sufficiently large dataset to capture the nuances of your specific use case. In general, diversity is more important than the size of the data. This means, the data should comprehensively represent the different variations across the use case. Make sure to clean and preprocess the data to eliminate noise and irrelevant information.

4. **Start with a Small Subset**: Begin with a small subset of your data. This allows for quicker iterations and helps in understanding how the model responds to fine-tuning. Gradually increase the dataset size based on initial results and identified needs.

5. **Regular Evaluation**: Use a separate validation set to regularly evaluate the model's performance during fine-tuning. Monitor for signs of overfitting or underfitting and adjust your approach accordingly.

6. **Incorporate Domain Expertise**: Where possible, involve domain experts in reviewing and annotating the fine-tuning dataset. Use expert feedback to refine the model iteratively.

7. **Ethical and Bias Considerations**: Actively look for and mitigate biases in both the training data and the model's outputs. Consider the ethical implications of the model in your specific domain and strive for responsible AI use.

8. **Testing with Real-World Scenarios**: Test the fine-tuned model with real-world scenarios to ensure it performs well in practical applications. Gather user feedback to further refine the model.

Fine-tuning an FM is a delicate process that balances enhancing the model's performance on specific tasks with maintaining the model's general capabilities. By following these best practices, you can effectively tailor the model to your specific needs while ensuring its reliability and ethical use.

4.6.4 RAG vs. Fine-Tuning

Table 4-1 summarizes key distinction between RAG and LLM fine-tuning. At a high level, the guidance is to

- Use RAG when you need real-time, dynamically updated responses (e.g., compliance updates, financial news analysis).
- Use Fine-Tuning when your AI application requires deep expertise in proprietary or historical financial data (e.g., risk modeling, fraud detection).
- Use a Hybrid Approach when combining RAG for dynamic information retrieval with fine-tuning for specialized financial reasoning.

Table 4-1. *RAG vs. Fine-Tuning*

Feature	RAG	LLM fine-tuning
Approach	Dynamically retrieves external data	Modifies model parameters through retraining
Data Dependency	Requires access to an external knowledge base	Requires high-quality labeled datasets
Accuracy	High accuracy when reliable sources are available	High accuracy in specialized tasks
Adaptability	Easily updates with new data	Requires retraining for updates
Cost and Complexity	Lower cost, no need for retraining	Higher cost, requires computational resources
Transparency	Provides citations and sources	Less transparent, as knowledge is embedded
Use Cases	Regulatory compliance, real-time market analysis	Risk assessment, fraud detection

In many financial applications, a **hybrid approach** leveraging both RAG and fine-tuning yields the best results. This involves

- Fine-tuning an LLM on proprietary financial datasets to develop domain expertise
- Enhancing responses with RAG by fetching real-time regulatory and market data
- Implementing a validation layer where human experts verify critical AI-generated insights

4.7 GenAI Application Architecture

So far we have discussed some important concepts such as prompts, RAG and agents that are needed to handle some of the complexities and nuances of a GenAI application. Fig 4-5 depicts the application architecture of such an application.

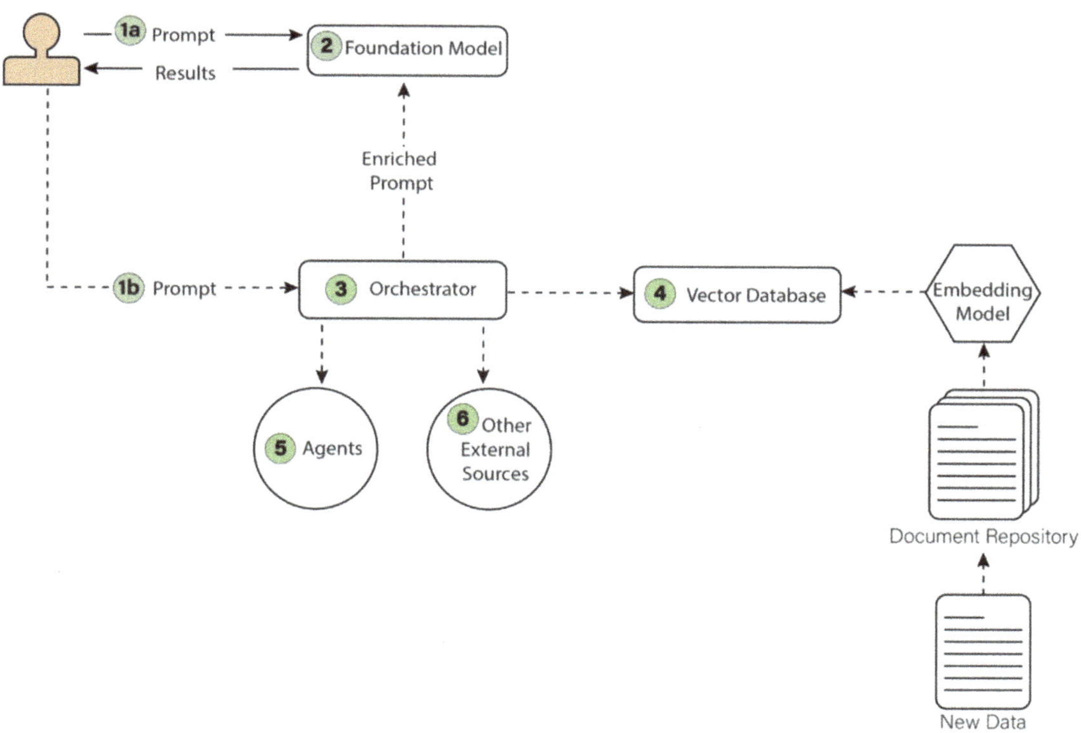

Figure 4-5. GenAI Application Architecture

Let's discuss each step of the architecture. Some steps are optional, depending on your business needs and the model you're considering. For example, text-to-image generation models may not need components 3, 4, and 5.

1. **Prompt**: As discussed earlier, the prompt contains instructions as well as additional information to help the model provide a relevant answer. The prompt can be sent (1a) directly to the FM or (1b) to the Orchestrator.

2. **FM**: The FM that performs your generation task. It receives the prompt directly from the user or from an orchestrator and generates a response, passed either directly back to the user or to the orchestrator. It is important to evaluate and select the right model for your use case. The FM itself could be pretrained or fine-tuned depending on your domain and the characteristics of the task at hand. See Chapter 3, section "Building an FM or Selecting a Pretrained FM," for additional guidance on selecting a model.

3. **Orchestrator**: We discussed the orchestrator briefly in our section on RAG. In the case of RAG, the orchestrator sends a prompt enriched with the relevant context to the FM. Orchestrators may also add additional statements to the prompt sent by the user. This may include guardrails or statements that ensure that the FM does not provide answers to questions deemed as harmful by the organization. Orchestrators also help with other complex activities such as handling multiple FMs, handling agents, or making an external API call.

4. **Vector Database**: As an FSO, you typically store a lot of information in documents. Examples are financial documents, risk assessments, customer transactions, equity and market reports, contracts, procedures, federal policies information, and so on. As discussed earlier in the RAG section, you can store these documents in the vector database for retrieval. FSO uses an embedding model to convert data from documents, databases, and repositories to LLM-aware embeddings.

5. **Agents**: Agents, will help you work with an LLM on complex reasoning problems.

6. **Other External Sources**: These are additional sources outside the organization such as websites and APIs that the orchestrator can call, depending on the use case.

This architecture lays the foundation for building GenAI applications for a variety of tasks, including document and image generation, chatbots, and summarization and reporting. In later chapters, we explore variations in this architecture specific to these tasks and use cases.

4.8 Agents and Agentic AI

The evolution of GenAI in financial services is not limited to static models that generate responses based on user prompts. The next frontier involves *AI agents*, which are autonomous systems that can perceive, reason, and act to achieve specific financial objectives. These agents go beyond simple text generation by dynamically interacting with systems, retrieving real-time data, executing tasks, and continuously improving their decision-making.

An even more advanced paradigm is *Agentic AI*, where AI-driven agents exhibit higher levels of autonomy, adaptability, and contextual understanding. In this section, we'll explore the distinctions between GenAI, AI agents, and Agentic AI, illustrating their differences through a financial services analogy.

As we have learned in this book so far, the key characteristics of GenAI include

- **Static Output Generation**: generates responses based on trained knowledge but lacks real-time decision-making capabilities
- **No Execution Capability**: cannot take actions beyond generating text or predictions
- **Limited Autonomy**: requires continuous user input to function

4.8.1 AI Agents

AI agents are an advanced form of AI that perceive their environment, interact with external systems, retrieve real-time information, and perform actions autonomously. Unlike GenAI, which passively responds to prompts, AI agents can execute workflows, automate financial operations, and integrate with enterprise systems.

4.8.1.1 Key Characteristics

Autonomous Decision-Making: agents can trigger predefined workflows without human intervention.

- **Real-Time Data Retrieval**: agents fetch live data from APIs, databases, and financial markets.
- **Multistep Reasoning**: agents can break down complex financial tasks into smaller steps and execute them systematically.

4.8.1.2 Example in Financial Services

A financial analyst asks an AI agent

> *"Analyze the latest market trends and adjust our investment strategy accordingly."*

The AI agent

1. Retrieves live stock market data
2. Analyzes performance trends
3. Generates an updated investment strategy
4. Automatically integrates recommendations into the portfolio management system

Unlike GenAI, which would only generate a textual response, the AI agent *performs* specific tasks based on its understanding of the market.

4.8.2 Agentic AI

Agentic AI represents the next level of AI systems; they are *fully autonomous agents* that exhibit goal-driven behavior, continuous learning, and adaptability. These agents go beyond simple task execution and can self-improve, self-correct, and handle unforeseen situations without explicit programming. At a high level, Agentic AI is focused on goal-oriented autonomy, as depicted in Figure 4-6.

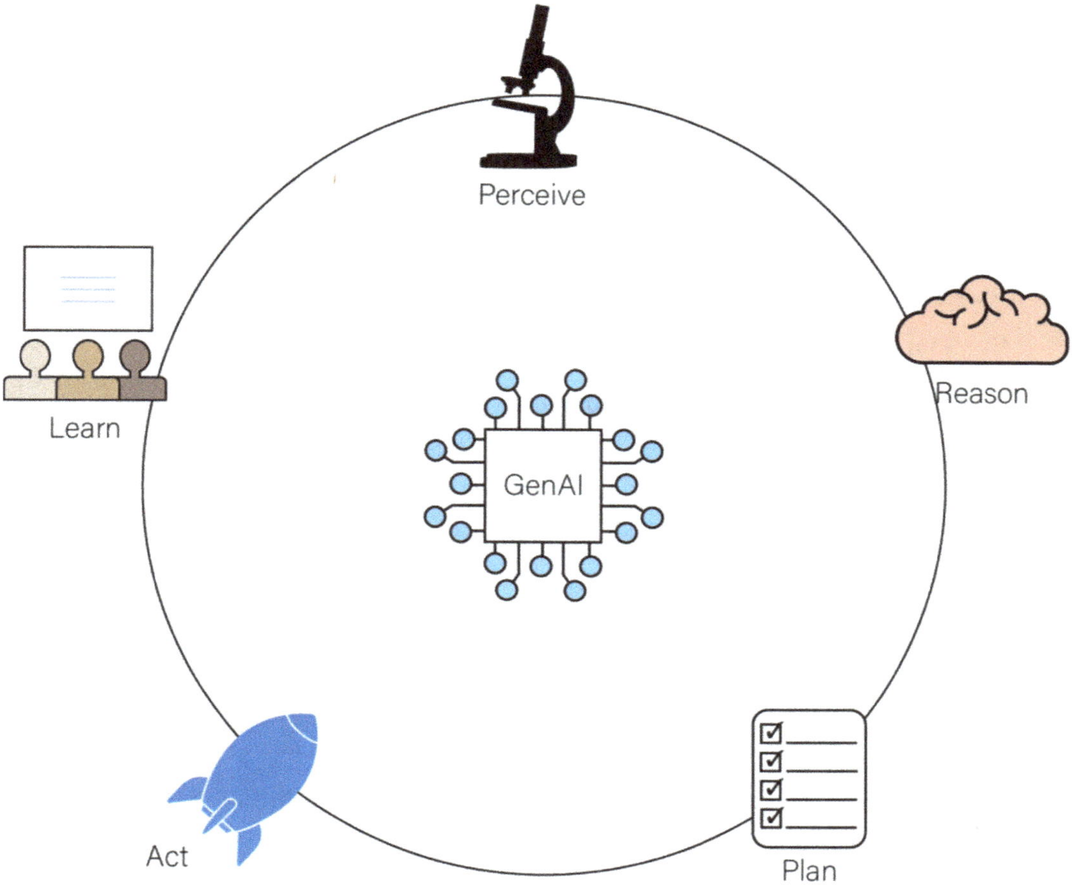

Figure 4-6. *Agentic AI (Goal-Oriented Autonomy)*

4.8.2.1 Key Characteristics

- **Long-Term Autonomy**: works toward high-level financial goals rather than executing isolated tasks
- **Adaptive Learning**: improves performance based on historical data and feedback loops
- **Decision-Theoretic Reasoning**: weighs risks and rewards before making decisions

4.8.2.2 Example in Financial Services

A wealth management firm deploys an Agentic AI-powered financial advisor. Instead of reacting to individual queries, the AI proactively

1. Monitors the client's portfolio 24/7
2. Detects macroeconomic changes affecting investments
3. Simulates potential risks based on real-time data
4. Adjusts asset allocations autonomously
5. Notifies the client about portfolio changes with justifications

Unlike AI agents that follow predefined rules, Agentic AI evolves and adapts, making intelligent, long-term decisions without explicit human intervention.

As you can imagine, Agentic AI will be the next frontier in GenAI. The evolution from GenAI to AI agents and ultimately to Agentic AI represents a paradigm shift in financial services. While GenAI enhances customer interactions, AI agents take it a step further by retrieving live data and executing actions. Agentic AI, the most advanced form, autonomously manages financial operations, continuously learning and adapting.

For financial institutions, embracing these AI advancements can lead to

- Hyper-personalized financial services tailored to individual customer needs
- Automated risk management and compliance reducing human oversight
- Proactive AI-driven investment strategies that outperform static models

As financial firms move toward a future where AI is not just reactive but proactive, the adoption of Agentic AI will redefine how wealth is managed, risks are mitigated, and customer relationships are enhanced.

4.8.3 Key Paradigm Shifts with Agentic AI

The following characteristics outline the key paradigm shifts with Agentic AI:

1. **From Reactive to Proactive**: Systems now anticipate and prevent issues rather than just respond.
2. **From Product-Centric to Goal-Oriented**: Focus shifted to achieving customer objectives through integrated solutions.

3. **From Discrete Services to Ecosystem Orchestration**: Agents coordinate across multiple financial stakeholders.
4. **From Standardized to Personalized**: AI develops unique strategies tailored to individual circumstances.
5. **From Human-Dependent to Autonomous**: Systems operate with sustained independence while maintaining human alignment.

Table 4-2 summarizes the key features and the distinction between GenAI, AI agents, and Agentic AI.

***Table 4-2.** Gen AI, AI Agents, and Agentic AI Feature Comparison*

Feature	GenAI	AI Agents	Agentic AI
Primary Function	Generates content	Retrieves data and executes tasks	Autonomously adapts and optimizes decisions
Data Retrieval	Based on pretrained knowledge	Real-time API and database access	Continuous data learning and adaptation
Task Execution	No execution	Executes predefined workflows	Self-directed decision-making
Autonomy	Low – responds to prompts	Medium – executes structured tasks	High – evolves and self-corrects
Learning Ability	No learning after training	Can incorporate external knowledge	Continuously learns and optimizes
Example Use Case	Chatbots, report generation	Automated trading, compliance monitoring	AI-powered wealth management

4.9 Anatomy of an Agentic AI Application

Figure 4-7 illustrates the various components of an Agentic AI application.

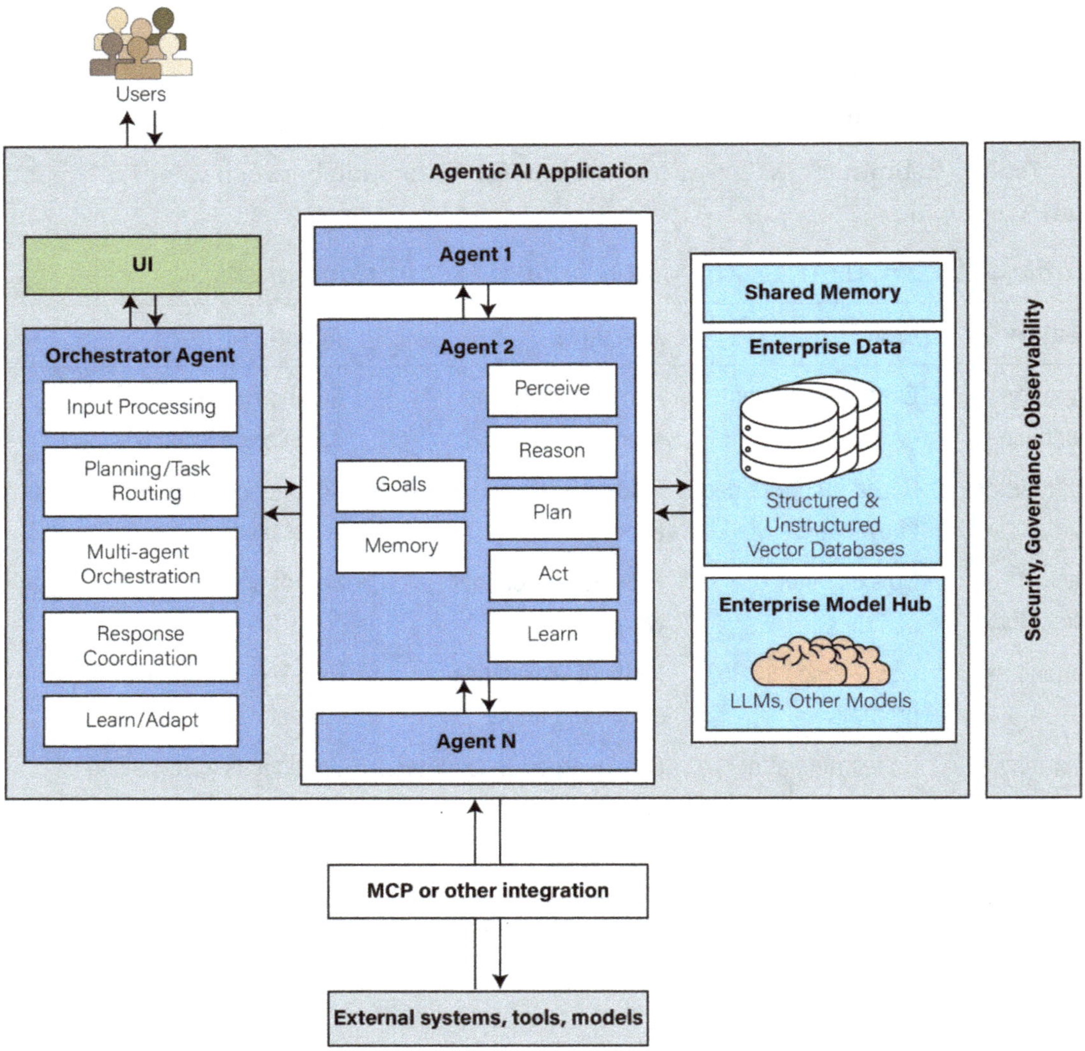

Figure 4-7. *Anatomy of an Agentic AI Application*

This architecture and the components are further described in this section.

4.9.1 User Interface (UI) Layer

The UI layer is the primary interaction point between users and the Agentic system - the main role of the UI is to capture user requests, display responses, and provide real-time feedback.

4.9.2 Orchestration Layer

The Orchestration layer consists of the Orchestrator agent that is responsible for the following functionality:

- **Input Processing:** (1) Interprets and standardizes incoming user requests and system inputs; (2) performs initial validation and context extraction; and (3) routes information to appropriate specialized agents
- **Planning/Task Routing:** (1) Decomposes complex tasks into manageable subtasks; (2) determines optimal agent assignment based on task requirements; and (3) creates execution sequences and dependency mapping
- **Multi-agent Orchestration:** (1) Coordinates activities across multiple specialized agents; (2) manages inter-agent communication and data flow; and (3) ensures coherent execution of distributed tasks
- **Response Coordination:** (1) Aggregates outputs from multiple agents into unified responses; (2) handles conflict resolution between competing agent recommendations; and (3) maintains response quality and consistency standard
- **Learn/Adapt:** (1) Continuously improves orchestration strategies based on outcomes; (2) adapts routing decisions based on agent performance patterns; and (3) evolves coordination mechanisms for enhanced efficiency

4.9.3 Agent Execution Layer

The agent execution layer consists of individual Agents (Agent-1, Agent-2, Agent-N) that have a structured cognitive framework including

- **Goals:** (1) Maintains specific objectives and success criteria; (2) aligns individual agent goals with overall system objectives; and (3) provides measurable targets for performance evaluation
- **Memory:** (1) Stores agent-specific knowledge and experience; (2) maintains context across interactions and sessions; and (3) enables learning from past decisions and outcomes
- **Perceive:** (1) Gathers and interprets relevant environmental information; (2) monitors data sources and system states; and (3) identifies patterns and anomalies in available data
- **Reason:** (1) Applies logical analysis to available information; (2) evaluates options and potential consequences; and (3) makes informed decisions based on goals and constraints
- **Plan:** (1) Develops step-by-step execution strategies; (2) creates contingency plans for potential obstacles; and (3) optimizes resource allocation and timing
- **Act:** (1) Executes planned actions within defined parameters; (2) interacts with external systems and data sources; and (3) implements decisions while maintaining safety constraints
- **Learn:** (1) Captures feedback from actions and outcomes; (2) updates knowledge base and decision-making models; and (3) improves future performance through experience

4.9.4 Data and Model Infrastructure

The data and model infrastructure consists of the following components:

- **Shared Memory**: Shared memory acts as a centralized knowledge repository accessible by all agents. It consists of the Common facts, policies, procedures, and shared learnings. This component ensures consistency and enables knowledge sharing across the system.

- **Enterprise Data**: Enterprise data consists of structured, unstructured, and vector databases. This provides a comprehensive data foundation for agent decision-making and has real-time access to current business information and historical data.
- **Enterprise Model Hub**: Enterprise model hub consists of LLMs for natural language processing and generation and also includes specialized models for specific domain tasks (analytics, prediction, classification).

4.9.5 External Integration Layer

The external integration layer includes Model Context Protocol (MCP) and/or other integrations. The objective is to utilize standardized protocols for external system connectivity. The scope includes APIs, microservices, and third-party platform integrations and this layer extends agent capabilities beyond internal systems.

4.9.6 Foundation Layer/Cross-Cutting Capabilities

The foundation layer includes the following horizontal system capabilities:

- **Security**: Authentication, authorization, encryption, and threat protection
- **Governance**: Policy enforcement, compliance monitoring, and audit trails
- **Observability**: System monitoring, performance tracking, and diagnostic capabilities

4.10 Agentic AI in the Financial Services Sector

The following practical examples highlight how Agentic AI is transforming the financial services domain. Some of these examples are outlined from FinAI.[2]

[2] https://finai.blog/2025/03/01/agentic-ai-the-future-of-banking-transforming-financial-services-through-autonomous-intelligence/

4.10.1 Algorithmic Trading and Portfolio Management

4.10.1.1 Renaissance Technologies

- **Implementation**: Implementation consists of autonomous trading agents that continuously analyze market conditions and execute complex strategies.
- **Agentic Capabilities**: Agents don't just react to signals but actively develop and test novel market hypotheses across multiple asset classes.
- **Autonomy Level**: Higher level systems operate independently to identify patterns and execute trades.

4.10.1.2 BlackRock (Aladdin Platform)

- **Implementation**: Evolved beyond traditional portfolio management to incorporate autonomous rebalancing capabilities
- **Agentic Capabilities**: Integrates macroeconomic indicators, geopolitical analysis, and market sentiment for independent allocation decisions
- **Key Innovation**: Provides detailed explanations for decisions, addressing AI transparency concerns

4.10.2 Advanced Fraud Prevention

4.10.2.1 Mastercard (Decision Intelligence)

- **Implementation**: Dynamic risk assessment framework that autonomously evolves with emerging fraud patterns
- **Agentic Capabilities**: Correlates unrelated transactions across global networks to identify coordinated fraud attempts
- **Autonomous Actions**: Implements countermeasures before damage occurs without human intervention

4.10.2.2 HSBC (Financial Intelligence Unit)

- **Implementation**: Predictive fraud prevention system analyzing behavioral patterns across millions of interactions
- **Agentic Capabilities**: Proactively implements customized security protocols for at-risk accounts
- **Paradigm Shift**: Moved from reactive detection to preventative security models

4.10.3 Regulatory Compliance and Risk Management

4.10.3.1 Standard Chartered (Regulatory Intelligence)

- **Implementation**: Monitors regulatory developments across 70+ jurisdictions automatically
- **Agentic Capabilities**: Analyzes implications and implements operational adjustments without human intervention
- **Advanced Features**: Autonomously initiates clarification processes with regulatory authorities.

4.10.3.2 Goldman Sachs (Risk Assessment Agent)

- **Implementation**: Continuously stress-tests bank positions against thousands of simulated scenarios
- **Agentic Capabilities**: Autonomously implements hedging strategies within defined tolerance parameters
- **Innovation**: Shifted from periodic human-led testing to continuous autonomous risk management

4.10.4 Customer Experience Transformation

4.10.4.1 DBS Bank Singapore

- **Implementation**: Persistent financial agent managing complex processes from initiation to completion
- **Agentic Capabilities**: Guides customers through entire home-buying process autonomously
- **Learning System**: Continuously improves service experience based on customer interactions

4.10.4.2 Ant Group

- **Implementation**: Autonomous financial advisor for previously unbanked populations in China
- **Agentic Capabilities**: Analyzes alternative data, establishes creditworthiness, and provides financial guidance
- **Adaptive Communication**: Adjusts approach based on user comprehension levels

4.10.5 Future Development Initiatives

4.10.5.1 JPMorgan Chase (Cognitive Banking Prototype)

- **Implementation**: Specialized agents handling distinct financial management aspects with central orchestration
- **Agentic Vision**: Comprehensive financial life cycle management through agent collaboration
- **Integration**: Coordinates spending optimization, investment management, debt reduction, and tax efficiency

4.10.5.2 BBVA (Financial DNA Project)

- **Implementation**: Personalized financial optimization through reinforcement learning
- **Agentic Capabilities**: Develops novel financial strategies optimized for individual circumstances
- **Continuous Learning**: Refines recommendations based on actual outcomes

4.10.5.3 UBS (Financial Foresight Initiative)

- **Implementation**: Predictive system analyzing spending behavior and economic indicators
- **Agentic Capabilities**: Predicts significant financial events before they occur
- **Proactive Optimization**: Suggests adjustments and identifies optimal timing for major financial decisions

4.10.5.4 Bank of America (Advisory Intelligence Research)

- **Implementation**: Personal financial advisor for every customer regardless of account balance
- **Agentic Vision**: Democratizes sophisticated financial guidance previously limited to high-net-worth clients
- **Contextual Analysis**: Analyzes spending patterns, income stability, and life stage indicators

4.10.5.5 Morgan Stanley (Financial Inclusion Initiative)

- **Implementation**: Specialized agents for customers with limited financial resources

- **Agentic Approach**: Incorporates understanding of economic vulnerability factors
- **Social Impact**: Builds pathways toward financial stability for underserved populations

4.10.5.6 Citibank (Autonomy Framework)

- **Implementation**: Five-level agent authority system from "advisory only" to "fully autonomous"
- **Graduated Approach**: Progressive expansion of agent autonomy as technical capabilities mature
- **Risk Management**: Progressive security and oversight requirements at each autonomy level

4.11 Chapter Summary

In this chapter, we explored the essential building blocks of creating a GenAI application, with a particular focus on the FSS. We began by examining the anatomy of prompts and the art of prompt engineering, highlighting how crafting clear and strategic inputs is fundamental to guiding FMs toward desired outcomes. We also delved into the evaluation of LLMs, emphasizing the importance of robust metrics and benchmarks, especially within the context of regulatory compliance and industry-specific requirements in financial services.

The chapter further introduced the concept of agents and Agentic AI, showcasing their potential to facilitate complex reasoning and multistep problem-solving, thus enhancing automation and operational efficiency in areas such as investment analysis, risk management, and customer service. We explored advanced data handling techniques, including Retrieval Augmented Generation (RAG) and model fine-tuning, which empower GenAI applications to leverage domain-specific knowledge and provide accurate, context-aware outputs.

Finally, we presented a generic application architecture, emphasizing scalability, security, and compliance; these are important considerations for deploying GenAI solutions in the financial sector.

By understanding these core concepts, you are now equipped with the foundational knowledge required to design and build effective GenAI applications tailored to the financial services industry. This chapter lays the groundwork for the more advanced technical implementation and strategic deployment strategies that we will explore in the upcoming chapters.

CHAPTER 5

Risk and Compliance Management with GenAI

In Chapter 4, we explored the key concepts for building GenAI applications. In this chapter, we outline the Risk and Compliance Management Framework for FSOs and how GenAI can enable the overall risk management. Let's discuss further context on why Risk and Compliance management is one of the most critical aspects in the Financial Services Sectors (FSS).

In 2008, the world witnessed one of the most devastating financial crises in modern history,[1] a crisis born out of unchecked risk-taking and inadequate risk management. Subprime mortgage lending, driven by the relentless pursuit of profit, spiraled out of control as financial institutions packaged risky loans into complex securities. These companies were convinced that rising housing prices would shield them from default. When the housing bubble burst, the domino effect was catastrophic; banks collapsed, credit markets froze, and millions lost their homes and livelihoods. Trillions of dollars evaporated overnight, exposing a harsh reality: when financial institutions fail to properly assess and manage risk, the consequences can be devastating, not only for the firms involved but for the global economy as a whole.

This cautionary tale serves as a sobering reminder that risk is inherent to the FSS. Banks, credit card issuers, investment firms, and wealth managers operate in a domain where taking calculated risks is fundamental to generating profit. Yet, without a disciplined approach to managing credit risk, market volatility, operational failures, liquidity constraints, and regulatory demands, the line between success and failure becomes thin. The challenge lies not in avoiding risk altogether but in comprehensively understanding and mitigating it to safeguard assets, ensure compliance, and maintain market stability.

[1] https://www.fdic.gov/media/18636

S. Godavarthi, R. Nagvekar, *Transforming Financial Services with Generative AI*,
https://doi.org/10.1007/979-8-8688-2053-3_5

GenAI has emerged as an enabling technology, offering unprecedented capabilities to enhance risk management. By analyzing vast and diverse data sources, GenAI can detect early warning signals and subtle patterns that traditional models might overlook. Whether it is predicting credit defaults or identifying emerging fraud risks, GenAI empowers Financial Services Organizations (FSOs) to take proactive measures rather than merely reacting to crises.

FSOs are expected to have a corporate risk and governance strategy in accordance with the Office Of the Comptroller of the Currency (OCC), which defines a framework for corporate Risk and Governance.[2] Based on the OCC guidance, the types of risks include

- **Credit Risk**: Customer and counterparty credit risk across retail and wholesale banking. This occurs when borrowers or counterparties fail to meet their obligations, potentially leading to financial losses.
- **Market Risk**: Exposure to market fluctuations impacting trading and investment portfolios.
- **Operational Risk**: Risks arising from business operations, cybersecurity, and third-party dependencies. Includes losses incurred due to inadequate internal processes, people, systems, or external events.
- **Regulatory and Compliance Risk**: Adhering to international regulations such as Basel III, Dodd-Frank, General Data protection regulation (GDPR), and Anti Money Laundering (AML) requirements. The risk of legal or regulatory sanctions resulting from a failure to comply with laws, regulations, or standards.
- **Reputational Risk:** Safeguarding brand reputation amidst public scrutiny and geopolitical tensions. The potential for negative public opinion or loss of confidence to adversely impact a financial institution's operations or capital.
- **Liquidity Risk**: The risk of incurring losses when certain assets cannot be traded without impacting their market price, or when a bank is unable to meet its cash obligations.

---

[2] https://www.occ.treas.gov/publications-and-resources/publications/comptrollers-handbook/files/corporate-risk-governance/pub-ch-corporate-risk.pdf

- **Strategic Risk**: This relates to the risk of losses arising from poor business decisions or inadequate implementation of business strategies.

5.1 Challenges in Risk and Compliance Management

The Global Fiscal Group (GFG), our fictitious FSO that we introduced in Chapter 2, faces a number of challenges with Risk and Compliance Management that have resulted in heavy financial losses, reputational loss, and hefty fines from federal agencies due to non-compliance in certain areas.

Note that in FY 2023, the US Securities and Exchange Commission (SEC) alone has filed 784 enforcement actions, obtained orders for nearly $5 billion in financial remedies and distributed nearly $1 billion to harmed investors.[3] Additionally, in the AML space, nearly 50 fines were issued by US regulators in 2024, with North America accounting for an overwhelming 95% of the $4.6 billion in global financial penalties.[4]

Additionally, SEC regulations[5] 17-a3, 17-a4 require broker-dealers to make and keep current records of all communications related to their business, including electronic communications. These rules specify the format, medium, retention period, and production requirements for such records.

In 2022, SEC and Commodity Futures Trading Commission (CFTC) each announced charges and fines against 11 financial institutions for failures to comply with recordkeeping, supervision, and monitoring regulations for business communications conducted outside permitted channels, including communications conducted on personal devices, text messaging, and apps. The enforcement actions and fines, which total over $1.8 billion in the aggregate, range from $16 million to $225 million for each financial institution.[6]

---

[3] https://www.sec.gov/newsroom/press-releases/2023-234

[4] https://resources.fenergo.com/newsroom/fenergo-study-regulatory-penalties-in-north-america-account-for-95-of-global-financial-penalties-in-2024

[5] https://www.sec.gov/rules-regulations/2001/10/books-records-requirements-brokers-dealers-under-securities-exchange-act-1934

[6] https://www2.deloitte.com/content/dam/Deloitte/us/Documents/Advisory/us-advisory-ecomms.pdf

GFG's CIO outlined a vision to address some of the challenges by utilizing GenAI and other emerging technologies. The vision is to "*Become a market leader in leveraging cutting-edge technologies for risk resilience and sustainable growth.*" The CIO directed the Senior Leadership Team to minimize the reputational and financial loss by outlining a plan that includes specific objectives and key results (OKRs).

For the rest of this chapter, we outline these challenges via use cases and OKRs that help address these challenges. Note that these OKRs are mostly directional and ambitious; each FSO may have their own mandates depending on varying conditions.

5.2 Use Case 1: Transforming AML Compliance and Suspicious Activity Reporting (SAR) with GenAI

5.2.1 Problem Statement

At GFG, detecting suspicious financial activity and generating SARs remains a time-consuming and error-prone process. Currently, AML analysts rely on traditional rule-based systems to identify potential suspicious activity, which often results in high false-positive rates and missed patterns of complex money laundering schemes. Additionally, generating SARs is a manual task that can take several days due to the need for detailed analysis and cross-referencing of multiple data sources. Furthermore, the lack of sufficient high-quality training data hampers the development of more accurate detection models.

5.2.2 Current State and Challenges

Some of the challenges include

- AML analysts spend 30–40 hours per week manually reviewing transactions flagged as suspicious.
- Compliance officers and auditors spend 15–20 hours per SAR report, which includes gathering evidence, writing narratives, and ensuring regulatory compliance.

- The ML model training for fraud detection and pattern recognition is hampered by the lack of diverse and comprehensive data, requiring 10–15 hours per week of manual data generation and curation.
- Siloed data and fragmented workflows slow investigations and increase regulatory risk.

5.2.3 Objective

Utilize GenAI and Agentic AI to transform suspicious activity detection and reporting by automating investigation, narrative generation, and regulatory filing. Deploy a collaborative, multi-agent system to improve detection accuracy, accelerate SAR generation, and synthesize high-quality training data. The ultimate goal is to enable GFG to proactively combat complex money laundering schemes.

5.2.4 Key Results

- **Increase Detection Accuracy**: Improve detection accuracy of suspicious activity by 50% by integrating GenAI-powered anomaly detection to identify previously overlooked patterns.
- **Reduce Report Generation Time**: Automate 80% of SAR report generation, reducing the average time to generate a report from 10 hours to 2 hours per report.
- **Improve Data Coverage**: Generate 90% of synthetic transaction data required for training, addressing gaps in the current model training dataset and boosting model performance.
- **Enhance Investigative Efficiency**: Reduce manual review time for flagged transactions by 60% (saving 20+ hours per week per AML analyst).
- **Boost Model Training Speed**: Reduce the time to generate high-quality synthetic training data by 70%, accelerating the development and iteration of anti-money laundering models.

5.2.5 Solution Overview

The challenges faced by GFG in AML operations represent a critical opportunity for transformation through GenAI. This section outlines a detailed solution architecture that addresses the identified challenges and meets the specified objectives and key results.

The proposed solution integrates multiple GenAI components to create a comprehensive AML enhancement system with four key pillars:

1. **Advanced Suspicious Activity Pattern Detection Engine**: Utilize advanced GenAI models (e.g., GPT-5, Claude SONET, and Gemini) to detect complex money laundering patterns.
2. **Automated SAR Generation System**: Implement LLM-based automation for generating SARs, significantly reducing manual effort and ensuring compliance with regulatory standards.
3. **Investigative Assistant Framework**: Use Retrieval Augmented Generation (RAG)-powered analysis and query to investigate and conduct case management.
4. GenAI/AI-augmented SAR filing that includes human-in-the-loop evaluation.

Our primary implementation framework is Agentic AI which we described earlier in Chapter 4. In this framework, multiple agents coordinate to complete an objective which is to file SAR for those customers who fall under the SAR guidelines.

5.2.6 High-Level Solution Architecture

Figure 5-1 shows the high-level architecture of the solution.

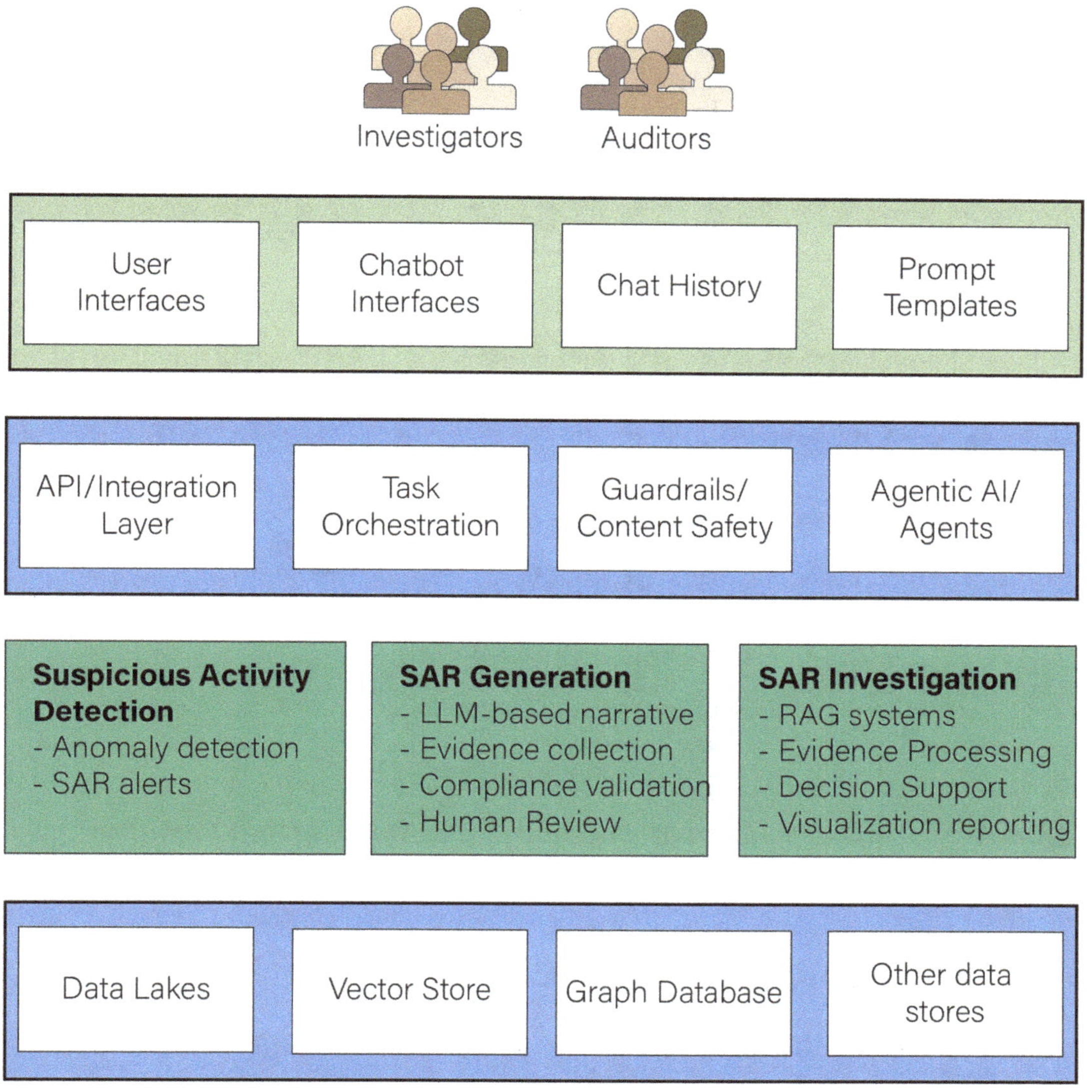

Figure 5-1. *High-level Solution Architecture for the AML and SAR Initiatives Use Case*

5.2.7 Detailed Solution Architecture

Figure 5-2 represents the detailed solution architecture for the AML and SAR initiatives at GFG.

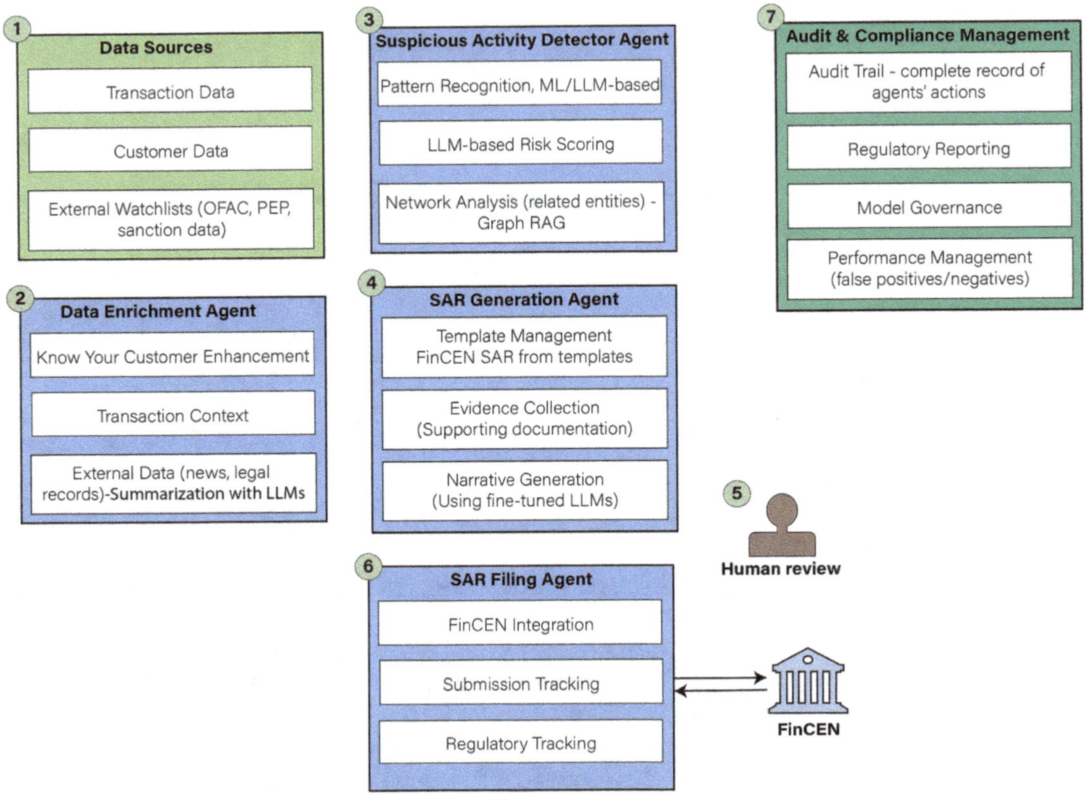

Figure 5-2. *Detailed Solution Architecture for the AML and SAR Initiatives Use Case*

5.2.8 Key Components of the Solution

5.2.8.1 Data Sources

The data sources include customer data, transaction data, and external watchlists such as Office of Foreign asset control (OFAC), Politically Exposed Persons (PEP), and Sanctions data[7] from Treasury.gov. This includes specially designated nationals (SDN) lists.[8]

[7] https://ofac.treasury.gov/sanctions-list-search-tool

[8] https://sanctionslist.ofac.treas.gov/Home/SdnList

5.2.8.2 Advanced Data Enrichment

The data enrichment agent automatically gathers and synthesizes relevant information with the following approach:

- Collects customer data across multiple internal systems and lines of business
- Retrieves external data from public records, news sources, and business registries
- Identifies and resolves entity information across disparate data sources
- Standardizes and normalizes data from multiple formats and structures

The intelligent Know Your Customer (KYC) component builds comprehensive customer profiles and (1) identifies ultimate beneficial owners through complex corporate structures, (2) discovers undisclosed relationships between customers and external entities, (3) assesses business activities against stated purpose and industry norms, and (4) evaluates customer risk profiles based on enriched information.

Contextual Analysis provides deeper understanding of transaction patterns:

- Determines business purpose and economic rationale for unusual transactions
- Identifies industry-specific risk factors relevant to the customer
- Evaluates geographic risk based on transaction counterparties
- Compares activity against peer groups and industry benchmarks

Real-time Information Gathering ensures decisions are based on current data with the following process:

- Monitors news and regulatory updates for emerging risks
- Tracks changes in corporate structures and ownership
- Updates customer profiles with recent activity across products
- Identifies new relationships as they form between entities

5.2.8.3 Intelligent Suspicious Activity Detection

Suspicious activity detection agent analyzes transaction patterns and customer behavior to identify potential suspicious activities using the following approach:

- Processes unstructured data, including transaction descriptions and customer communications
- Identifies anomalies by comparing activity against expected customer behavior profiles
- Generates detailed explanations of why specific activities triggered alerts
- Adapts detection parameters based on feedback from confirmed cases

As we discussed in Chapter 4, Graph RAG can be used to capture relationships - it can help reveal hidden connections between accounts, businesses, and individuals that traditional systems miss using the following process:

- Maps multi-hop relationships that span across multiple entities and transactions
- Identifies circular transaction patterns indicative of layering activities
- Detects structuring attempts across multiple accounts and time periods
- Reveals beneficial ownership structures that may indicate shell company arrangements
- Knowledge Graphs map complex relationships to detect sophisticated money laundering schemes

5.2.8.4 Professional SAR Generation

The SAR generation agent creates clear, compliant SAR narratives in alignment with FinCEN guidelines with the following actions:

- Structures narratives with the 5 W's (Who, What, When, Where, Why) format
- Generates clear descriptions of suspicious activity patterns

- Avoids conclusory language while clearly stating suspicious factors
- Adapts writing style to meet regulatory expectations

RAG ensures consistency with previous filings and regulatory expectations:

- References similar past cases for consistent treatment
- Incorporates language from regulatory guidance documents
- Maintains consistent terminology for specific activity types
- Aligns with examiner expectations based on previous feedback

Graph visualization illustrates complex relationships for better reporting:

- Creates transaction flow diagrams showing movement of funds
- Visualizes entity relationships to demonstrate beneficial ownership
- Highlights key nodes in complex transaction networks
- Provides timeline visualizations of structured transactions

5.2.8.5 Streamlined Filing with Human Oversight

The SAR filing agent completes FinCEN forms accurately and consistently with the following approach:

- Auto-populates all required fields with appropriate formatting and ensures proper categorization of suspicious activity types
- Generates consistent subject information across multiple filings and adapts to form changes without requiring system updates
- Validates and checks currency transactions that are suspicious and prepares the report in compliance with Bank Secrecy Act (BSA)
- Checks completed forms against latest FinCEN requirements and validates narrative against regulatory expectations
- Ensures consistency with previous filings on related subjects and identifies potential gaps or areas needing enhancement

AI-assisted review highlights key areas for human validation:

- Flags high-risk elements requiring special attention
- Identifies unusual narrative elements for verification
- Suggests areas where additional detail may be beneficial
- Provides confidence scores for different components

5.2.9 Business Benefits

The Agentic AI-powered AML and SAR platform delivers transformative value through the following results:

- **Efficiency:** Automates 80% of SAR generation, saving millions in compliance costs and reclaiming 20–24 analyst hours per week. This allows them to focus on complex investigations and strategic risk management
- **Accuracy:** Reduces false positives and uncovers sophisticated laundering schemes, improving detection by 50%.
- **Scalability:** Handles 40% more transaction volume without additional headcount.
- **Regulatory Readiness:** Ensures consistent, compliant filings with comprehensive audit trails, reducing regulatory risk and penalties.
- **Agility:** Accelerates model training and adaptation to new threats via synthetic data generation and continuous agent learning.

Overall, the GenAI-powered AML and SAR solution delivers substantial financial and operational benefits to GFG. Beyond direct cost savings, the solution significantly reduces regulatory risk exposure by improving the quality and consistency of SAR filings. With automated narrative generation following FinCEN guidelines, compliance and comprehensive audit trails, GFG strengthens its defensibility during regulatory examinations and reduces the risk of penalties, which averaged $125 million per financial institution in recent AML enforcement actions.

The solution's ability to identify complex relationship patterns through Graph RAG technology has already uncovered previously undetected money laundering schemes, potentially preventing millions in financial losses and associated regulatory penalties. Together, these benefits position GFG as an industry leader in financial crime compliance, enhancing both regulatory standing and market reputation.

5.2.10 Other Challenges and Considerations

The deployment of GenAI in AML presents complex data protection challenges, particularly when operating across multiple jurisdictions with varying regulatory frameworks such as GDPR, CCPA, and local banking secrecy laws. Privacy-preserving AI techniques become essential, including federated learning approaches that enable AML model training without centralizing sensitive customer data, differential privacy mechanisms that add statistical noise to protect individual privacy while maintaining analytical utility, and homomorphic encryption that allows computations on encrypted data without decryption. For cross-border operations, organizations must implement data localization strategies using regional AI model deployments, pseudonymization and tokenization of customer identifiers before cross-border transfer, and consent management frameworks that ensure compliance with varying jurisdictional requirements.

Additionally, synthetic data generation using GenAI can create realistic but non-personal training datasets that eliminate privacy concerns while maintaining model effectiveness, while zero-knowledge proof systems can enable AML compliance verification without revealing underlying customer information. These approaches ensure that GenAI-powered AML systems can operate effectively across global financial networks while maintaining the highest standards of customer data protection and regulatory compliance, transforming potential privacy constraints into competitive advantages through innovative privacy-by-design architectures.

5.2.11 Summary

GFG's GenAI-powered AML and SAR solution represents a transformative approach to financial crime compliance, moving beyond traditional rule-based systems to an intelligent, adaptive framework. By integrating advanced LLMs, Graph RAG technology, and Agentic AI architecture, the solution creates a comprehensive ecosystem capable of detecting complex money laundering schemes across disparate data sources. The multi-agent approach, with specialized components for data enrichment, suspicious activity detection, SAR generation, and filing enables a seamless workflow that maintains human oversight while dramatically reducing manual effort.

The solution's strength lies in its ability to understand context and relationships rather than merely flagging threshold violations. By analyzing transaction patterns in conjunction with beneficial ownership structures, business purposes, and external data sources, the system identifies sophisticated money laundering techniques that previously went undetected. The automated SAR generation capability ensures consistent, compliant narratives that follow FinCEN's 5W format[9] while avoiding conclusory language and addresses a common regulatory criticism of manual reports. The human-in-the-loop approach maintains appropriate oversight while leveraging AI to handle routine tasks, creating a balanced framework that satisfies both efficiency and compliance requirements.

As financial institutions face increasing regulatory scrutiny and more sophisticated financial crime threats, solutions such as GFG's AML and SAR will become essential for maintaining effective compliance programs. This case study demonstrates how GenAI can transform compliance from a cost center into a strategic capability that enhances risk management while optimizing resource allocation. This is a model that financial institutions can follow as they modernize their financial crime compliance programs.

5.3 Use Case 2: Risk Identification and Measurement, Real-Time Analysis of Regulatory Updates

5.3.1 Problem Statement

GFG struggles with identifying emerging risks due to the manual interpretation of regulatory changes and updates. Delays in assessing the impact of new regulations compromise the firm's compliance posture.

[9] https://www.fincen.gov/sites/default/files/shared/sarnarrcompletguidfinal_112003.pdf

5.3.2 Current State, Challenges

- Compliance Advisors and Analysts spend around 15–20 hours per month manually interpreting and summarizing regulatory documents.
- Risk Advisors and Analysts spend an additional 10–12 hours analyzing the impact on existing policies.

5.3.3 Objective

Accelerate the identification of regulatory changes and their implications for GFG, enhancing real-time decision-making.

5.3.4 Key Results

- Automate the summarization of 90% of new regulatory updates within 24 hours of release.
- Reduce the time spent on manual analysis by 80% (saving 20+ hours/ month per analyst).
- Improve response time to regulatory changes by 50%.

5.3.5 Solution Overview

To address these GFG challenges, we propose a GenAI-driven solution that leverages **RAG** and **vector databases** to transform how compliance and risk teams manage regulatory intelligence. This solution automates the ingestion, summarization, and contextualization of complex regulatory updates by combining the power of large language models with domain-specific retrieval from a regulatory knowledge base. Through intelligent document processing, semantic search, and AI-grounded reasoning, GFG can accelerate its response to emerging regulations, reduce manual workload, and improve the accuracy and timeliness of risk impact assessments. The architecture is designed to be scalable, explainable, and compliant with model risk governance standards, enabling real-time decision-making and operational resilience across the enterprise.

5.3.6 Detailed Solution Architecture

The following diagram provides a high level solution overview.

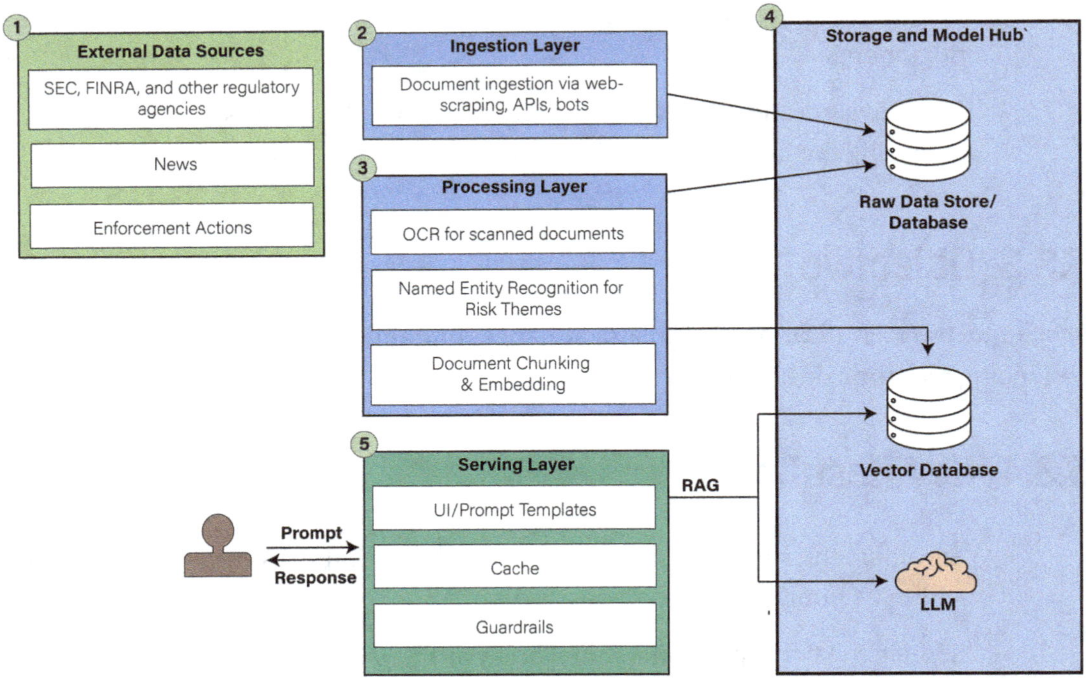

***Figure 5-3.** Detailed Solution Architecture for the Real-time Analysis of Regulatory Updates*

5.3.7 Key Components of the Solution

5.3.7.1 External Data Sources

These include regulatory agencies, including SEC and FINRA, financial news organizations, those agencies that provide enforcement actions, etc.

5.3.7.2 Data Ingestion Layer

This layer has APIs or bots that scrape the web for specific and relevant financial regulations and other news/enforcement actions, collect the documents and store them in a database or an object store (such as Amazon S3).

5.3.7.3 Processing Layer

This includes data pre-processing and converting unstructured data into embeddings. The features in this layer include OCR for scanned documents, Named Entity Recognition (NER) for identifying risk themes, and document chunking/embedding, in other words, it splits documents into semantically meaningful chunks (for example, by clause or paragraph).

5.3.7.4 Storage and Model Hub

This layer consists of data stores such as a data lake for storing files, images, etc., and others such as the vector database. The models are hosted on the model hub.

5.3.7.5 Serving Layer

This layer provides the primary interface for the users to interact with the system via prompts. This helps the risk advisors and compliance advisors who look into actionable summaries grounded in facts, uses the RAG pipeline that we discussed earlier in Chapter 4. The key features include a chat interface where the advisors can ask questions similar to the following:

- *"Which controls need review based on this SEC ruling?"*
- *"How does this update compare to GDPR Article 33?"*
- *"Which operational controls are impacted by this ruling?"*
- *"What are the historical precedents for this clause?"*

Analysts can provide thumbs-up or down on AI outputs to further fine-tune the models.

5.3.7.6 Future Enhancements

- **Multimodal Regulatory Input**: Include webinars, audio commentary, or visual regulatory updates
- **Proactive Alerting**: Transformer-based time-series models to predict regulatory focus areas
- **Self-Updating Policy Templates**: Use LLM agents to draft revised policy paragraphs ready for analyst review

5.3.8 Business Benefits

The GenAI-powered Regulatory Platform delivers substantial financial and operational benefits to GFG. By automating 90% of regulatory update summarization and reducing manual analysis time by 80%, the organization achieves an estimated annual cost savings of millions of dollars through more efficient resource allocation. Compliance and Risk Advisors reclaim approximately 20–25 hours monthly previously spent on document interpretation and impact analysis, allowing them to focus on strategic risk management and proactive compliance initiatives. This efficiency gain enables GFG to monitor 3.5 times more regulatory sources without additional headcount, providing comprehensive coverage across global jurisdictions and specialized financial regulations.

Beyond direct cost savings, the platform significantly reduces regulatory risk exposure by improving response time to regulatory changes by 50%. This enhanced responsiveness allows GFG to implement required controls and policy updates before compliance deadlines, avoiding potential penalties that averaged $185,000 per violation in recent enforcement actions. The platform's comprehensive audit trail of regulatory interpretations strengthens GFG's defensibility during examinations, while the factually grounded outputs ensure consistent application of regulatory requirements across business units. The interactive chat interface democratizes access to regulatory expertise throughout the organization, enabling frontline staff to quickly understand compliance implications without specialist intervention. Additionally, the platform's ability to identify cross-regulatory impacts (such as overlaps between SEC requirements and GDPR provisions) helps GFG develop more efficient, harmonized compliance approaches rather than siloed solutions for each regulation. Together, these benefits transform regulatory compliance from a reactive cost center into a strategic capability that enhances decision-making and competitive positioning.

5.3.9 Summary

GFG faces significant challenges in managing regulatory updates, with compliance and risk advisors spending 25–30 hours monthly on manual interpretation and impact analysis of new regulations. This labor-intensive process creates delays in identifying emerging risks and compromises the firm's compliance posture. To address these challenges, GFG implemented a GenAI-driven solution leveraging RAG and vector databases to automate the ingestion, summarization, and contextualization of regulatory updates.

This comprehensive approach enables GFG to automate 90% of regulatory update summarization within 24 hours of release, reduce manual analysis time by 80%, and improve response time to regulatory changes by 50%.

5.4 Use Case 3: Trade and Market Surveillance for Insider Trading and Compliance

5.4.1 Problem Statement

At GFG, monitoring trading activities and related communication for potential insider trading and other compliance violations is a critical task. One of the main challenges includes processing large amounts of unstructured data such as emails, attachments, images, and audio to find patterns for insider trading. GFG follows a rule-based trade monitoring system which is similar to that of a number of other FSOs. However existing rule-based trade monitoring systems are unable to distinguish between suspicious and legal trades effectively.[10] In fact, according to a survey of 17 FSOs, the ratio of actual suspicious transactions to total identified suspicious transactions can be as low as 0.01%.[11]

The rule-based approach is limited in its ability to detect complex patterns or subtle indications of insider trading activities. Additionally, compliance analysts spend a significant amount of time reviewing audio call recordings manually to detect suspicious discussions, which is a labor-intensive process.

5.4.2 Current State, Challenges

- Compliance officers and surveillance analysts spend 25–30 hours per week reviewing flagged communications (emails, chats, internal messaging, social media) and manually investigating potential patterns of insider trading.

[10] https://www.infosys.com/iki/perspectives/effective-trade-market-surveillance.html

[11] https://www.niceactimize.com/compliance/blog-winning-the-compliance-battle-on-multiple-fronts-tackling-market-abuse-and-false-positives.html

- Rule-based systems are limited in scope, generating high false-positive rates, leading to inefficiencies in investigation and a 25% increase in review times.
- Manual context analysis of flagged communications consumes 15–20 hours per week per analyst, further delaying the identification of potential insider trading schemes.
- Audio call monitoring is particularly time-consuming, with analysts spending 40–50 hours per week listening to and transcribing flagged calls to detect potential insider trading discussions. This process is inefficient and resource-draining, especially when calls contain a large volume of irrelevant information.

5.4.3 Objective

Use GenAI to enhance corporate communication surveillance by identifying complex patterns indicative of insider trading or other compliance violations. This approach should move beyond rule-based systems to include contextual analysis and pattern recognition that can detect subtle signs of illicit activities.

5.4.4 Key Results

- **Increase Detection Accuracy**: Improve the accuracy of insider trading detection by 40% by using context-based analysis and advanced pattern recognition rather than traditional keyword searches.
- **Reduce False Positives**: Cut the false-positive rate by 30%, allowing for more efficient resource allocation by only flagging truly suspicious communications.
- **Enhance Efficiency**: Reduce the time spent on manual review of flagged communications by 50% (saving 15+ hours per week per compliance officer).

- **Automate Contextual Summarization**: Automate the generation of 90% of communication summaries, reducing time spent on manual reporting and investigation by 60%.
- **Improve Insider Trading Detection**: Detect previously undetected insider trading patterns by identifying subtle anomalies and complex communication dynamics, leading to a 30% increase in early detection.
- Automatically transcribe audio calls and reduce the time spent by compliance analysts by 90%.

5.4.5 Solution Overview

The challenges faced by GFG in corporate electronic communications surveillance represent a critical opportunity for transformation through GenAI. This section outlines a detailed solution architecture that addresses the identified challenges and meets the specified objectives and key results. The proposed solution to address the limitations of rule-based surveillance and manual review at GFG is a comprehensive, GenAI-powered intelligent surveillance platform.

To address these challenges, this solution leverages GenAI, including advanced LLMs, RAG, and vector databases, to enhance the accuracy, efficiency, and scalability of communication surveillance. By implementing context-aware AI models, automated transcription, and anomaly detection systems, GFG can significantly improve detection accuracy, reduce false positives, and streamline compliance workflows. This solution not only ensures regulatory compliance but also mitigates the risk of hefty fines.

5.4.6 Detailed Solution Architecture

Figure 5-4 represents the detailed solution architecture.

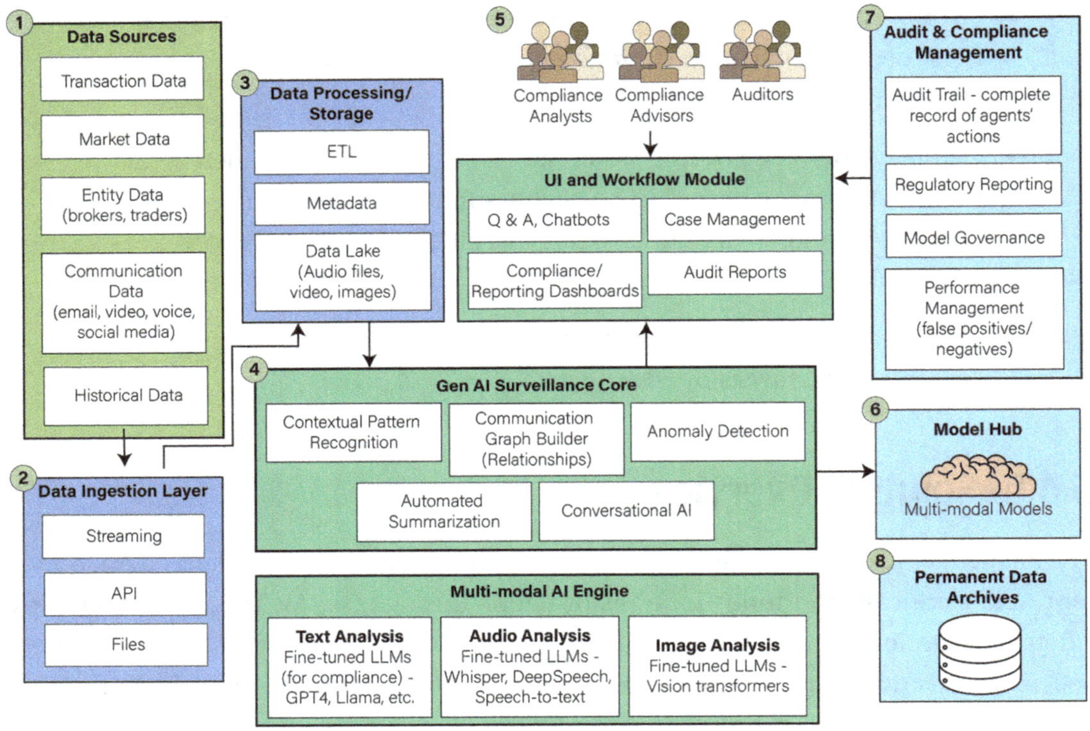

***Figure 5-4.** Detailed Solution Architecture for Insider Trading Surveillance*

5.4.7 Key Components of the Solution

5.4.7.1 Data Sources

The data sources include structured transaction data, entity data, including brokers, traders; market data, including news, events, announcements, etc.; and communication data (voice, video, chat, email, social media, etc.). Note that overall, there could be millions of messages across all these channels.

5.4.7.2 Data Ingestion and Integration Layer

This includes integration of the data sources with the surveillance platform through various methods such as API integration, streaming integration and file-based integration.

5.4.7.3 Data Processing and Storage Layer

This includes extracting and preprocessing and processing data. The preprocessing includes data normalization, language detection, Entity Extraction (NER), metadata enrichment (timestamps, sender, etc.) and attachment/image extraction. The meta data as well as the data such as the raw files, images, and audio/video are stored for further analysis

5.4.7.4 GenAI Surveillance Core and Multimodal AI Engine

This includes the core of the GenAI functionality and the following components.

- **Text Analysis**: LLMs (e.g., GPT-5, Llama 4, fine-tuned for compliance) - this functionality helps analyze the vast amount of unstructured data for any insider trading patterns.
- **Audio Analysis**: Speech-to-Text (e.g., OpenAI Whisper, DeepSpeech) - meetings generate audio and video. These should be translated to text for further analysis. Several GenAI models will help achieve this functionality.
- **Image Analysis**: Vision Transformers (e.g., CLIP, BLIP).
- **Multimodal Fusion**: Joint embedding models for cross-modal context.
- **Contextual Pattern Recognition**: LLMs, prompt engineering, few-shot learning.
- **Anomaly Detection**: Autoencoders, clustering, graph neural networks.
- **Communication Graph Builder**: Relationship and information flow mapping. There may be communication chains across various channels that may be indicative of insider trading patterns. Graph databases and graph RAG can help detect these patterns.
- **Automated Summarization**: Generative models for concise summaries of the conversations.
- **Conversational AI**: Dialogue analysis for collusion detection.

5.4.7.5 Surveillance Workflow Module

This module consists of the following components:

- **Case Management**: Users, including compliance advisors and analysts, primarily interact with the surveillance system using the case management. The users investigate the potential insider trading alerts and notifications within this component.
- Q/A chatbots help the investigators to retrieve insights into potential trading patterns. Rather than manually investigating various sources of data, the users can utilize LLM-based chatbots to gather information and conduct potential investigations.
- Compliance Dashboards help track whether the organization is compliant with the regulations from SEC, FINRA, and other regulatory agencies.
- The human-in-the loop review provides an option to the users to help fine-tune the models further based on whether a given alert is a false positive or not.

5.4.7.6 Model Hub

The model hub hosts both third party models such as Llama3, GPT4, etc., and first party models such as those fine-tuned by the organization for specific compliance needs.

5.4.7.7 Audit and Compliance Management

- Immutable Logging (blockchain or WORM storage)
- Regulatory Reporting (SEC, FINRA, FCA templates)
- Privacy and Access Controls (GDPR/CCPA compliance)

5.4.7.8 Permanent Data Archives

As discussed earlier in this section, for SEC compliance, data retention policies for communication surveillance are stringent and highly prescriptive. Under SEC Rules 17a-3 and 17a-4, broker-dealers must retain all business-related electronic communications for a minimum of three years. These records must be preserved in a non-rewritable, non-erasable (WORM) format to prevent tampering or deletion, and firms must be able to promptly produce them upon regulatory request.

The solution includes a permanent data archive that stores the messages in compliance with these regulations (e.g., WORM compliance).

5.4.8 Business Benefits

The GenAI-powered intelligent surveillance platform delivers substantial financial and operational benefits to GFG. By reducing false positives by 30% and automating 90% of communication summarization, the organization achieves an estimated annual cost savings in millions of dollars through efficient resource allocation and reduced manual review time. Compliance officers and surveillance analysts reclaim approximately 20–25 hours per week previously spent on manual reviews, allowing them to focus on high-value investigative work and strategic compliance initiatives. This efficiency gain translates to a 40% increase in analyst productivity and enables GFG to handle a 35% growth in communication volume without additional headcount.

Beyond direct cost savings, the platform significantly reduces regulatory risk exposure by improving detection accuracy by 40% and identifying previously undetected insider trading patterns. This enhanced detection capability helps GFG avoid potential regulatory penalties. The platform's comprehensive audit trail and immutable logging capabilities strengthen GFG's defensibility during regulatory examinations, while the 90% reduction in audio review time ensures complete coverage of communication channels which addresses a critical gap in traditional surveillance approaches. Together, these benefits position GFG as an industry leader in compliance technology, enhancing both regulatory standing and market reputation.

5.4.9 Summary

GFG's GenAI-powered Intelligent Surveillance Platform represents a paradigm shift in financial services compliance monitoring, moving beyond traditional rule-based systems to context-aware, multimodal surveillance. By integrating advanced LLMs, speech-to-text conversion, image analysis, and graph-based relationship mapping, the platform creates a comprehensive surveillance ecosystem capable of detecting subtle patterns across diverse communication channels. The solution's strength lies in its ability to understand context and relationships rather than merely flagging keywords, enabling it to identify complex insider trading schemes that previously went undetected.

The platform's implementation demonstrates how GenAI can transform labor-intensive compliance processes while simultaneously improving effectiveness. The human-in-the-loop approach ensures continuous improvement through analyst feedback, while immutable logging and comprehensive audit trails maintain regulatory defensibility. As financial institutions face increasing communication volumes across multiple channels, solutions such as GFG's platform will become essential for maintaining compliance with SEC and FINRA regulations while efficiently managing surveillance resources. This case study illustrates how GenAI can address the dual challenges of compliance effectiveness and operational efficiency that have long plagued financial services surveillance programs.

5.5 Use Case 4: GenAI-Powered Technology Risk Management Platform

GFG faces significant operational risk exposure due to its fragmented technology landscape. With legacy core banking systems operating alongside newer cloud applications, the organization struggles with system integration, security vulnerabilities, and operational inefficiencies. This section outlines a comprehensive GenAI-powered solution to address these challenges and transform GFG's technology risk management capabilities.

5.5.1 Problem Statement

At GFG, the aging technology infrastructure and fragmented systems landscape create significant information systems and technology risk exposure. Legacy core banking systems, some over 40 years old, operate alongside newer cloud applications with inadequate integration. This fragmentation results in data silos, security vulnerabilities, and operational inefficiencies. System outages have increased by 35% in the past year, with recovery times averaging 4–6 hours per incident. Additionally, the lack of comprehensive API governance and monitoring capabilities has led to unauthorized access attempts increasing by 25%, creating regulatory compliance concerns and potential data breaches.

5.5.2 Current State, Challenges

- IT operations teams spend 45–50 hours weekly addressing system performance issues and unplanned outages, with incident resolution taking 30% longer than industry benchmarks.
- Security teams manually review 2,000+ daily security alerts across disconnected monitoring tools, with 65% of critical vulnerabilities taking more than 30 days to remediate.
- Technology governance committees spend 25+ hours monthly reconciling conflicting data from various systems to produce regulatory reports.
- System integration requires custom code maintenance that consumes 40% of development resources, delaying strategic initiatives by an average of 3 months.
- Disaster recovery testing reveals 30% of critical systems fail to meet recovery time objectives, with data loss potential exceeding acceptable thresholds.

5.5.3 Objective

Implement a GenAI-powered technology risk management platform that provides real-time system monitoring, predictive maintenance, automated vulnerability detection, and intelligent incident response to reduce operational disruptions, strengthen security posture, and ensure regulatory compliance.

5.5.4 Key Results

- **Reduce System Downtime**: Decrease unplanned system outages by 75% through AI-powered predictive maintenance and proactive issue detection.
- **Accelerate Incident Response**: Reduce mean time to resolution for critical incidents from 4 to 6 hours to under 60 minutes using AI-driven root cause analysis.

- **Enhance Security Posture**: Identify and remediate 90% of critical vulnerabilities within 7 days (down from 30+ days) through automated vulnerability detection and prioritization.
- **Improve Regulatory Compliance**: Automate 85% of technology risk reporting, reducing manual effort by 20+ hours monthly while improving accuracy by 40%.
- **Optimize Resource Allocation**: Reduce maintenance workload by 35% through intelligent automation, redirecting 25% of IT resources to strategic innovation initiatives.
- **Strengthen Disaster Recovery**: Achieve 99.5% success rate in disaster recovery testing with AI-optimized recovery procedures and automated failover capabilities.

5.5.5 Solution Overview

The GFG GenAI-powered technology risk management platform represents a paradigm shift in how financial institutions can address information systems and technology risk. This integrated solution leverages cutting-edge AI and GenAI technologies to provide real-time system monitoring, predictive maintenance, automated vulnerability detection, and intelligent incident response capabilities.

The platform's architecture consists of four primary layers:

1. **Data Integration Layer**: Connects disparate systems and aggregates data from across the technology landscape
2. **AI and GenAI Processing Layer**: Applies traditional and GenAI models to analyze data and generate insights
3. **Application Layer**: Provides specialized applications for risk management, incident response, and compliance
4. **Presentation and Governance Layer**: Delivers insights to stakeholders and manages governance workflows

5.5.6 Solution Architecture

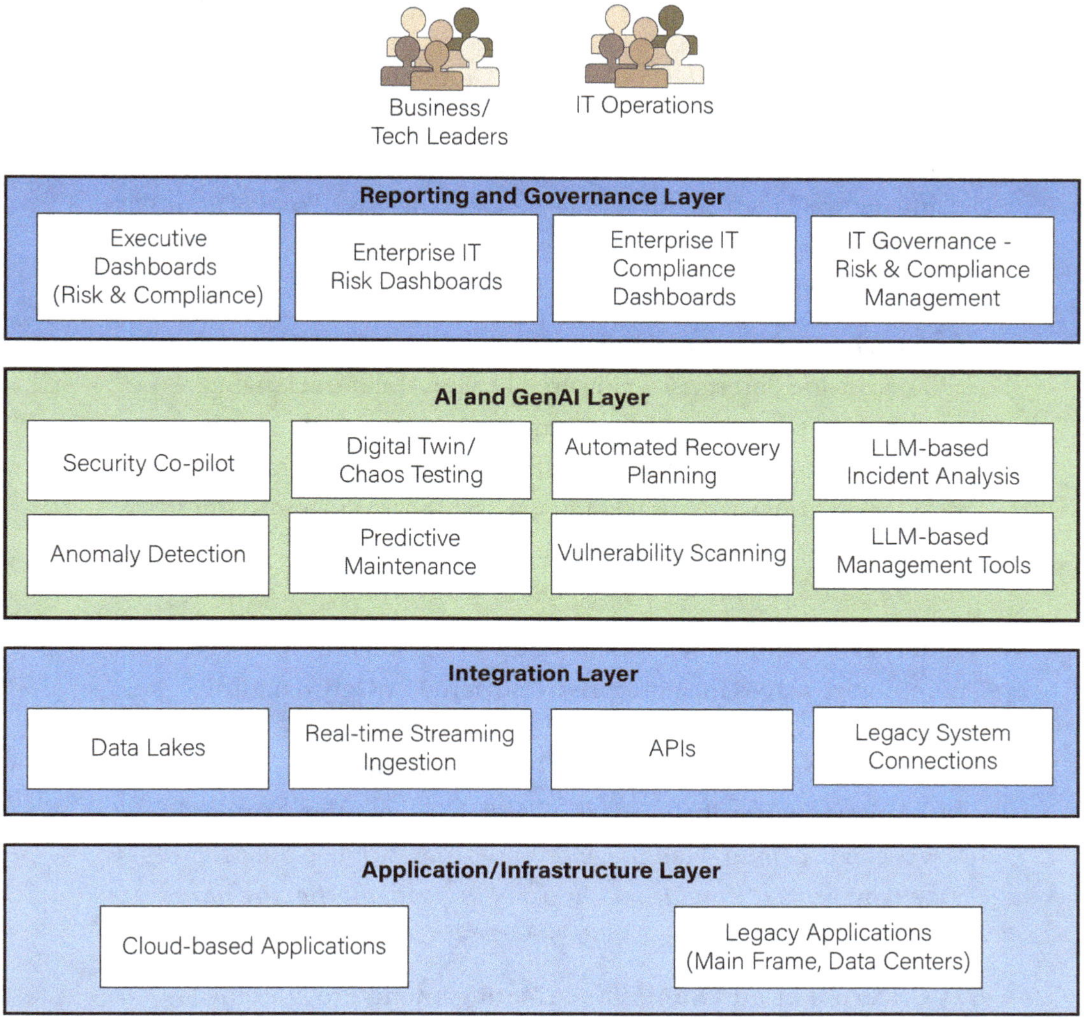

Figure 5-5. *Detailed Solution Architecture for the GenAI-powered Technology Risk Management Platform Use Case*

5.5.7 Key Components of the Solution

5.5.7.1 Presentation and Governance Layer

- **Executive Dashboards**: Powered by GenAI natural language search capabilities, it provides high-level technology risk metrics for leadership. The business leaders can customize their own reports using natural language prompts - for example, say "*Provide me a pie chart report of all the high, medium, and low IT specific risks created across the enterprise over the last 30 days.*"
- **Enterprise IT Risk Dashboards**: Consolidated view of technology risk across the enterprise - powered by GenAI natural language search. These provide IT operations staff across the enterprise with insights into technology risks, including cyber and operational risks. Users can use natural language prompts to customize their reports - for example, say "*Provide me the list of DDOS attacks and the originating countries using a world map format.*"
- **Enterprise Compliance Dashboards**: Consolidated view of IT compliance across the enterprise - powered by GenAI natural language search. These provide business leaders and IT operations staff across the enterprise with insights into compliance, including regulations such as the PCI DSS, GDPR, NIST, or other standards. Users can use natural language prompts to customize their reports - for example, say "*Provide me the list of PCI systems that are non-compliant in the AML line of business.*"
- **IT Governance and Compliance Management**: Provides the IT staff with the ability to view and fix compliance issues - for example, if there is a non-compliant system with a vulnerability, an IT staff member can use the prompt "*Install the latest operating system patch for all non-production environments, run the automated system tests and provide an updated compliance report.*"

5.5.7.2 AI and GenAI Layer

- **Anomaly Detection**: ML models that identify unusual system behavior patterns.
- **Predictive Maintenance**: AI algorithms that forecast potential system failures.
- **LLM-Based Incident Analysis**: GenAI that performs root cause analysis and produces a detailed set of actions for the operations teams. This component analyzes system logs, error messages, and performance metrics, generates comprehensive root cause analysis reports and recommends remediation steps with specific implementation details.
- **Vulnerability Scanner**: AI-powered security assessment tools that scan for vulnerabilities as well as any potential PII or PCI data.
- **Digital Twin Simulator, Synthetic Data, and Chaos Test Generators**: Virtual replicas of critical systems for scenario testing – also generates test cases and synthetic data for various scenarios, including system downtime and security attacks.
- **LLM-Based Management Tools**: These tools interpret the natural language prompts from the IT staff and implement the corresponding actions. These can be coordinating agents to accomplish a goal such as "*Fix the current system vulnerabilities*" – that includes various agents to (1) run a vulnerability scan; (2) remediate the vulnerability; and (3) generate a detailed report for the fixes.
- **Automated Recovery Planner**: GenAI tools that create optimal recovery plans and procedures. This planner develops detailed recovery procedures for various failure scenarios, optimizes recovery sequences to minimize downtime, and generates step-by-step instructions for operations teams.

- **Security Copilot**: GenAI assistant for security teams to accelerate threat response. This will help guide the security teams with incident, event and threat management via chatbots. The security co-pilot assists security analysts in investigating alerts, generates security policy recommendations and creates documentation for security procedures.

5.5.7.3 Data Integration Layer

- **Legacy System Connectors**: Custom adapters for integrating core banking systems
- **APIs**: For other applications and systems to send data to the GenAI IT Risk management platform
- **Data Lake**: Unified repository for structured and unstructured data from all systems
- **Real-Time Streaming**: Incident and Event processing pipeline for immediate detection of anomalies

5.5.8 Business Benefits

The GenAI-powered technology risk management platform delivers substantial business value beyond technical improvements, directly impacting GFG's bottom line and competitive positioning. By reducing system outages by 75% and accelerating incident resolution to under 60 minutes, the platform minimizes operational disruptions that previously cost the organization millions of dollars annually in lost productivity and customer dissatisfaction. The enhanced security posture and 85% automation of compliance reporting translate to approximately several million dollars in annual savings from avoided regulatory penalties and reduced audit preparation costs, while simultaneously strengthening customer trust and brand reputation in an increasingly security-conscious market.

Furthermore, the platform transforms GFG's technology organization from a cost center to a strategic enabler by redirecting 25% of IT resources from maintenance to innovation initiatives. This reallocation, combined with the platform's ability to optimize infrastructure spending through predictive capacity planning, yields an estimated

25% reduction in total technology ownership costs while accelerating time-to-market for new financial products. The resulting competitive advantage positions GFG as an industry leader in both operational resilience and innovation agility, creating sustainable differentiation in the crowded financial services marketplace.

5.5.9 Summary

The GFG GenAI-powered technology risk management platform represents a transformative approach to addressing information systems and technology risk in financial institutions. By leveraging the power of both traditional AI and cutting-edge GenAI technologies, GFG has created a solution that not only mitigates current risks but also adapts to emerging threats.

The platform's ability to continuously learn from system behavior, generate synthetic data for testing, create digital twins for simulation, and provide AI-assisted incident response fundamentally changes how technology risk is managed. Rather than relying on reactive approaches and manual processes, GFG now has a proactive, automated system that identifies and addresses risks before they impact the business.

As financial institutions continue to face increasing technology complexity and regulatory scrutiny, solutions such as the GFG's platform will become essential components of operational risk management. The combination of traditional AI capabilities with GenAI's creative problem-solving abilities creates a powerful toolset for addressing the challenges of modern financial technology environments.

5.6 Chapter Summary

The 2008 financial crisis serves as a stark reminder of the devastating consequences when financial institutions fail to properly manage risk. This global economic catastrophe, triggered by unchecked risk-taking in subprime mortgage lending, demonstrated how inadequate risk management can lead to widespread financial devastation affecting millions of lives. For FSOs, risk is inherent to their business model; the challenge lies not in avoiding risk entirely but in understanding and mitigating it effectively to protect assets, ensure compliance, and maintain market stability.

GenAI emerges as a transformative technology for risk management in financial services, offering unprecedented capabilities to analyze vast data sources, detect subtle patterns, and predict potential issues before they escalate into crises.

As we discussed throughout this chapter, GenAI solutions across multiple risk domains demonstrate the technology's versatility and impact. From enhancing Anti-Money Laundering operations and suspicious activity reporting to revolutionizing regulatory compliance monitoring, trade surveillance, and technology risk management, GenAI is enabling more accurate, efficient, and proactive risk management. These solutions leverage advanced techniques including RAG, multimodal AI processing, and digital twin simulation to transform traditionally reactive, manual processes into automated, predictive systems that identify and address risks before they impact the business. These solutions help financial institutions avoid hefty fines, protect their reputation, and maintain regulatory compliance in an increasingly complex environment.

CHAPTER 6

Retail Banking with GenAI

In Chapter 5, we laid the groundwork by exploring the foundations of GenAI and its early impact on the financial industry, with a focus on risk and compliance. We covered advancements in Anti-Money Laundering (AML) compliance, Suspicious Activity Reporting (SAR) automation, real-time regulatory analysis, and risk management. This chapter shifts to retail banking, where GenAI is driving innovation in customer-facing operations. We explore three core applications: intelligent customer support and digital assistants, credit risk profiling and loan decisioning for thin-file customers, and AI-powered Know Your Customer (KYC) and compliance automation. Together, these use cases highlight how GenAI is enabling more personalized, efficient, and scalable retail banking services.

Retail banking represents the foundation of the global financial services industry. This sector is responsible for delivering critical day-to-day financial products and services such as savings and checking accounts, personal loans, mortgages, and digital payments to billions of individuals and businesses. As of 2024, the global retail banking market is estimated at US$ 2,039.25 billion, with a projected compound annual growth rate (CAGR) of 5.8% through 2033.[1] The industry is at a pivotal point, driven by accelerated digitization, increasing customer expectations for around-the-clock service, growing regulatory complexity, and heightened competition from agile fintechs and digital-only banks.[2]

Global surveys by firms such as Accenture and Deloitte reveal that over 75% of banking customers expect hyper-personalized experiences, seamless digital onboarding, and instant service across channels.[3] Simultaneously, traditional institutions face

---

[1] https://www.grandviewresearch.com/industry-analysis/retail-banking-market

[2] https://www.emerald.com/insight/content/doi/10.1108/978-1-83797-130-520241015/full/html

[3] https://www.deloitte.com/uk/en/Industries/financial-services/research/hp-future-of-retail-banking.html

S. Godavarthi, R. Nagvekar, *Transforming Financial Services with Generative AI*,
https://doi.org/10.1007/979-8-8688-2053-3_6

rising operational costs, fragmented data ecosystems, and intensifying cybersecurity threats. To remain competitive and compliant in this dynamic landscape, leading banks are turning to advanced technologies such as GenAI to reimagine core banking services, improve efficiency, and redefine customer engagement.[4] Within this shifting global landscape, Global Fiscal Group (GFG), our fictitious FSO that we introduced in Chapter 2 has embarked on a strategic transformation journey to future-proof its retail banking operations. GFG provides a full suite of services, including checking and savings accounts, mortgage services, personal and auto loans, credit cards, electronic wallets, and real-time payments. Historically rooted in traditional branch-based banking, GFG is now at the forefront of integrating next-generation technology into its core service model.

Recognizing the urgent need to deliver speed, personalization, and intelligent service at scale, GFG is leveraging GenAI as a foundational driver of its multi-year transformation agenda. The bank's strategic vision is to "change the current banking experience by making everyday banking intelligent, predictive, and personalized through Agentic AI." Tools such as GPT-5, Claude, Retrieval-Augmented Generation (RAG) pipelines, and multi-agent orchestration platforms, such as LangChain, and CrewAI, are being deployed to modernize how GFG understands customer context, manages risk, ensures compliance, and scales omnichannel support.[5]

Unlike investment banking, retail banking deals with millions of highly personalized, low-value transactions daily. GFG's legacy systems, similar to many in the industry, suffer from data silos, manual intervention points, and static service protocols. By integrating GenAI into its operating model, GFG aims to convert both structured and unstructured data into actionable intelligence, streamline onboarding and credit evaluation, proactively support financial wellness, and ultimately, redefine retail banking as a scalable, customer-centric, AI-powered ecosystem.

This chapter explores how GenAI is transforming retail banking operations at institutions such as GFG, focusing on customer experience enhancement, support automation, lending operations, and marketing optimization. We'll examine both current implementations and emerging possibilities, highlighting the tangible benefits these technologies bring to both financial institutions and their customers.

---

[4] https://www.mckinsey.com/industries/retail/our-insights/personalizing-the-customer-experience-driving-differentiation-in-retail

[5] https://arxiv.org/html/2505.10468v4

6.1 Current Challenges in Retail Banking

There is a tectonic change in retail banking in North America, and GFG is leading this change initiative in its stride. The mix of customer behavior change, growth in the digital channels, intensifying regulatory environment, as well as the growing complexity of operations makes it a set of circumstances which the legacy banking infrastructure cannot effectively address.[6] The following is a list of the main obstacles the current retail banking business of GFG has to offer and reasons to invest in the use of GenAI as a groundbreaking technology.

6.1.1 Increasing Demands in Individual and Around-the-Clock Service

Today, customers want personalized responses to their financial needs immediately and they do not care whether they get them through their mobile phone, the web, the bank branch, or via a voice call. Nevertheless, legacy systems have little context-awareness and personalization.[7] Long customer support turnaround times, canned marketing messages, and static FAQs all diminish the engagement and fail to build trust. At GFG, over 60% of contact center interactions involve repetitive queries that could be automated if systems understood context and intent.

6.1.2 Data Silos and Disjointed Customer Perspectives

The retail consumers are exposed to GFG at various points of contact but the transactional, behavioral, and engagement information are all usually in different systems. Such fragmentation does not allow GFG advisors to develop a united impression of the customer or provide them with the same cross-channel experiences. Consequently, personalization initiatives are not proactive and are restricted to demographic groups rather than situational, real-time wisdom.

[6] https://www.researchgate.net/publication/377748651_The_Impact_of_Digital_Marketing_Management_on_Customers_Buying_Behavior_Case_Study_of_Soran_City

[7] https://www.mdpi.com/2078-2489/14/11/608

6.1.3 Missing Appropriate Credit Risk Analysis of Thin-File Applicants

At GFG, about one-third of the people asking to take out loans are first-time credit users or lack the history required to automatically approve their loan. Conventional credit scoring methods are rule-based and usually cannot measure behavior and other forms of credit-worthiness.[8] The latter causes a high rate of rejections among underserved groups and depreciates the capacity of GFG to advance financial inclusion through minimizing risk exposure.

6.1.4 Lending, Onboarding, and Compliance Operational Inefficiencies

Retail functions, such as loan generation, KYC/AML work, as well as account onboarding, are labor-intensive and include manual checks. Personal loan application processing time takes an average of five to seven business days to go through, due to the iterations between the internal systems and the human analysts.[9] Similarly, KYC compliance checks and fraud alerts produce high number of false positives and flood compliance units with unnecessary reviews.

6.1.5 Increasing Digital Fraud and Regulatory Pressure

With the emergence of digital banking, fraud detection has become complicated. The threats to GFG include the growing presence of identity fraud, account takeovers, and transactional anomalies that develop much faster than the conventional rule-based detection systems can keep up with. Regulatory agencies such as the Consumer Financial Protection Bureau (CFPB), the Office of the Comptroller of the Currency (OCC), and the Financial Crimes Enforcement Network (FinCEN) demand stricter compliance, where hefty fines are imposed on oversight malpractices.[10] In 2023, the

---

[8] http://repository.kyu.ac.ke/handle/123456789/1114

[9] https://www.fourthline.com/blog/how-long-does-kyc-verification-take

[10] https://heinonline.org/HOL/Page?handle=hein.journals/ielr40&div=138&g_sent=1&casa_token=

average penalty assessed against North American financial institutions for failure to conduct KYC and transaction monitoring was more than $219 million.[11]

6.2 Use Case 1: Enhancing Customer Experience via Intelligent Customer Support and Digital Banking Assistant

6.2.1 Problem Statement

GFG's retail banking division receives millions of customer service requests each month across phone, email, web, mobile, and in-branch channels. A significant portion, over 65%, comprises low-complexity queries such as balance checks, password resets, card activations, and transaction status updates. These repetitive tasks overwhelm contact center agents, increase operational costs, and erode customer satisfaction due to long wait times and inconsistent responses. Despite deploying traditional chatbots, GFG has faced challenges in achieving human-level understanding, contextual awareness, and emotional intelligence especially when handling follow-ups or multi-turn conversations.

6.2.2 Current State, Challenges

GFG's customer support operations suffer from several legacy limitations:

- **Low Automation Coverage**: Existing rule-based chatbots can only resolve 20% of queries end-to-end. The rest are escalated to live agents, resulting in high queue times and support costs.
- **Fragmented Knowledge Base**: Information is spread across various systems product manuals, policy docs, FAQs, and compliance memos, making it difficult to retrieve timely, accurate responses.
- **No Contextual Memory**: Current systems lack long-term memory, leading to disconnected customer journeys across channels.

[11] https://resources.fenergo.com/newsroom/global-financial-institution-aml-and-regulatory-fines-soar-in-2023

- **Lack of Sentiment Awareness**: There is no active detection of customer frustration, urgency, or satisfaction during digital or voice interactions.
- **Scalability Challenges**: The contact center workforce is already stretched, and scaling through human hiring is economically unsustainable.
- **Compliance Risk**: Improper handling of sensitive information or providing inaccurate advice could violate regulatory guidelines and lead to penalties.[12]

In Q4 2023, GFG's internal audit revealed that the average support resolution time was 22 hours via email and more than 15 minutes via voice call. Customer satisfaction for digital support channels was 36% below the benchmark for Gen Z customers.

6.2.3 Objective

To transform customer service into an intelligent, scalable, and emotionally responsive experience, GFG aims to deploy an Agentic AI-powered omnichannel assistant. The system must provide 24/7 contextual support, resolve 80% of common issues autonomously, reduce live-agent dependency, and deliver personalized interactions that align with each customer's financial profile and emotional state.

6.2.4 Key Results

GFG defined the following strategic OKRs for this transformation:

1. **Resolution Efficiency**: Increase the self-service resolution rate from 20% to 80% within 12 months by deploying an AI agent capable of resolving routine and mid-complexity inquiries through intelligent, context-aware interactions.
2. **Time Reduction**: Reduce the average support resolution time by 70% across all digital channels through AI-assisted summaries, context carry-over, and pre-drafted responses.

[12] https://heinonline.org/HOL/Page?handle=hein.journals/upjlel25&div=21&g_sent=1&casa_token=

3. **Customer Satisfaction**: Improve Customer Satisfaction (CSAT) scores by 40% by delivering faster, more accurate, and personalized support experiences powered by Large Language Models (LLMs) and real-time learning.

4. **Agent Productivity**: Reduce call volume to live agents by 50%, allowing support teams to focus on escalated, high-value cases that require human empathy and decision-making.

5. **Multilingual Support**: Enable real-time multilingual support in five major languages (including English, Spanish, and French) within six months using LLM translation and Natural Language Understanding (NLU) capabilities.

6. **Regulatory Compliance**: Achieve 100% compliance alignment with data privacy and audit trail regulations such as the Gramm-Leach-Bliley Act (GLBA) and the California Consumer Privacy Act (CCPA) by embedding governance controls into the AI agent's architecture.

6.2.5 Solution Overview: Agentic AI-Powered Banking Assistant

GFG can launch the OmniAssist Platform, an Agentic AI-driven customer engagement engine built on a multi-agent architecture. It combines GenAI (GPT-5, Claude), RAG, and LangChain orchestration to understand, process, and respond to customer requests across channels with near-human fluency and contextual awareness.

This AI-powered system includes a conversational assistant agent that supports multi-turn dialogues and natural language interactions, a knowledge retrieval agent that fetches real-time answers from GFG's dynamic enterprise content repository using vector search and RAG, a sentiment and emotion detection agent to modulate tone and escalate sensitive issues, a memory agent that maintains session continuity and historical context across interactions, a compliance monitor agent to ensure every interaction adheres to legal, ethical, and regulatory standards.

The OmniAssist platform is deployed across web, mobile app, Interactive Voice Response (IVR), and in-branch kiosks to ensure true omnichannel continuity.

6.2.6 Detailed Solution Architecture

Figure 6-1 depicts the detailed solution architecture for the OmniAssist platform.

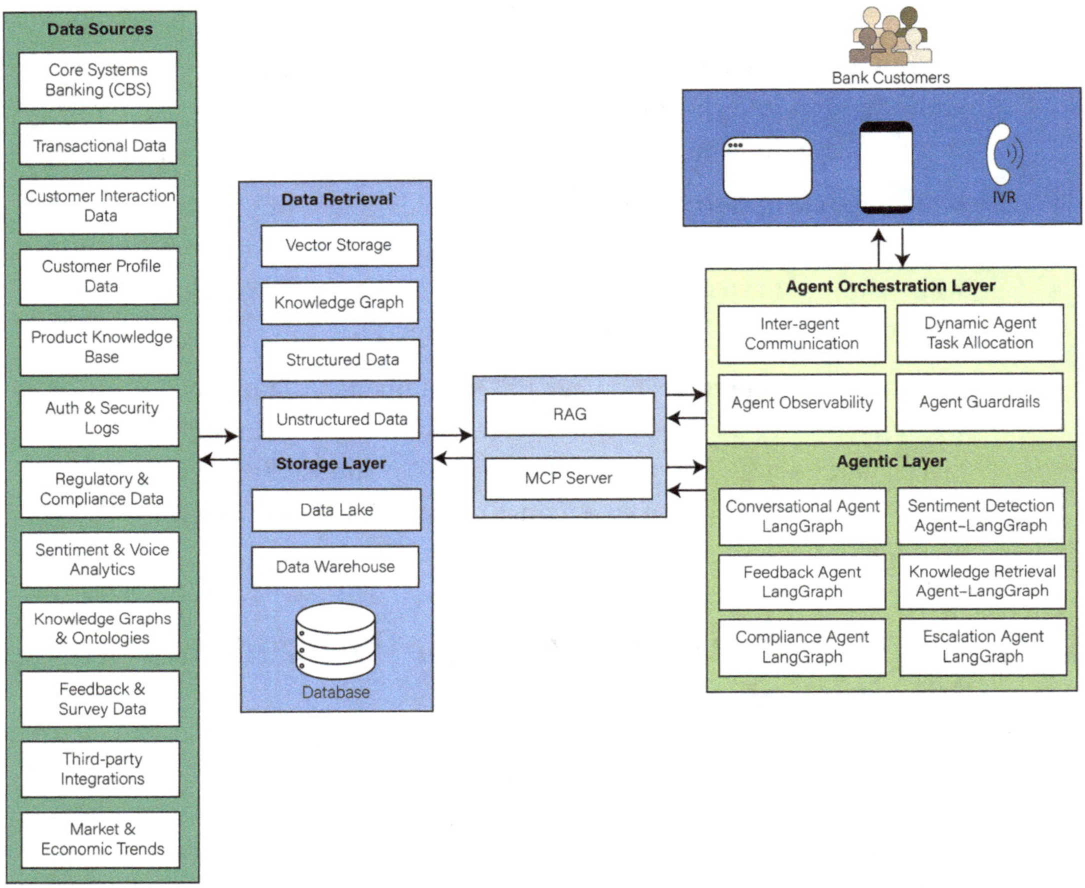

***Figure 6-1.** Detailed Solution Architecture for the OmniAssist Platform*

6.2.7 Key Components of the OmniAssist Platform Solution

6.2.7.1 Input Layer

- **Web Interfaces and In-application Widgets**: Deliver support via embedded chatbots and contextual widgets within banking websites and applications.

- **Mobile Chat Interfaces**: Facilitate real-time assistance through chat features in native mobile banking applications.
- **Voice Assistants and IVR Systems**: Handle spoken queries via phone-based support using speech-to-text technologies.
- **Input Normalization and Preprocessing**: To ensure accurate and context-aware responses, all customer inputs (whether from voice, text, or in-app interactions) are first normalized into a structured format. This includes automatic language detection and translation, speech-to-text conversion for voice inputs, and text cleaning as well as tokenization for LLM readiness. Metadata such as customer ID, channel source, and timestamps are also captured to enrich context. This step ensures downstream agents receive clean, actionable input for effective resolution.
- **Session Management and Context Preservation**: The system maintains multi-turn conversational context by tracking session history, prior responses, and user preferences. This continuity enables the Conversational Agent and Sentiment Detection Agent to respond with greater personalization, emotional awareness, and consistency across channels, delivering a more seamless and human-like experience.

6.2.7.2 Data Sources

- **Core Banking Systems (CBS)**: Access to real-time balances, account status, transaction limits, and loan repayment schedules enables assistants to provide accurate, up-to-date support and transaction execution capabilities.
- **Transactional Data**: Bank account activity, credit and debit card usage, bill payments, transfers, and ATM withdrawals provide insight into financial behavior and are essential for offering personalized support, fraud detection, and financial recommendations.
- **Customer Interaction Data**: Historical and real-time records of customer engagements across channels such as mobile applications, chatbots, call centers, emails, and branch visits. This data helps the AI assistant understand user intent, behavioral patterns, and preferences.

- **CRM and Customer Profile Data**: Demographic information, customer segmentation, account history, life events, and relationship tenure stored in Customer Relationship Management (CRM) systems are used to tailor conversations, predict needs, and enhance personalization.
- **Banking Product Knowledge Base**: Internal documentation, FAQs, product brochures, policy guides, and procedural manuals that allow AI assistants to accurately answer queries about products such as savings accounts, credit cards, loans, and mortgages.
- **Authentication and Security Logs**: Data from biometric systems, OTP logs, and device fingerprinting systems helps the AI assistant validate user identity and detect potential fraud during interactions.
- **Regulatory and Compliance Data**: Data repositories containing information on KYC, AML, and other compliance policies guide the assistant to operate within legal and regulatory frameworks.
- **Sentiment and Voice Analytics**: Derived from call recordings, live chat logs, and feedback forms, sentiment data enables the AI to assess customer mood and adapt responses accordingly, escalating issues when necessary.
- **Knowledge Graphs and Ontologies**: These represent relationships between banking concepts, products, and customer intents, enabling the assistant to reason across multiple topics and deliver coherent responses.
- **Feedback and Survey Data**: Insights collected through post-interaction surveys, Net Promoter Scores (NPS), and customer satisfaction (CSAT) ratings are used to train and refine AI models for continuous improvement.
- **Third-Party Integrations**: APIs from fintech partners (such as credit scoring agencies, payment platforms, financial wellness platforms) provide additional context for AI-powered recommendations and cross-product support.

- **Market and Economic Trends**: Publicly available macroeconomic indicators (such as interest rates and inflation) from sources, including Federal Reserve Economic Data (FRED) or central bank reports, to contextualize financial advice.

6.2.7.3 Agentic Layer

The Agentic Layer comprises modular, task-specific AI agents that collaborate to handle complex customer interactions in a flexible and intelligent manner. Each agent is built on a foundation of LLMs and orchestrated using tools such as LangGraph for state and logic management.

- **Conversational Agent**: Serves as the frontline interface, maintaining multi-turn dialogue with customers. It leverages LLMs to generate natural responses and incorporates memory to retain context across a session, offering a personalized, fluid experience.
- **Knowledge Retrieval Agent**: Uses RAG to fetch precise information from internal sources such as product documentation, compliance manuals, or policy databases, ensuring accurate responses to customer queries.
- **Sentiment Detection Agent**: Analyzes the emotional tone of customer inputs using Natural Language Processing (NLP) and tone modeling. It helps the system adapt its conversational tone and flags interactions that indicate frustration, urgency, or distress.
- **Escalation Agent**: Identifies when a query is too complex or risky for automation, such as disputes, fraud, or regulatory complaints, and routes the conversation to a human agent in real time, ensuring continuity and context handover.
- **Feedback Agent**: Engages post-interaction to gather satisfaction ratings, comments, and suggestions. This agent feeds user feedback back into the training loop, supporting reinforcement learning and continual model improvement.

- **Compliance Agent**: Enforces data privacy and regulatory compliance by redacting sensitive information (such as PII and card numbers), validating response accuracy, logging interactions, and maintaining audit trails in alignment with policies such as GLBA, PCI-DSS, and CCPA.

6.2.7.4 Agent Orchestration Layer

The *Agent Orchestration Layer* is responsible for coordinating and supervising the behavior of individual agents in the Agentic Layer. It ensures that each agent works within its domain while contributing to the overall customer experience. Key components include

- **Inter-Agent Communication**: Facilitates data exchange and coordination among agents using shared context, memory, and standardized protocols. For example, the Sentiment Detection Agent may alert the Escalation Agent if customer frustration is detected, triggering a real-time handover.
- **Dynamic Agent Task Allocation**: Adapts workflows dynamically based on the conversation's context, determining which agent(s) should be invoked at any given time. This prevents unnecessary computation and ensures task relevance.
- **Agent Observability**: Enables real-time monitoring of AI agent performance, including metrics such as latency, confidence scores, escalation rates, and task success. This observability is crucial for debugging, optimization, and trust.
- **Agent Guardrails**: Applies business rules, ethical guidelines, and security filters to constrain agent behavior. This includes grounding LLM responses, ensuring factual correctness, and preventing hallucinations or policy violations.

6.2.8 Business Benefits

The implementation of OmniAssist delivered measurable business outcomes within the first six months of deployment. One of the most immediate benefits is a significant reduction in contact center operating expenses - by 35%, resulting in annualized savings of approximately $9 million. Additionally, customer satisfaction scores across digital channels improved markedly, rising from 56% to 82%, indicating a more responsive and seamless service experience. OmniAssist also transformed agent productivity, freeing up 50% of live agents to focus on higher-value, complex advisory interactions rather than routine inquiries. The platform demonstrated remarkable scalability by seamlessly handling a fourfold increase in peak traffic during the tax season, without any degradation in system performance.

From a regulatory standpoint, all AI-generated responses are fully logged and auditable, ensuring continuous compliance with financial services regulations such as GLBA and CCPA. Most notably, the consistency and reliability of the AI-driven interactions led to a 25% improvement in repeat engagement rates, strengthening long-term customer loyalty.

6.3 Credit Risk Profiling and Loan Decisioning for Thin-File Customers

6.3.1 Problem Statement

A significant challenge in GFG's North American retail banking portfolio lies in credit underwriting for thin-file or new-to-credit applicants. Despite strong demand for personal loans, credit cards, and buy-now-pay-later products, a sizable portion of applicants lack traditional credit history. According to GFG's internal data, nearly 30% of North American loan applications fall into the "thin-file" category, comprising students, gig workers, recent immigrants, and young professionals. These applicants are often denied due to insufficient historical credit bureau data, despite possessing potential indicators of financial stability. This results in lost business opportunities, poor customer experience, and reduced financial inclusion.

6.3.2 Current State, Challenges

Traditional risk models at GFG rely heavily on structured data sources such as FICO scores, debt-to-income ratios, and repayment history obtained from credit bureaus. These models are limited in their ability to evaluate applicants with unconventional income sources, fragmented work histories, or those transitioning from cash-based lifestyles to formal banking.

Key challenges include

- **High Rejection Rates**: Thin-file applicants face a 60–70% rejection rate due to incomplete, insufficient, or credit profiles that cannot be scored.
- **Manual Underwriting Burden**: Underwriters spend excessive time reviewing borderline cases due to a lack of automation or contextual intelligence.
- **Limited Alternative Data Use**: Behavioral, transactional, and digital footprint data is underutilized, despite its potential to signal creditworthiness.
- **Bias and Fairness Risks**: Existing scoring models may reinforce systemic bias, unintentionally excluding certain demographic groups.
- **Compliance Constraints**: Any new decision-making model must be explainable, auditable, and compliant with US fair lending laws, including the Equal Credit Opportunity Act (ECOA) and Fair Credit Reporting Act (FCRA).[13]

These limitations hinder GFG's ability to serve emerging market segments and diversify its lending portfolio without increasing risk exposure.

6.3.3 Objective

GFG aims to implement a GenAI-powered credit decision-making system that enhances risk profiling of thin-file applicants by integrating alternative data sources, behavioral signals, and predictive analytics. The goal is to promote responsible financial inclusion while maintaining high risk standards and regulatory compliance.

[13] https://www.fdic.gov/resources/supervision-and-examinations/consumer-compliance-examination-manual/documents/4/iv-1-1.pdf

6.3.4 Key Results

The strategic OKRs for this initiative are

- **Approval Expansion**: Increase approval rate for thin-file applicants by 50% without increasing default rates
- **Decision Speed**: Reduce loan decision turnaround time from 5 to 7 days to under 24 hours
- **Model Explainability**: Ensure 100% of credit decisions are auditable and explainable under ECOA and FCRA[14]
- **Bias Mitigation**: Reduce adverse action notices due to missing or biased data by 40%
- **Cross-Sell Uplift**: Improve downstream product adoption (such as savings accounts and auto loans) by 30% for newly onboarded thin-file customers

6.3.5 Solution Overview: Agentic AI Credit Assessment Engine

To meet these objectives, GFG developed the FairScore AI Engine, a multi-agent GenAI system designed to evaluate creditworthiness using both traditional and alternative data.[15] The architecture incorporates

- GenAI models to simulate financial scenarios and fill gaps in applicant data.
- RAG pipelines pull insights from customer interactions, transaction logs, and third-party behavioral data.
- Fairness and Bias Detection Agents to ensure equitable treatment across demographic segments.

[14] https://www.consumercomplianceoutlook.org/2013/second-quarter/adverse-action-notice-requirements-under-ecoa-fcra/

[15] https://arxiv.org/abs/2502.07254

- Explainability Agents that automatically generate plain-language rationales for each credit decision, aligned with regulatory disclosure requirements.

By combining GenAI with predictive analytics and ethical AI principles, FairScore enables data-rich, compliant, and inclusive credit evaluation at scale.

6.3.6 Detailed Solution Architecture

The FairScore AI Engine operates as an Agentic AI pipeline, orchestrated through LangChain and LangGraph, and comprises the following layers depicted in Figure 6-2.

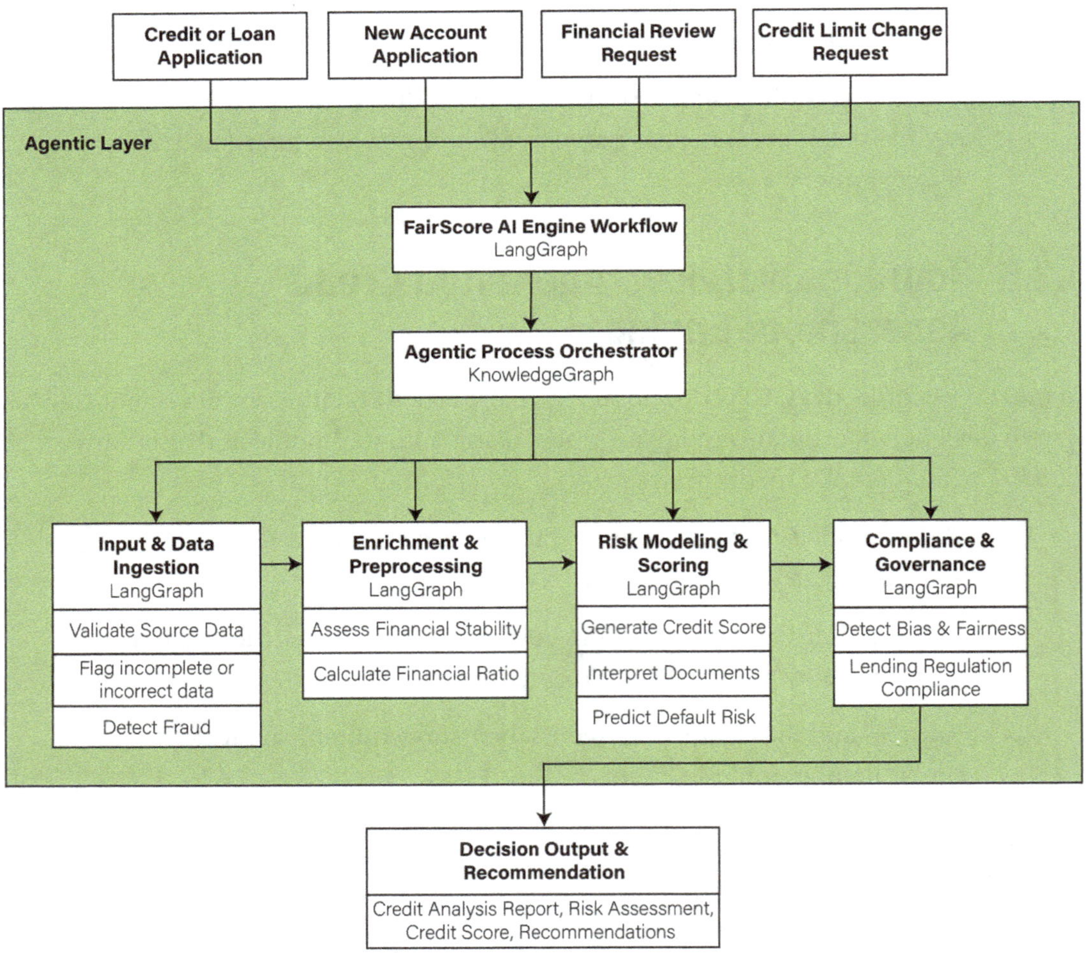

Figure 6-2. *Technology Solution Architecture*

6.3.6.1 Input and Data Ingestion Layer

This layer collects loan applications from multiple customer touchpoints, including mobile applications, web portals, and in-branch systems. It integrates seamlessly with internal enterprise systems such as CRM platforms, historical transaction data repositories, and payroll databases. In addition, it connects with external alternative data providers such as Plaid and Yodlee and ingests non-traditional data from sources such as utility bills and telecom providers. It also incorporates digital behavioral data, including clickstream activity, mobile app engagement metrics, and patterns in bill payments, providing a rich, contextual foundation for downstream processing.

6.3.6.2 Enrichment and Preprocessing Agents

To address data gaps and enhance the quality of incoming applications, several AI-powered agents operate within this layer. The Synthetic Data Agent uses GPT-5 to intelligently fill missing application fields by simulating plausible financial behaviors based on contextual cues. The Income Estimator Agent analyzes transaction patterns and gig economy signals to estimate both income level and stability. Meanwhile, the Spending Analyzer Agent segments customer expenses into fixed and discretionary categories and calculates a financial resilience score, which gauges a borrower's ability to withstand financial shocks.

6.3.6.3 Risk Modeling and Scoring Layer

This component employs a hybrid modeling approach, combining the strengths of multiple techniques. Gradient Boosting Machines (such as XGBoost) capture structured, nonlinear relationships, while deep learning models built in TensorFlow generate credit scores by learning complex patterns in applicant data. Additionally, LLMs are used to interpret unstructured documents such as pay stubs, landlord letters, and employment contracts. Scoring occurs in real time, using over 100 structured and unstructured features, enabling instant credit decisions. An integrated Explainability Engine generates transparent, customer-facing reason codes using tools, such as LIME and SHAP, that support regulatory requirements and build trust with applicants.

6.3.6.4 Compliance and Governance Layer

A suite of governance agents ensures the platform remains compliant with lending regulations. The Bias Detection Agent proactively flags any disparate impact or proxy discrimination risk across applicant segments. An Audit Trail Generator captures data inputs, model parameters, and decision logic for each application, supporting audit readiness and regulatory transparency. Furthermore, the Fair Lending Compliance Monitor continuously validates that credit decisions, whether approvals or denials, adhere to GFG's internal fairness criteria, pre-deployment, and ongoing tests across protected and intersectional groups. The checks also include statistical parity difference, disparate-impact ratio (alert if <0.80), equal opportunity/TPR gap, calibration, and counterfactual flips of protected attributes, with bootstrap confidence intervals and drift alarms (PSI > 0.10).

6.3.6.5 Decision Output and Recommendation Layer

This final layer delivers the lending decision in real time, categorizing outcomes into approvals, referrals for further review, or denials. For applicants who are denied, the system doesn't simply reject the request, it suggests alternative pathways such as starter credit products or credit-building programs tailored to their financial profile. Personalized communication is automatically generated using GenAI-powered templates, ensuring each applicant receives clear and empathetic messaging aligned with their outcome.

6.3.7 Key Components of the Solution

- **Synthetic Data Generator**: Fills missing application fields by simulating plausible financial behaviors using GenAI, ensuring thin-file customers are not unfairly penalized for data gaps. This agent leverages contextual cues and peer group analysis to enrich applicant profiles for more accurate risk assessment.
- **Risk Scoring Agent**: Combines traditional and alternative data including utility payments and digital behavior, using advanced machine learning to produce a unified, real-time credit score for each applicant. It adapts dynamically to new data sources, enabling instant, data-rich credit decisions even for applicants with limited credit history.

- **Bias Detection Agent**: Monitors the credit assessment process for demographic or geographic bias, using fairness metrics to flag and help correct any discriminatory patterns. Continuous auditing ensures compliance with fair lending regulations and supports ethical AI practices.
- **Explainability Agent**: Automatically generates clear, regulator-ready, and customer-friendly explanations for every credit decision, translating complex model outputs into actionable reason codes. This transparency builds trust with applicants and streamlines bank regulatory reporting.
- **Income Estimator Agent**: Analyzes transaction data and gig economy signals to estimate both the level and stability of income, enabling fair assessment for applicants with non-traditional earnings. It distinguishes between regular and irregular income streams, providing a nuanced view of financial resilience.
- **Product Recommendation Agent**: Suggests tailored credit-building products or upsell options based on each applicant's risk profile, supporting financial inclusion and customer satisfaction. By aligning offers with individual needs, it increases cross-sell opportunities and long-term customer engagement.

6.3.8 Business Benefits

The deployment of FairScore has delivered measurable performance improvements within its first year:

- **Increased Approvals**: Thin-file loan approvals rose by 52%, with no increase in 90-day delinquencies.
- **Faster Decisions**: Average decision time fell to 6 hours, accelerating onboarding and customer satisfaction.
- **Inclusive Lending**: 65% of approved thin-file applicants had never received formal credit before.
- **Regulatory Readiness**: GFG passed third-party fairness audits with 100% transparency in model explainability and data usage.

- **Operational Savings**: Underwriting time dropped by 60%, enabling reallocation of staff to high-risk loan categories.
- **Portfolio Diversification**: GFG expanded its lending base into underserved regions, contributing to a 9% increase in overall net interest income from personal loans.

6.4 AI-Powered KYC and Retail Bank Compliance Automation

6.4.1 Problem Statement

KYC and AML regulations are fundamental to ensuring the security, legality, and integrity of financial operations. However, for GFG, similar to many retail banks, KYC remains a complex, expensive, and slow process. Onboarding new clients requires extensive manual verification of identity documents, address proof, and employment records, often involving disconnected systems and human validation at every step.

- Internal audits at GFG revealed that more than 20% of customer onboarding delays were directly linked to KYC bottlenecks. Moreover, false positives from rule-based screening systems triggered over 40% of unnecessary escalations to compliance teams. The sheer volume of regulatory requirements, combined with legacy document processing tools, limit GFG's ability to offer a seamless onboarding experience especially for digitally savvy, mobile-first users. This has led to higher dropout rates during onboarding and growing operational strain on compliance analysts.

6.4.2 Current State, Challenges

GFG's KYC infrastructure is predominantly rule-based, relying on a mix of Optical Character Recognition (OCR) tools, manual checks, and form-driven decision flows. While functionally compliant, it presents multiple inefficiencies:

- **Manual Document Review**: Human analysts verify documents, such as passports, driver's licenses, and tax IDs, which increases processing time and error rates.

- **Fragmented Data Sources**: Information comes from disparate sources, customer uploads, public records, and third-party identity services without integration into a unified view.
- **Static Screening Systems**: AML and sanctions screening rely on keyword-based searches, which generate a high volume of false positives and miss nuanced risks.
- **Lack of Explainability**: Compliance teams struggle to justify decision outcomes to regulators, especially when using opaque risk-scoring models.
- **Audit Fatigue**: Regulatory audits require exhaustive data logs and explanation of every rejected or flagged application, which strains resources.

In an age when onboarding speed and regulatory accuracy are both essential, GFG's KYC process lags behind customer expectations and competitive benchmarks.

6.4.3 Objective

GFG aims to modernize its KYC process using a GenAI-powered platform that automates identity verification, reduces false positives, and enables real-time risk classification while ensuring regulatory compliance and full auditability.

The system, called KYC-AI, will integrate LLMs with multi-agent workflows to process unstructured documents, extract relevant entities, cross-check with watchlists, and generate clear, explainable justifications for onboarding decisions.

6.4.4 Key Results

GFG has defined the following strategic OKRs for the KYC-AI initiative:

- **Onboarding Speed**: Reduce the average onboarding time from 4 days to under 12 hours. This acceleration enhances operational efficiency and customer satisfaction.
- **False Positive Reduction**: Lower KYC/AML false alerts by 50% within 6 months. Fewer false positives reduce unnecessary compliance escalations and resource strain.

- **Analyst Efficiency**: Free up 40% of compliance team capacity through automation. This allows analysts to focus on high-risk cases and strategic oversight.
- **Regulatory Readiness**: Ensure 100% of KYC decisions are explainable and audit-ready. This supports compliance with evolving regulatory frameworks and internal governance standards.
- **Customer Experience**: Improve onboarding satisfaction scores by 35%. A smoother onboarding process builds early trust and reduces customer drop-off.
- **Coverage Expansion**: Enable onboarding of previously excluded segments, such as freelancers and migrants, using alternative document intelligence. This expands the addressable market while maintaining compliance integrity.

6.4.5 Solution Overview: Agentic AI for KYC

The KYC-AI platform uses a modular, agent-based architecture to orchestrate multiple GenAI components for document processing, identity verification, fraud risk analysis, and compliance reporting.

The core capabilities include

- **Automated Document Understanding**: LLMs extract names, dates, addresses, ID numbers, and validity data from photos, scans, or PDFs using OCR + GPT-5.
- **Watchlist Matching**: Cross-checks applicant data with OFAC, FinCEN, Interpol, and internal fraud databases using RAG.
- **Risk Scoring and Justification**: Generates dynamic, risk-based recommendations with regulator-friendly explanations (such as "High match probability with sanctioned entity").
- **Real-Time Escalation and Audit Logging**: Automatically routes flagged cases to human analysts while logging decision rationale for every application.

This system ensures decisions are not only fast and accurate but also transparent and aligned with evolving compliance mandates.

6.4.6 Detailed Solution Architecture

Figure 6-3 depicts the detailed solution architecture for the KYC-AI platform.

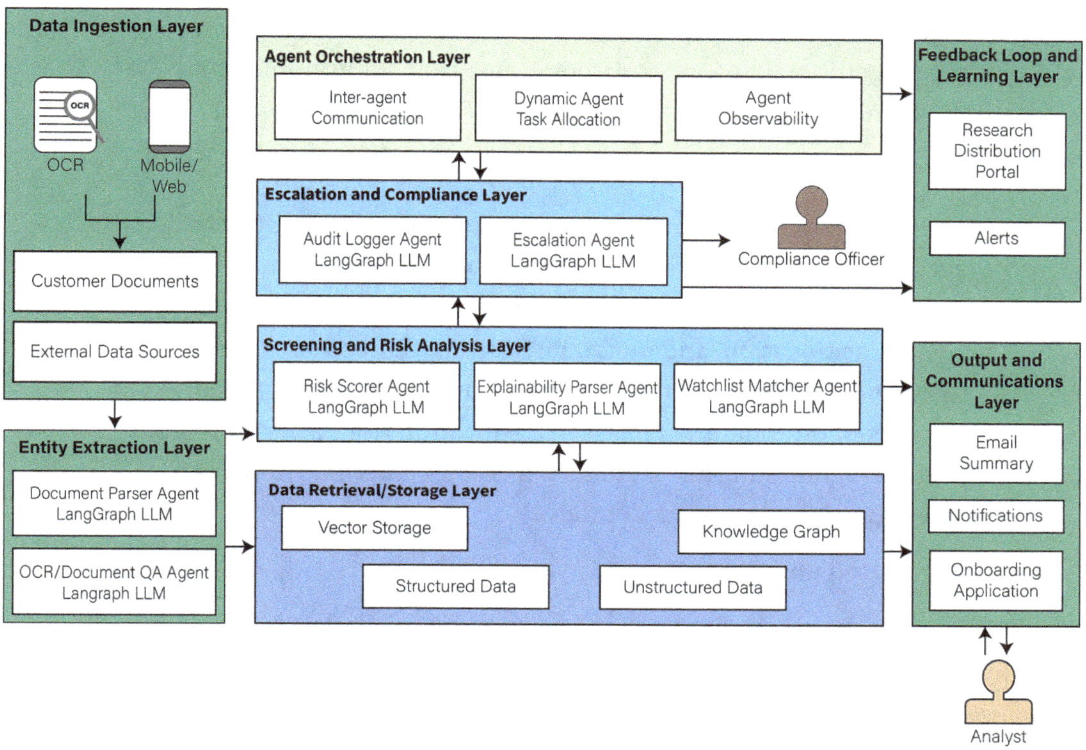

Figure 6-3. *KYC Process Automation Using GenAI*

The KYC-AI platform is structured across six functional layers, each playing a key role in automating and securing the onboarding and compliance process.

1. **Input and Document Capture Layer**:

   Customers initiate onboarding by uploading identity documents, proof of address, tax records, and other required documentation through web or mobile interfaces. Optical Character Recognition (OCR) engines process these documents to extract raw text, laying the groundwork for downstream data analysis.

2. **Entity Extraction and Verification Layer**:

   This layer includes the Document Parser Agent, which leverages GPT-5 to convert varied document formats into structured, machine-readable data. The Entity Validator Agent then checks this structured data for consistency, ensuring, for example, that the name and date of birth match across all submitted forms.

3. **Screening and Risk Analysis Layer**:

   The Watchlist Matcher Agent scans the applicant's identity details against global sanction and watchlists to detect any known risks. Simultaneously, the Risk Scorer Agent evaluates behavioral signals, geolocation, and metadata from submitted documents to assign a risk level. To promote transparency, the Explainability Agent generates natural language justifications for each risk score, such as highlighting anomalies such as login attempts from high-risk regions or expired credentials.

4. **Escalation and Compliance Layer**:

   In cases where elevated risk is detected, the Escalation Agent routes those profiles to human compliance officers for manual review. Alongside this, the Audit Logger Agent continuously records every agent action and decision path, ensuring that the entire process remains traceable and audit-ready for regulatory reviews.

5. **Feedback Loop and Learning Layer**:

   This layer enables continuous improvement by feeding human analyst decisions back into the system to retrain models and enhance risk evaluation accuracy. Additionally, updates in regulatory frameworks are dynamically reflected in the system through RAG, allowing the platform to stay compliant with evolving requirements.

6. **Output and Communication Layer**:

   Finally, customers are proactively informed of their application status via real-time notifications. Internally, compliance teams can monitor operational performance using dashboards that present key metrics such as onboarding throughput, risk profiles, and process bottlenecks in the form of compliance KPIs and heatmaps.

6.4.7 Key Components of the Solution

- **Document Parser Agent**: Extracts structured information from unstructured documents such as IDs, utility bills, and contracts. Uses advanced OCR and NLP to accurately capture key fields, reducing manual data entry and errors.
- **Entity Validator Agent**: Checks for consistency and accuracy across all uploaded records and data sources. Automatically flags discrepancies or mismatches, ensuring data integrity and compliance with regulatory standards.
- **Watchlist Matcher Agent**: Performs AI-enhanced name and pattern matching against global sanctions and PEP lists. Adapts to spelling variations, aliases, and transliteration, improving detection of high-risk individuals and entities.
- **Risk Scorer Agent**: Generates a dynamic risk score for each customer, incorporating contextual insights from multiple data sources. Continuously updates risk profiles as new information is ingested, supporting proactive compliance management.
- **Explainability Agent**: Produces clear, regulator-compliant rationales for every KYC and compliance decision. Translates complex AI outputs into understandable explanations for auditors, regulators, and customers.
- **Audit Logger Agent**: Maintains a complete, tamper-proof record of all inputs, outputs, and agent actions throughout the KYC process.
- Enables end-to-end traceability and supports rapid response to regulatory audits or internal reviews.

6.4.8 Business Benefits

- **Faster Onboarding**: Over 80% of applicants are now verified within 10 hours, dramatically reducing onboarding time from the previous 4-day average and accelerating customer acquisition.
- **Reduced Manual Effort**: Compliance analyst workload dropped by 43%, allowing teams to redirect their focus toward handling high-risk or exceptional cases rather than routine checks.
- **Lower False Positives**: The system reduced false alerts by 55% through intelligent, context-aware entity matching, minimizing unnecessary escalations and compliance friction.
- **Increased Coverage**: GFG successfully onboarded 18% more first-time applicants, including freelancers and migrants, by accepting and intelligently parsing alternative documentation.
- **Improved Compliance**: The platform demonstrated strong regulatory performance, passing audits with zero compliance breaches, thanks to fully explainable and traceable decision-making.
- **Enhanced Customer Experience**: Onboarding satisfaction scores rose by 38%, particularly among Gen Z and mobile-first users, who benefited from the smoother, faster verification flow.

6.5 Chapter Summary

The leap that GFG made to use GenAI in retail banking to benefit from intelligent, scalable, and personalized commercial services is a game-changer. With increasing customer demands, poor efficiencies in operations, and increasing regulatory pressures, GFG has been able to effectively use Agentic AI to overcome the operational issues across levels of customer support, credit risk assessment, and automation of regulatory processes. Such solutions as OmniAssist, FairScore, and KYC-AI also help not only increase the accuracy of decisions and the speed of services provided but also cut down on manual work, enhance financial inclusion, and enhance regulatory compliance. This chapter showed that GenAI will enable GFG to reinvent the retail banking model and transform from reactive provision of services to proactive and context-based interactions, where prospective adaptation to the continually more digital and competitive banking world prevails.

CHAPTER 7

Investment Banking with GenAI

In Chapter 6, we explored how GenAI is transforming retail banking through customer-facing applications. In this chapter, we discuss how GenAI can help transform investment banking by streamlining complex, information-heavy workflows. Key use cases include AI-powered trade surveillance, automated investment research and insight generation, and deal structuring with client intelligence. These applications enhance decision making, compliance, and operational efficiency across high-stakes functions.

Investment banking forms the cornerstone of global capital markets, enabling capital formation, strategic advisory, risk management, and securities underwriting. The global investment banking market is projected to exceed US$765 billion by 2034, driven by rising corporate restructuring, cross-border mergers and acquisitions, and the growth of emerging markets.[1] The industry plays a critical role in facilitating complex financial transactions for institutional clients, sovereign entities, and multinational corporations, particularly in an era defined by heightened market volatility and technological disruption.[2]

Traditionally, investment banking is distinguished from retail banking by its high-value, low-volume transactional nature that demands real-time decision-making, data-rich modeling, and deep financial expertise. However, global investment banks now face mounting challenges, including regulatory tightening, shrinking margins, data explosion, and client demand for hyper-personalized services. These pressures have led to a structural rethink of legacy workflows and digital capabilities across the industry.

[1] https://www.precedenceresearch.com/investment-banking-and-trading-services-market

[2] https://www.frontiersin.org/journals/marine-science/articles/10.3389/fmars.2024.1463843/full

S. Godavarthi, R. Nagvekar, *Transforming Financial Services with Generative AI*,
https://doi.org/10.1007/979-8-8688-2053-3_7

Operating at this intersection is Global Fiscal Group (GFG), our fictitious Financial Services Organization (FSO) that we introduced in Chapter 2. Yet, as its global peers do, GFG reports that over 70% of analyst time is consumed by data aggregation and formatting, while compliance reporting cycles are lengthening under increasing regulatory scrutiny.

To address these challenges, GFG plans to embed GenAI at the core of its investment banking infrastructure. Moving beyond traditional automation, GFG is investing in Agentic AI systems powered by Large Language Models (LLMs), Retrieval Augmented Generation (RAG), and orchestrators such as LangGraph and CrewAI. These intelligent agents help transform core workflows, enabling scalable decision-making, proactive compliance, and client-specific insights. This chapter outlines the challenges and use cases driving this strategic transformation.

7.1 Challenges in Investment Banking

The investment banking division at GFG operates at the intersection of complex financial modeling, market volatility, and regulatory scrutiny. Unlike retail operations, investment banking relies heavily on expert analysis, bespoke client interactions, and rapid, high-stakes decision-making.[3] However, the division faces mounting operational inefficiencies and structural bottlenecks that are no longer sustainable in an increasingly digital and data-intensive capital markets ecosystem. GFG's internal performance audits and market benchmarking exercises have surfaced five primary challenge areas where traditional systems fall short and where GenAI presents an opportunity for disruptive improvement.

7.1.1 Data Explosion and Analysis Bottlenecks

GFG's investment bankers and analysts must process enormous volumes of unstructured data daily, ranging from earnings calls and SEC filings to industry reports, geopolitical news, and social sentiment. Despite access to premium data feeds, 70% of analysts' time is still consumed by manual data extraction, comparison, and formatting tasks, leaving little bandwidth for high-value judgment and synthesis.[4]

[3] https://jaibdd.com/index.php/jaibdd/article/view/38

[4] https://www.oecd.org/content/dam/oecd/en/publications/reports/2002/12/economic-surveys-and-data-analysis_g1gh2e61/9789264099074-en.pdf

The latency between event occurrence (for example, earnings releases, M&A rumors) and internal insight generation has widened due to siloed systems, fragmented dashboards, and inconsistent tagging of knowledge assets. In trading environments where seconds matter, this information lag translates directly into missed opportunities and competitive disadvantage.

7.1.2 Regulatory Compliance and Surveillance Complexity

Global investment banks, including GFG, must operate within overlapping and often contradictory regulatory frameworks across jurisdictions, such as MiFID II (EU), Dodd-Frank (US), and MAR (UK), among others. Surveillance systems must continuously monitor communication logs, trade flows, and client interactions for signs of insider trading, market manipulation, and conduct risk.

Currently, GFG's trade surveillance systems generate a 4:1 ratio of false positives to true alerts, overwhelming compliance teams and triggering unnecessary investigations. Audit trail generation is semi-manual, requiring weeks to compile defensible reports.[5] With rising penalties and zero-tolerance regulatory enforcement, the cost of non-compliance has become an existential risk.

7.1.3 Research and Deal Origination Inefficiencies

Deal teams at GFG spend excessive time preparing pitchbooks, reviewing historical transactions, and manually screening targets or acquirers based on public and proprietary data. Due to a lack of unified systems, insights often reside in isolated documents, emails, and individual analyst notes.

Furthermore, market and industry research is duplicated across teams, as there is no unified, intelligent layer to consolidate findings or learn from past deal cycles. This slows down origination efforts and reduces time-to-client for proposals, especially in fast-moving sectors such as tech, healthcare, and green finance.

[5] https://www.technologynetworks.com/informatics/articles/audit-trail-requirements-for-a-digitalized-regulated-laboratory-401729

7.1.4 Real-Time Risk Modeling Under Market Volatility

Investment banking thrives on accurate pricing, predictive modeling, and timely risk mitigation.[6] However, GFG's current frameworks are still based on preset models that often lack real-time responsiveness. In volatile markets, delays in recalibrating pricing models or stress testing scenarios can expose the firm to significant losses.

Risk officers frequently cite slow model adaptation, manual scenario planning, and fragmented data pipelines as bottlenecks.[7] Furthermore, modeling unstructured risks (such as, geopolitical events, natural disasters, or policy shocks) remains highly judgment-based, leading to inconsistent decisions across regions.

7.1.5 Process Fragmentation and Talent Bottlenecks

Despite a highly skilled workforce, GFG struggles with operational scalability due to process fragmentation and over-dependence on junior analysts for repetitive tasks such as financial data input, company comparisons, and document summarization.

Turnover among entry-level analysts remains high due to workload burnout and the perceived lack of strategic engagement. Moreover, domain expertise remains locked in siloed teams and is lost when key employees transition or retire. Without intelligent knowledge capture and task orchestration, institutional learning remains minimal and workflow resilience is at risk.

These challenges collectively hinder GFG's ability to move with speed, precision, and agility in a highly competitive investment banking environment. To overcome them, the firm has started integrating Agentic AI systems not merely for process automation but for intelligent collaboration capable of enhancing regulatory compliance, accelerating research cycles, and empowering client-facing bankers with real-time, contextual intelligence.

[6] https://www.mckinsey.com/~/media/mckinsey/dotcom/client_service/risk/pdfs/the_future_of_bank_risk_management.pdf

[7] https://www.sciencedirect.com/science/article/pii/S2212096320300243

7.2 Use Case 1: GenAI-Powered Trade Surveillance

In Chapter 5, we discussed trade and market surveillance for insider trading and compliance use cases from a risk and compliance perspective; in this chapter, we focus on the investment banking line-of-business perspective.

7.2.1 Problem Statement

Trade surveillance and regulatory compliance have become operational pressure points within GFG's investment banking division. With trading volumes growing across equities, derivatives, and fixed-income desks, the need to detect potential misconduct such as insider trading, market manipulation, or collusion has never been more urgent.[8] GFG currently monitors over 10 million daily trade events and 200,000 internal communications spanning voice calls, emails, and chat logs during daily trading hours. However, its existing surveillance infrastructure, built primarily on static rule-based systems, suffers from low signal-to-noise ratios, reactive alerting mechanisms, and limited contextual understanding.

Compliance investigations are frequently delayed due to overwhelming volumes of false positives, incomplete audit trails, and manual log analysis. The firm's 2023 compliance audit noted that only 22% of alerts led to actionable follow-up, while the remainder consumed valuable human resources without producing regulatory or ethical insights. In a financial environment where regulators demand both responsiveness and transparency, these inefficiencies increase reputational and legal exposure.

7.2.2 Current State, Challenges

GFG's current trade surveillance systems exhibit the following limitations:

- **Fragmented Data Sources**: Trade logs, communications data, and market triggers exist in separate systems, reducing cross-contextual analysis accuracy.
- **High False Positive Rate**: Existing rule-based filters generate an unmanageable number of alerts with limited relevance.

[8] https://fmsb.com/wp-content/uploads/2022/05/22020525_BCA_Report_2022_FINAL.pdf

- **Delayed Investigations**: Manual triage and event correlation cause investigation delays of up to 72 hours, breaching internal SLA thresholds.
- **Compliance Burden**: Audit trail compilation and report generation for regulators requires 2–3 weeks per case.
- **Scalability Gaps**: Increased market volatility during earnings or geopolitical events can spike alerts by 5–7 times, overwhelming monitoring teams.
- **Lack of Interpretability**: Black box scoring mechanisms provide little explainability or auditability, both of which are critical under SEC and ESMA regulations.

These challenges make GFG's surveillance function reactive, compliance-heavy, and misaligned with the speed and complexity of modern financial markets.

7.2.3 Objective

GFG seeks to deploy a GenAI-powered trade surveillance and compliance intelligence platform that enables proactive detection of market abuse, contextual understanding of trading behavior, and automatic generation of audit-ready documentation. The system must significantly reduce false positives, improve investigation speed, and ensure regulatory transparency through explainable AI mechanisms.

7.2.4 Key Results

GFG's transformation initiative defines the following Objectives and Key Results (OKRs):

- **Alert Quality**: Reduce false positive alerts by at least 60% without increasing false negatives.
- **Investigation Speed**: Decrease average investigation time from 72 hours to under 12 hours.
- **Regulatory Readiness**: Enable on-demand generation of complete, timestamped audit trails.

- **Compliance Team Productivity**: Increase case throughput by 3 times without additional headcount.
- **Explainability**: Achieve 100% traceability and rationalization of alert scoring and recommendations.
- **Cross-market Intelligence**: Enable cross-asset and communication correlation for complex patterns.

7.2.5 Solution Overview: Agentic AI Surveillance System

GFG implemented the Agentic Surveillance Intelligence Engine (ASIE), a modular, GenAI-powered compliance platform built on a multi-agent architecture. ASIE operates as a real-time, context-aware monitoring system that continuously ingests, analyzes, and explains anomalies in trading and communication behaviors.

Key characteristics include

- **Agent Collaboration**: Multiple specialized AI agents simulate a compliance analyst team, detecting anomalies, generating summaries, and validating evidence.
- **Generative Case Reports**: Natural Language Generation (NLG) tools create case reports automatically, aligned to regulatory templates.[9]
- **Contextual Risk Scoring**: Combines trade data, communication logs, and market context for dynamic risk weighting.
- **Explainability Layer**: Uses LLMs and visualization tools to explain why an alert was triggered and how it aligns with regulatory standards.

7.2.6 Detailed Solution Architecture

Figure 7-1 depicts the detailed solution architecture of the Agentic AI surveillance system.

[9] https://www.techtarget.com/searchenterpriseai/definition/natural-language-generation-NLG

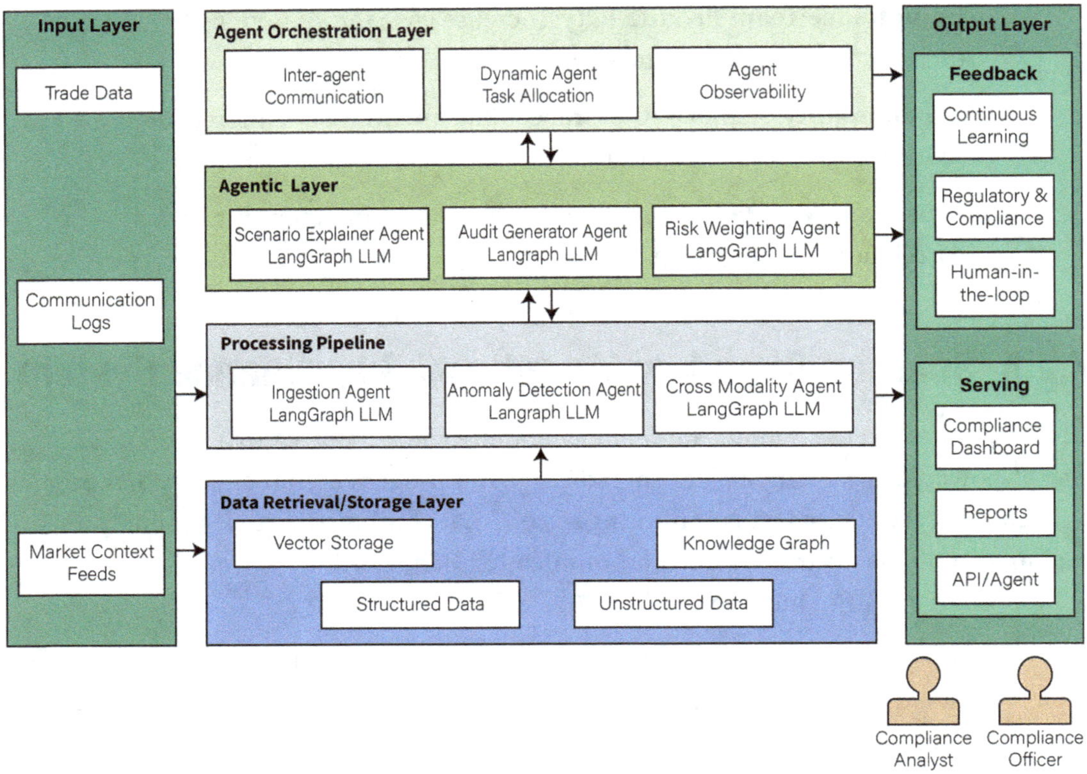

Figure 7-1. *Detailed Solution Architecture for Agentic AI Surveillance System*

The input layer includes the following types of data:

- Trade data (equities, FX, derivatives)
- Communication logs (emails, chat transcripts, call transcripts via ASR)
- Market context feeds (news sentiment, macro triggers)

The Data Retrieval/Storage Layer includes the following components:

- Vector databases, such as Pinecone, Weaviate, Qdrant/Milvus, Elasticsearch/OpenSearch (k-NN), along with BigQuery Vector Search store high-dimensional embeddings generated by models, such as Word2Vec, BERT, and CNNs, to convert text into vectors for fast similarity search and retrieval.

- Knowledge graphs, such as Amazon Neptune, Neo4j (Aura with vector index), Stardog, TigerGraph, and ArangoDB (multi-model), to provide graph-structured knowledge bases to represent and reason over entities and relationships.
- Structured and unstructured data retrieved from data lakes using Iceberg/Delta/Hudi, warehouses, such as Snowflake and BigQuery, and RDBMS platforms, such as Oracle and PostgreSQL.

The Processing Pipeline includes

- Ingestion Agents that parse and standardize trade and communications data
- Anomaly Detection Agents that run multi-dimensional checks across trade timing, pricing, and behavior sequences
- A Cross-Modality Correlator that links chat or voice content with trade activity

The Agentic Layer (powered by LangGraph + GPT-5) contains the following components:

- Scenario Explainer Agent that translates trade behavior into plain-language narratives
- Audit Generator Agent that auto-produces case files with embedded compliance references
- Risk Weighting Agent that scores each event against internal and external compliance thresholds

The Feedback and Compliance Layer contain

- A Continuous learning loop using investigator feedback
- Automatic compliance flag updates via LLM summarization of regulatory bulletins

7.2.7 Key Components of the Solution

The solution consists of the following key components:

- **Anomaly Detector Agent**: Uses GenAI models to learn normal trading behavior patterns and generate predictive baselines. It detects statistically abnormal trading activity by identifying deviations from these learned patterns, capturing subtle and novel anomalies beyond traditional threshold-based systems. The generative nature allows it to simulate potential suspicious scenarios and flag rare, unseen misconduct patterns.
- **Trade-Comms Correlator**: Applies LLMs to analyze and semantically link unstructured communication data, such as emails, chat logs, and voice transcripts, with trading events. This agent uncovers hidden correlations indicative of intent-based misconduct or collusion by generating context-aware embeddings and cross-referencing communication intent with trade actions.
- **Scenario Explainer Agent**: Leverages GenAI's natural language generation capabilities to transform complex, multidimensional anomaly data into coherent, investigator-ready narratives. These summaries articulate the sequence of events, contextual risk factors, and potential regulatory implications in clear, audit-friendly language that supports transparent decision making.
- **Regulatory Audit Agent**: Uses GenAI models fine-tuned on regulatory documentation, such as SEC 17a-4 and MiFID II reporting, to automatically compose detailed and trade compliance-aligned audit reports. It synthesizes findings, references applicable laws and precedents, and produces standardized reports formatted for regulator review and internal compliance workflows, accelerating report generation while ensuring accuracy.
- **Feedback Learning Agent**: Uses reinforcement learning with human-in-the-loop feedback to iteratively fine-tune generative detection models. This continuous learning loop reduces false positives, adapts to evolving trading behaviors, and aligns model outputs with evolving regulatory expectations and investigator insights.

- **Risk Scoring Agent**: Generates dynamic, explainable risk scores by synthesizing data from trades, communications, and market context using generative reasoning. It produces transparent risk rationales that consider asset class, trader profile, and temporal market factors, helping compliance teams prioritize cases based on AI-driven risk insights.

7.2.8 Business Benefits

The implementation of ASIE delivered immediate and scalable benefits, including

- **False Alert Reduction**: 62% fewer false positives, reducing analyst fatigue and focus drift. GFG averaged 320 false alerts per week before launch (6-month baseline). In the first 12 weeks after launch, that dropped to 120 per week.
- **Faster Investigations**: Average triage and reporting time reduced from 3 days to 9 hours.
- **Audit Efficiency**: Generated reports accepted without revision by three different regulators in 2024 Q1.
- **Cost Savings**: 40% reduction in overtime compliance hours, enabling reallocation to high-value advisory functions.
- **Risk Mitigation**: Early detection blocked a spoofing attempt, averting $11 million in losses estimated from trade exposure, a conservative adverse price move, and expected regulatory and remediation costs.
- **Regulatory Confidence**: SEC and FCA praised the explainability layer for meeting upcoming AI governance benchmarks.

7.2.9 Summary

This section demonstrates how GFG moves from isolated tools to agentic GenAI systems that combine contextual intelligence, automation, and interpretability, which turns unstructured signals into explainable, regulator-ready decisions and reframes compliance as proactive regulatory foresight rather than reactive policing. It situates a modular copilot architecture, LLMs with RAG and client-intent profiling, as an intelligent collaborator embedded across the investment-banking life cycle. In research, the copilot compresses cycle times from days to same-day outputs, scales personalization to hundreds of clients, and multiplies reuse of archival content while preserving 100% source traceability for audits. These shifts elevate analysts from data curators to insight architects and strengthen client trust through transparent, cited analysis.

In surveillance, the ASIE platform replaces brittle rules with a multi-agent engine that understands context across trades and communications, generates audit-ready narratives, and delivers measurable impact 62% fewer false alerts, faster investigations, and regulator-accepted reporting. Meanwhile, DSCIP unifies client intelligence and auto-generates compliant pitch materials in dealmaking, targeting a 60% reduction in pitch-prep time and consistent, personalized messaging at scale.

7.3 Use Case 2: Investment Research Automation and Insight Generation

7.3.1 Problem Statement

GFG's investment banking division produces thousands of internal and client-facing research reports each quarter across equities, fixed income, commodities, and private markets. These reports are vital for market insight, deal origination, and client advisory but the current research production cycle is time-consuming, inconsistent, and often reactive. Analysts are overwhelmed by the velocity and diversity of data inputs ranging from earnings calls, macroeconomic indicators, and regulatory filings to ESG disclosures and social sentiment.[10]

According to GFG's internal metrics, only 30% of produced research reaches clients within a 24-hour window following a key market event. Additionally, significant duplication occurs across sector teams due to siloed workflows and a lack of real-time collaboration. This results in lower analyst productivity, missed opportunities, and delayed strategic recommendations, particularly in volatile sectors such as technology, biotechnology, and energy.

[10] https://www.mdpi.com/2079-9292/13/22/4507

7.3.2 Current State, Challenges

GFG's traditional research pipeline faces the following bottlenecks:

- **Fragmented Source Data**: Analysts manually aggregate data from disparate feeds: Bloomberg, Reuters, SEDAR, EDGAR, and local sources, which are often unstructured or behind paywalls.[11]
- **Time Lag in Analysis**: Drafting and peer review cycles delay report distribution, especially for cross-border or multi-asset insights.
- **Limited Personalization**: Reports are standardized and lack contextualization based on client portfolio interests or current exposure.
- **Underutilized Content**: Historical research is rarely reused as retrieval systems lack semantic search and tagging.
- **Burnout Risk**: Junior analysts spend up to 60% of their day on summarization and formatting tasks, leading to attrition.
- **Compliance Burden**: Manual sourcing and quote attribution introduce risks around regulatory misrepresentation (such as SEC Reg FD, MAR).

7.3.3 Objective

GFG aims to deploy a GenAI-powered research copilot capable of automating data ingestion, synthesizing unstructured content, and delivering client-personalized research reports in real time. The goal is to elevate analysts from data curators to insight architects by accelerating workflows, reducing duplication, and enhancing the strategic value of every research interaction.

[11] https://arrow.tudublin.ie/busmas/32/

7.3.4 Key Results

The following OKRs were defined for the research copilot transformation:

- **Turnaround Time**: Reduce research production time by 70%, enabling analysts to deliver complete, client-ready reports within 6–8 hours of key market or corporate events. This acceleration ensures that insights remain timely and actionable, giving clients a competitive edge. It also minimizes the lag between data emergence and strategic decision-making.
- **Content Personalization**: Generate customized insight digests for more than 500 institutional clients within the first three months of deployment, each tailored to specific investment priorities, asset coverage, and market interests. The copilot dynamically adapts research outputs to align with client mandates, creating a differentiated and value-rich client experience. This personalization not only increases engagement but also strengthens client relationships through relevance and precision.
- **Analyst Efficiency**: Reallocate 50% of junior analyst time from repetitive data gathering, manual formatting, and content assembly tasks to higher-order activities such as scenario modeling, hypothesis testing, and strategic thematic research. By removing these bottlenecks, analysts can focus on generating differentiated insights rather than curating raw information. This transformation elevates the role of junior team members and accelerates their contribution to high-value work.
- **Content Reuse**: Achieve a 3X increase in the semantic reusability of archived research content, making it possible to rapidly assemble new reports from past analyses. This capability reduces duplication of effort while ensuring consistency in tone, structure, and data interpretation. It also allows analysts to build on prior work more effectively, enriching the depth and context of new deliverables.
- **Compliance Accuracy**: Maintain 100% source traceability and citation integrity through AI-driven tagging, ensuring that all generated insights are fully auditable and meet regulatory

standards. The system automatically links each claim or statistic to its originating data source, eliminating the risk of undocumented assertions. This not only safeguards compliance but also builds client trust in the accuracy and transparency of the research process.

7.3.5 Solution Overview – GenAI-Powered Analyst Copilot

GFG introduced the InsightSynth Platform, which is a modular, Agentic AI research ecosystem built on LLMs, RAG, and client intent profiling. The platform acts as an analyst copilot, operating alongside human research teams to ingest new information, track market signals, and generate reports in real time.

Key features include

- **Semantic Understanding**: GenAI models understand nuance, sentiment, and causality across financial documents.
- **Client Intent Matching**: Each report is scored against client interests and risk exposure to deliver tailored insights.
- **Voice-to-insight**: Transcribes and summarizes earnings calls and live market commentary within minutes.
- **Language Adaptation**: Generates content in multiple languages for cross-border client distribution.

7.3.6 Detailed Solution Architecture

The detailed solution architecture for the InsightSynth Platform is depicted in Figure 7-2.

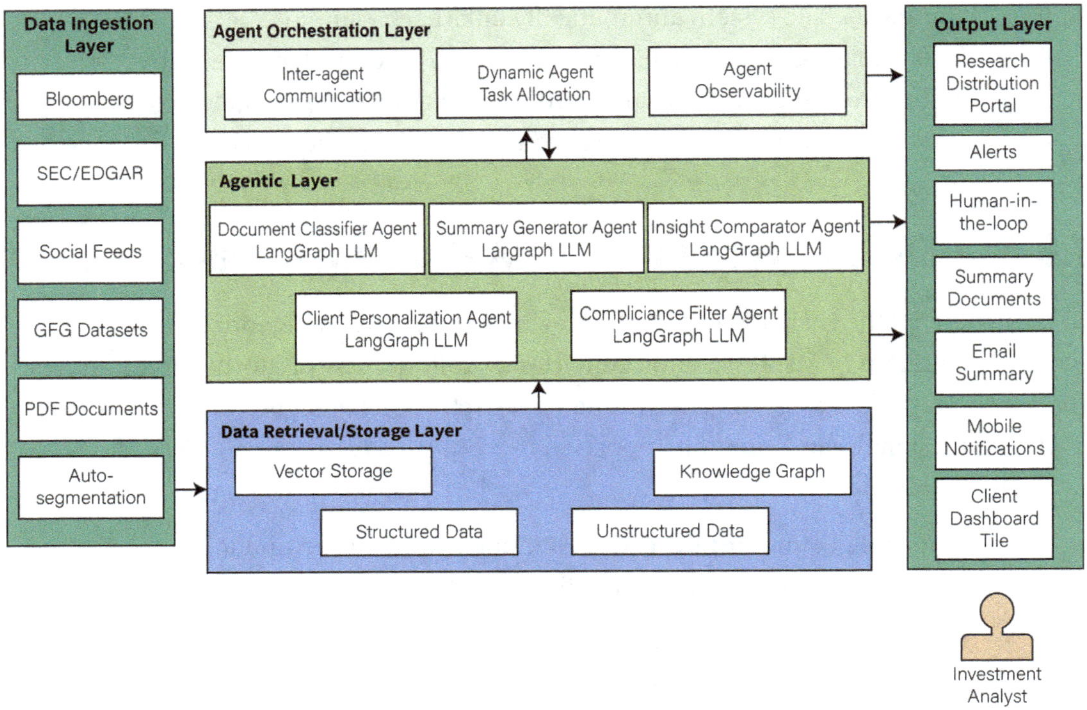

***Figure 7-2.** Detailed Solution Architecture for the GenAI-powered Analyst Copilot*

The InsightSynth Platform consists of the following major components: Data Ingestion Layer:

- Data aggregation. CFG pulls data from Bloomberg, Refinitiv, SEC/EDGAR, social feeds, and GFG into Kafka/Kinesis (one stream per source) and lands it in S3 with tags for PII, region, and retention.
- Call transcription (Whisper + Deepgram). CFG uses Deepgram for live captions and Whisper after the call for higher accuracy. Audio is chunked, speakers are labeled, word timestamps are kept, and Whisper text is preferred when confidence is ≥ 0.92.
- Document processing. CFG detects file type, runs OCR on scans (Amazon Textract with Tesseract/TrOCR fallback), and splits long documents into 1k-token chunks with 10–15% overlap.
- Semantic search. CFG creates text embeddings (bge-m3 or E5), indexes them with HNSW, and blends with keyword search (BM25).

Client/entity matching. CFG links names to companies/clients using IDs (LEI, CUSIP, ISIN, ticker) plus fuzzy checks (name and embedding similarity).

Agentic AI Pipeline (orchestrated via LangChain + LangGraph):

- **Document Classifier Agent**: Tags filings, reports, and calls by sector, region, and impact score
- **Summary Generator Agent**: Uses GPT-5 to produce executive summaries, SWOT tables, and key takeaways
- **Insight Comparator Agent**: Cross-references current data with prior GFG positions or analyst models
- **Client Personalization Agent**: Adapts tone, content, and focus based on portfolio preferences stored in CRM
- **Compliance Filter Agent**: Validates all statements against internal quote libraries and public sourcing

Output Layer:

- Integrates with GFG's research distribution portal
- Generates alerts for high-priority insights
- **Supports multi-format output**: PDF, email summary, mobile notification, or client dashboard tile

7.3.7 Key Components of the Solution

The solution consists of the following key components:

Document Classifier Agent: Automatically ingests and categorizes financial documents by asset class, geography, and impact level using NLP. Provides a metadata-rich knowledge base to streamline targeted analysis and minimize manual sorting. Feeds structured, tagged data into the downstream research automation pipeline.

Summary Generator Agent: Converts complex filings, earnings calls, and regulatory updates into clear, standardized summaries. Retains key metrics, sentiment signals, and guidance while removing irrelevant noise. Ensures uniform readability and format across the research team.

Insight Comparator Agent: Benchmarks new insights against historical forecasts, peer reports, and sector trends. Highlights deviations and contextualizes them with macro and microeconomic drivers. Supports analysts in refining assumptions and validating market outlooks.

Client Trade Ideas Agent: Personalizes research to each client's portfolio, risk profile, and trading history. It applies mean-variance optimization and factor-exposure checks and runs pre-trade VaR/Expected Shortfall with scenario stress tests. It then filters and prioritizes opportunities that fit the client's strategy, delivering targeted, actionable trade ideas aligned with the client's objectives.

Compliance Filter Agent: Validates all outputs against regulatory frameworks and firm disclosure policies. Ensures source attribution, proper disclaimers, and exclusion of restricted data. Prevents compliance breaches, reducing legal and reputational risk.

Feedback Loop Agent: Learns from analyst edits, client reactions, and trade outcomes to improve future outputs. Adapts to preferred tone, formatting, and prioritization criteria. Continuously increases accuracy and alignment with institutional research standards.

7.3.8 Business Benefits

Within six months of deployment, InsightSynth significantly improved GFG's research agility and strategic impact:

- **Speed to Market**: 80% of research reports are now published within 6 hours of major market events.
- **Analyst Productivity**: Report output per analyst rose by 2.5 times, enabling deeper sector coverage.
- **Client Engagement**: Customized research digests led to a 40% increase in client open rates and follow-ups.

- **Content Utilization**: Archived research reuse increased by 220%, reducing duplication and improving consistency.
- **Compliance Resilience**: Zero citation errors or compliance escalations in Q1 2024, improving audit performance.
- **Competitive Advantage**: GFG ranked in the top three for equity research timeliness in Greenwich Associates' 2024 buy-side survey.

7.3.9 Summary

The implementation of the Agentic Surveillance Intelligence Engine (ASIE) marks a transformative leap in how GFG approaches trade surveillance and regulatory compliance. Faced with fragmented data systems, overwhelming false positives, and delayed investigations, GFG needed a solution that could keep pace with the scale and complexity of modern financial markets while meeting the increasing demands for transparency from global regulators.

By integrating GenAI with a multi-agent architecture, ASIE replaces reactive, rule-based monitoring with a proactive, intelligence-driven system. It doesn't just detect anomalies; it understands context, links intent from communications, and produces audit-ready case narratives autonomously. Its explainability layer provides full traceability, and addresses regulatory interpretability which is one of the most critical gaps in legacy systems.

The results speak for themselves: a 62% reduction in false alerts, a drastic cut in investigation times, fully automated reporting accepted by top regulators, and millions saved through early risk detection. More importantly, ASIE has shifted compliance from a burdened cost center to a strategic function capable of identifying misconduct early, learning continuously, and scaling effortlessly during periods of market stress.

In essence, GFG's GenAI-powered platform is not just a technology upgrade; it represents a revolution in compliance philosophy. It proves that financial institutions can move beyond surveillance to achieve accurate regulatory foresight with the right blend of contextual intelligence, automation, and interpretability.

7.4 Use Case 3: Deal Structuring and Client Intelligence Automation

7.4.1 Problem Statement

One of the most time-intensive and critical functions in investment banking is deal structuring and pitch preparation.[12] At GFG, bankers spend weeks collecting client intelligence, building pitchbooks, and modeling valuation scenarios. This process involves manual consolidation of CRM data, regulatory filings, investor sentiment, historical deals, and macroeconomic context. Despite significant effort, proposals often lack personalization and may not reflect the most recent market developments.

Internal benchmarking showed that deal teams spent 40–50% of their time on repetitive data preparation, slowing response time in competitive pitches. Additionally, client knowledge is often fragmented across relationship managers, siloed Excel trackers, and disconnected systems, leading to inconsistent messaging and reduced deal conversion. As deal velocity increases and client expectations rise, GFG's traditional model is failing to keep pace.

7.4.2 Current State, Challenges

GFG's deal origination and structuring workflows face several critical challenges:

- **Manual Pitchbook Preparation**: Teams rely on slide libraries and custom Excel sheets, leading to version control issues.
- **Siloed Client Insights**: CRM, call transcripts, and meeting notes are scattered across systems and not searchable.
- **Delayed Opportunity Matching**: Bankers lack real-time tools to identify suitable deals for specific clients based on preferences or previous engagements.
- **Limited Personalization**: Pitchbooks often contain generic messaging, reducing client resonance.

[12] https://corporatefinanceinstitute.com/resources/career/investment-banking-job-description/

- **Compliance Risk**: Inconsistent language and unapproved templates risk breaching communications policies.
- **Knowledge Leakage**: Departing bankers take with them years of client nuance and deal knowledge.

These issues not only impact productivity but also affect win rates and client trust.

7.4.3 Objective

To address these inefficiencies, GFG launched the GenAI-Enhanced Deal Structuring and Client Intelligence Platform (DSCIP). The objective was to automate opportunity identification, personalization of pitch materials, and integration of structured and unstructured client intelligence, transforming every banker into a hyper-personalized deal maker.

7.4.4 Key Results

GFG's implementation goals were guided by the following outcomes:

- **Pitch Preparation Time**: Reduce pitch creation cycle by 60%.
- **Opportunity Mapping**: Auto-suggest relevant transactions or financing solutions based on the client profile.
- **Client Intelligence Accessibility**: Centralize relationship data with natural language search.
- **Personalized Messaging**: Tailor pitches to client tone, sector exposure, and recent activity.
- **Regulatory Alignment**: Ensure compliance-validated messaging across all materials.
- **Cross-Team Knowledge Sharing**: Increase reuse of historical pitch insights by 3 times.

7.4.5 Solution Overview – AI-Enhanced Deal Advisory Engine

The DSCIP system is powered by a GenAI-driven, agentic co-advisory framework that integrates GFG's internal data landscape with external market intelligence. The platform functions as an intelligent collaborator, provides deal structures, generates content, and delivers insights based on client context.

Key capabilities include

- **360° Client View Generator**: Aggregates call notes, CRM entries, ESG preferences, and industry positioning.
- **Dynamic Pitch Generator**: Produces editable pitch decks aligned to client interests, regulatory norms, and sector trends.
- **Scenario Modeler**: Tests valuation and transaction scenarios under varied economic inputs.
- **Feedback-responsive Refinement**: Learns from banker edits to improve future recommendations.

7.4.6 Detailed Solution Architecture

Figure 7-3 depicts the detailed solution architecture for the AI-enhanced deal advisory engine.

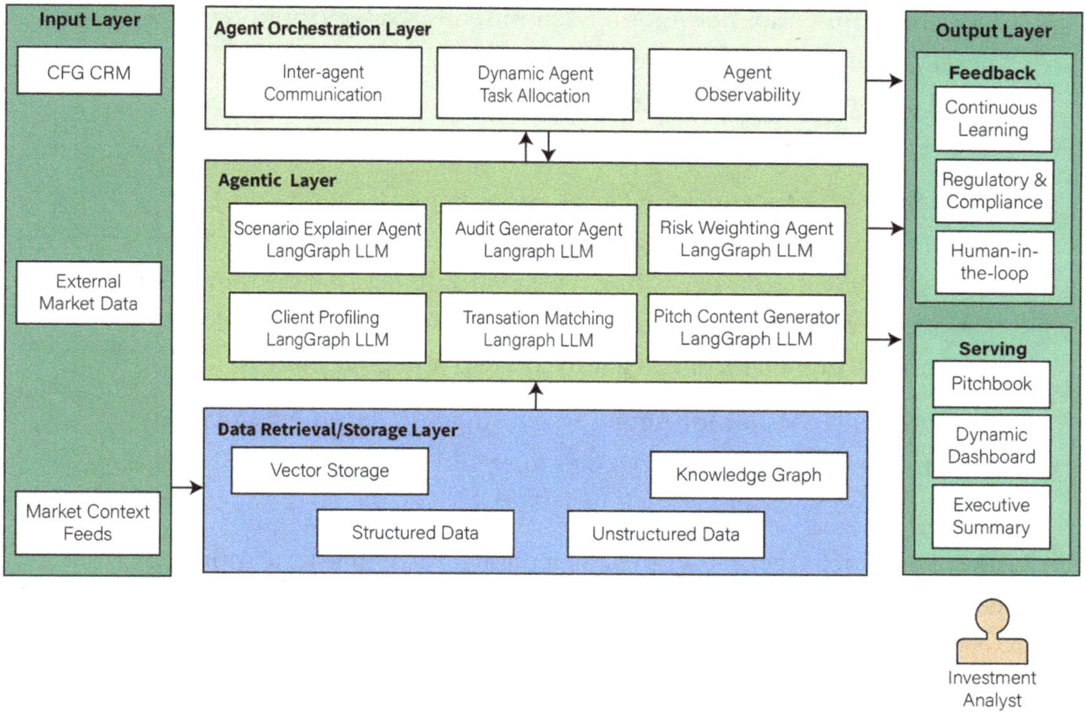

Figure 7-3. *Detailed Solution Architecture for the AI-enhanced Deal Advisory Engine*

7.4.7 Key Components of the Solution

7.4.7.1 Data Sources and Collection Infrastructure

Input Sources:

- GFG CRM, email logs, past deal archives, S&P Capital IQ, FactSet, public filings
- **External**: Industry news, analyst forecasts, M&A league tables

Agent Pipeline:

- **Client Profiling Agent**: Builds and updates a digital client dossier using internal and external data. Uses probabilistic entity resolution (Fellegi–Sunter with graph linking), profile embeddings, and both streaming and nightly refresh; quality is tracked via attribute-level F1 (≥ 0.95) and drift via the population stability index

- **Transaction Matcher Agent**: Recommends strategic options (buy, sell, equity, debt, joint venture) using similarity modeling with dual-encoder embeddings (E5 and FinBERT), cosine similarity, and a BM25 hybrid; targets Precision@10 ≥ 0.70 and nDCG@10 ≥ 0.80
- **Pitch Content-Generator Agent**: Auto-generates slides, deal rationale, valuation comparables, and ESG alignment. Powered by GPT-5 with RAG over filings and research; uses a slide template engine, tool calls to pricing/comparables/ESG APIs, and includes citations, provenance, and guardrails (PII and policy filters)
- **Compliance Validator Agent**: Scans language for policy violations or misrepresentation. Maps rules to FINRA 2210 and 2241, SEC Rule 10b-5, and SEC Marketing Rule 206(4)-1

Banker Feedback Agent: Captures the edit history to fine-tune future pitch versions. Uses edit-delta capture, bandit learning to update rankings and templates, and preference embeddings; key performance indicators include acceptance rate and cycle-time reduction.

- Output Formats:
- Customized pitchbooks (PPT/PDF)
- Executive summaries for emails
- Dynamic dashboards for live client meetings

7.4.7.2 Data Collection Agents

Client Profiling Agent

Aggregates structured and unstructured data such as CRM records, prior pitch decks, meeting notes, and news articles to build a holistic, dynamic profile of the client. It contextualizes business objectives, risk appetite, industry positioning, and recent activity.

Transaction Matcher Agent

Leverages historical transaction databases, industry trends, and strategic filters to recommend relevant deal ideas. It aligns proposals with the client's goals (e.g., M&A, capital raise) and benchmarks against peer activity for validation.

Pitch Content Generator

Automatically generates investment narratives, comparable company analysis (comps), charts, and PowerPoint slides in bank-approved formats. The content adapts to client tone and presentation style, saving analysts hours of manual formatting.

Compliance Validator

Scans all generated materials to ensure alignment with legal, regulatory, and branding standards. It flags prohibited language, ensures disclaimers are present, and verifies that confidential or restricted data is not unintentionally shared.

Knowledge-Learning Agent

Continuously improves through feedback by analyzing pitch outcomes, banker edits, and client reactions. Over time, it suggests stronger messaging, visual layouts, and storylines that have historically driven higher engagement or deal success.

7.4.8 Business Benefits

The deployment of DSCIP delivered a measurable impact within the first two quarters:

- **Faster Time-to-Pitch**: Average deck creation time dropped from 5 days to 2 days
- **Higher Client Engagement**: Personalized content increased client meeting conversion rates by 45%
- **Pitch Consistency**: All materials aligned with brand and regulatory standards across geographies
- **Opportunity Capture**: The Deal team surfaced 23% more relevant transactions using AI recommendations
- **Institutional Memory**: Departed banker's knowledge captured in reusable, searchable formats
- **Team Efficiency**: Analysts reported 50% less time spent on formatting and document prep

7.4.9 Summary

The implementation of the ASIE marks a transformative leap in how GFG approaches trade surveillance and regulatory compliance. Faced with fragmented data systems, overwhelming false positives, and delayed investigations, GFG needed a solution that could keep pace with the scale and complexity of modern financial markets while meeting the increasing demands for transparency from global regulators.

By integrating GenAI with a multi-agent architecture, ASIE replaces reactive, rule-based monitoring with a proactive, intelligence-driven system. It doesn't just detect anomalies, it understands context, links intent from communications, and produces audit-ready case narratives autonomously. Its explainability layer provides full traceability, addressing one of the most critical gaps in legacy systems: regulatory interpretability.

The results speak for themselves with a 62% reduction in false alerts, a drastic cut in investigation times, fully automated reporting accepted by top regulators, and millions saved through early risk detection. More importantly, ASIE has shifted compliance from a burdened cost center to a strategic function capable of identifying misconduct early, learning continuously, and scaling effortlessly during periods of market stress.

In essence, GFG's GenAI-powered platform is not just a technology upgrade; it represents a revolution in compliance philosophy. It proves that financial institutions can move beyond surveillance to achieve accurate regulatory foresight with the right blend of contextual intelligence, automation, and interpretability.

7.5 Key Takeaways

- **GenAI augments analyst workflows** by automating time-consuming tasks across surveillance, research, and deal preparation, freeing teams to focus on strategic decision making.
- **Agentic AI systems** (e.g., ASIE, InsightSynth, DSCIP) enable real-time insight generation, cross-modal correlation, and explainable outputs aligned with compliance frameworks.
- **Trade surveillance modernization** reduced false positives by 60% and enabled sub-12-hour investigations with auto-generated audit trails.

- **Investment research automation** cut report production time by 70%, increased content reuse, and improved client engagement through tailored insights.
- **AI-enhanced deal structuring** shortened pitchbook cycles by 60% and surfaced 23% more relevant opportunities via intelligent matching and personalization.
- **Knowledge retention and reuse** through GenAI agents helps preserve institutional memory and scale expertise across teams.
- **Additional AI-driven opportunities** include dynamic risk modeling and scenario simulation for volatile markets, automated regulatory reporting, enhanced due diligence via natural language understanding, and ESG and geopolitical risk monitoring.
- **Client engagement can be further improved** through AI-powered chatbots and virtual assistants that provide timely, context-aware support throughout the deal life cycle.

Investment banks embedding GenAI throughout their operations will gain critical advantages in speed, accuracy, federal compliance, and client service, positioning themselves to thrive in an increasingly complex and fast-paced financial landscape.

7.6 Chapter Summary

Investment banking is undergoing a fundamental transformation as GenAI reshapes how institutions handle surveillance, research, and client engagement. At GFG, GenAI is not simply optimizing tasks, it is re-architecting critical workflows through Agentic AI systems that combine reasoning, personalization, and automation. Trade surveillance has evolved from static rule-based alerts to proactive, explainable intelligence. Research workflows are now accelerated and contextualized through real-time insight synthesis. Deal structuring is being redefined with AI-generated pitchbooks, personalized messaging, and client-aware recommendations.

Beyond these core areas, GenAI holds promise for numerous other investment banking applications, including dynamic risk modeling, scenario simulation under volatile markets, automated regulatory reporting, enhanced due diligence through natural language understanding, and real-time monitoring of geopolitical or ESG factors impacting deals. AI-driven chatbots can also support client relationship management by providing timely, contextual responses. As the technology matures, the potential to integrate AI across the entire deal life cycle and capital markets operations will continue to expand, driving greater efficiency, insight, and competitive advantage.

Collectively, these capabilities enable GFG to operate with greater precision, speed, and regulatory confidence essential in a fast-evolving, high-stakes market landscape.

CHAPTER 8

Wealth and Asset Management with GenAI

In Chapter 7, we explored how GenAI is transforming investment banking by streamlining complex, information-heavy workflows. In this chapter, we discuss how GenAI can help transform wealth and asset management.

The wealth and asset management industry stands at a pivotal crossroads. As global investable assets are projected to reach US$3.67 trillion by 2030, growing at a CAGR of 36.4% from 2024 to 2030,[1] the sector faces mounting pressure to deliver superior returns, personalized experiences, and operational efficiency in an increasingly complex environment. At the same time, client expectations are evolving rapidly; according to the Ernst and Young (EY) 2025 global wealth research report,[2] 45% of clients believe their investing needs are more complicated than two years ago. According to this study, clients also see key wealth management processes as becoming more complex, such as: financial planning for taxes (53%), financial planning for inheritance or wealth transfer (45%), financial planning for retirement (43%), and capturing a holistic view of one's wealth (41%).

Yet, the industry's ability to meet these demands is hampered by legacy systems, rising regulatory complexity, and a persistent talent shortage. Meanwhile, the competitive landscape is intensifying, with fintech disruptors and robo-advisors capturing nearly US$1.5 trillion in assets under management globally.[3] Overall, the global wealth management industry is under increasing pressure.

---

[1] https://www.grandviewresearch.com/industry-analysis/asset-management-market

[2] https://www.ey.com/content/dam/ey-unified-site/ey-com/en-gl/noindex/documents/ey-2025-global-wealth-research-report.pdf

[3] https://www.statista.com/outlook/fmo/wealth-management/digital-investment/robo-advisors/worldwide

S. Godavarthi, R. Nagvekar, *Transforming Financial Services with Generative AI*,
https://doi.org/10.1007/979-8-8688-2053-3_8

However, GenAI has emerged as a pivotal technology, offering unprecedented capabilities to transform wealth and asset management. By analyzing vast and diverse datasets, from market trends and economic indicators to individual client preferences and risk profiles, GenAI can help create hyper-personalized investment strategies. It can help automate complex portfolio adjustments, and enhance client engagement in ways previously unimaginable.

Whether creating customized financial plans, predicting market movements with greater accuracy, or identifying emerging investment opportunities, GenAI empowers wealth and asset managers to deliver superior value and build stronger client relationships. Wealth managers are increasingly evaluating using GenAI to address some of the challenges. According to a 2024 EY survey,[4] 98% of wealth and asset managers are investing in or planning to invest in GenAI.

In this chapter, we outline the key applications of GenAI in wealth and asset management and explore how it can enable a more proactive, personalized, and efficient approach to serving clients. By understanding both the opportunities and the risks, industry leaders can chart a path toward sustainable growth and enduring client trust in the age of AI.

8.1 Challenges in Wealth and Asset Management

The Global Fiscal Group (GFG), our fictitious Financial Services Organization (FSO) that we introduced in Chapter 2, operates in a highly competitive and rapidly evolving wealth and asset management landscape. In recent years, GFG has faced mounting challenges that have impacted client satisfaction, operational efficiency, and regulatory compliance. These challenges have resulted in missed growth opportunities, increased operational costs, and, in some cases, regulatory scrutiny. Some of these challenges include

- **Market Analysis and Forecasting**: GFG's advisors struggle to keep pace with rapidly changing markets and to provide timely, data-driven insights to clients. Manual analysis is time-consuming and often lacks the precision needed for optimal decision-making.

[4] https://www.ey.com/content/dam/ey-unified-site/ey-com/en-gl/industries/wealth-asset-management/documents/ey-gl-genai-wam-survey-highlights-03-2024.pdf

- **Hyper-Personalization:** GFG's clients increasingly expect advice and solutions tailored to their unique financial goals, life events, and risk profiles. Traditional segmentation and manual customization are insufficient to meet these expectations at scale.
- **Portfolio Management Automation:** Portfolio rebalancing and optimization are often reactive, with delays in responding to market shifts or changes in client circumstances. This can lead to suboptimal performance and increased risk exposure.
- **Client Segmentation and Lead Generation, Marketing, and Onboarding**: GFG faces mounting pressure to grow its client base and deliver seamless onboarding experiences in an increasingly digital and competitive marketplace. Traditional client segmentation methods, often based on static demographic data, fail to capture the nuanced behaviors, preferences, and life events that drive client needs. As a result, marketing campaigns are less targeted, conversion rates are suboptimal, and high-potential prospects are frequently overlooked. Additionally, the onboarding process itself is often fragmented, involving multiple manual steps, redundant data entry, and compliance checks that slow down the client journey. This leads to frustration, higher abandonment rates, and lost revenue opportunities

GFG's Chief Information Officer has set a vision to "Lead the industry in client-centric, data-driven wealth management by harnessing GenAI." The leadership team has been tasked with identifying the core challenges and aligning them with strategic objectives and key results (OKRs) to drive transformation.

For the rest of this section, we outline these challenges in the form of use cases and OKRs that help address these challenges. Note that these OKRs are mostly directional and ambitious. Each FSO may have their own mandates depending on varying conditions.

8.2 Use Case 1: Intelligent Portfolio Management, Market Analysis, and Forecasting

8.2.1 Problem Statement

At GFG, providing timely and accurate market analysis and forecasting remains a significant challenge. Advisors and portfolio managers currently rely on a combination of legacy analytics tools and manual research to interpret market trends, assess product suitability, and forecast outcomes. This fragmented approach often leads to delayed insights, inconsistent recommendations, and missed opportunities for clients.

The inability to process and synthesize large volumes of structured and unstructured data - such as economic indicators, news, and alternative data limits GFG's ability to deliver proactive, data-driven advice. As a result, clients may receive outdated or generic guidance, undermining trust and competitive positioning.

8.2.2 Current State, Challenges

- Advisors spend 10–15 hours per week manually gathering and analyzing market data from disparate sources, leading to inefficiencies and delayed decision-making.
- Only 30% of investment recommendations are based on real-time data, with the remainder relying on historical trends or static reports.
- The lack of advanced forecasting tools results in a 25% higher error rate in market predictions compared to industry benchmarks.
- Product suitability assessments are often generic, with limited ability to match clients to optimal investment products based on evolving market conditions.

8.2.3 Objective

Leverage GenAI to automate and enhance market analysis and forecasting, enabling advisors to deliver timely, precise, and highly relevant investment insights and product recommendations to clients.

8.2.4 Key Results

- **Reduce Analysis Time**: Decrease the time advisors spend on market research and analysis by 60%, freeing up 6–9 hours per week for client engagement and strategic planning.
- **Improve Forecast Accuracy**: Increase the accuracy of market forecasts by 40% through the integration of GenAI models that synthesize real-time and alternative data sources.
- **Enhance Product Suitability**: Ensure that 80% of investment recommendations are dynamically tailored to current market conditions and individual client profiles.
- **Boost Advisor Adoption**: Achieve a 70% adoption rate of AI-powered market analysis tools among advisors within 12 months.
- **Increase Client Satisfaction**: Improve client satisfaction scores related to investment advice and market insights by 25% as measured by post-interaction surveys.

8.2.5 Solution Overview: Agentic AI-Powered Market Intelligence Platform

The challenges faced by GFG in market analysis and forecasting present an opportunity to leverage not only GenAI but also the emerging paradigm of Agentic AI. This enhanced solution proposes a multi-agent system where specialized AI agents collaborate to deliver comprehensive market intelligence and personalized investment recommendations.

The Agentic AI-powered market intelligence platform uses a group of autonomous agents, each specialized for specific wealth management tasks. These agents work collaboratively under an orchestrator to gather data, analyze markets, generate insights, and deliver personalized recommendations. By leveraging frameworks such as LangChain, CrewAI, AutoGen, and LangGraph, the platform creates a dynamic, self-improving ecosystem that adapts to market conditions and client needs in real time.

8.2.6 Detailed Solution Architecture

Figure 8-1 depicts the detailed solution architecture.

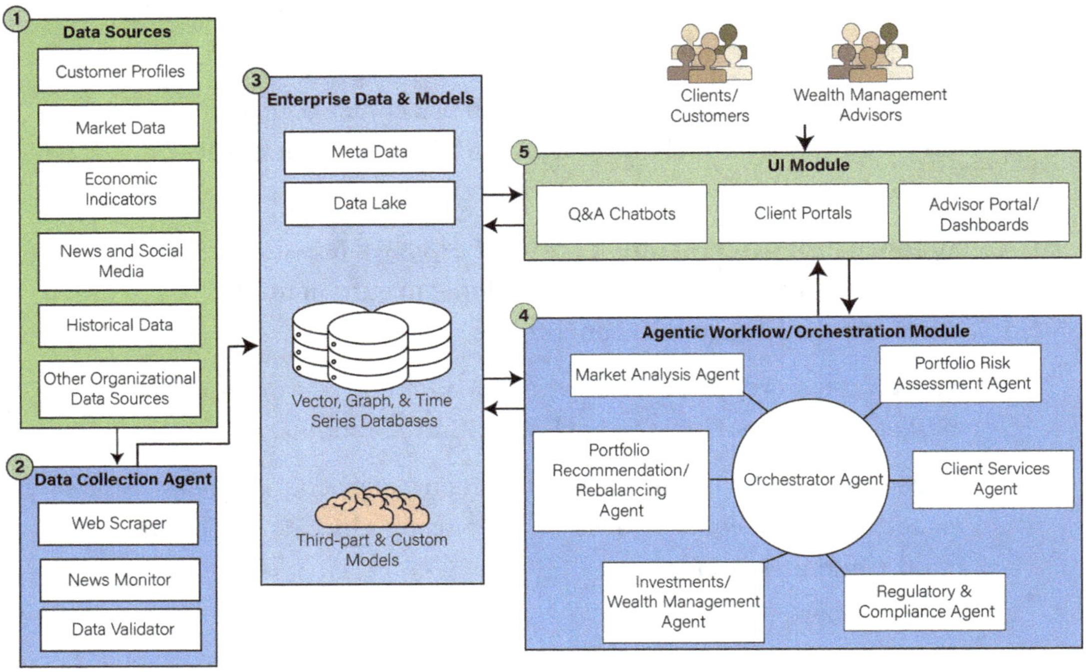

Figure 8-1. *Detailed Solution Architecture*

8.2.7 Key Components of the Solution

8.2.7.1 Data Sources

The data sources include diverse data streams utilized for market analysis, client insights, and investment decision-making. They consist of

- **Market Data Feeds**: Real-time and historical prices, volumes, and indices from providers, including Bloomberg, Reuters, and FactSet.
- **Economic Indicators**: Macroeconomic data (GDP, inflation, employment) from sources such as Federal Reserve Economic Data (FRED) and World Bank.

- **News and Social Media**: Unstructured data from news APIs, financial blogs, Twitter, Reddit, and earnings call transcripts. This includes sentiment analysis from social media sources.
- **Alternative Data**: ESG scores, satellite imagery, web traffic, and other non-traditional sources for deeper market insights.
- **Internal Product Databases**: Information on available investment products, historical performance, and suitability criteria.
- **Client Profiles**: Risk tolerance, investment goals, transaction history, and behavioral data.

8.2.7.2 Data Collection Agents

The data collection agents consist of the following:

- **Web scraper agent that has the following responsibilities**: (1) Real-time web scraping of financial news and analyst reports; (2) social media sentiment collection from platforms such as Twitter, Reddit, and LinkedIn; and (3) regulatory filing extraction from sources, including SEC EDGAR and company websites. The implementation framework/tools include LangChain + Scrapy + Beautiful Soup.
- **News monitor agent that has the following responsibilities**: (1) Continuous monitoring of breaking financial news; (2) event detection and impact assessment; and (3) real-time alert generation for market-moving events. The implementation frameworks/tools include LangChain + NewsAPI + RSS Feeds + Finnhub + Yahoo Finance API.
- **Data validator agent that has the following responsibilities**: (1) Data quality assessment and anomaly detection; (2) cross-source data validation and reconciliation; and (3) data lineage tracking and audit trails. The implementation framework includes: Great Expectations + Pandas.

8.2.7.3 Enterprise Data and Models

The enterprise data layer includes data lakes and databases for storing structured and unstructured enterprise data. This also includes Vector Databases (e.g., PineCone, Chroma), Graph Databases (e.g., Neo4j, ArangoDB), and Time Series Databases (e.g., InfluxDB, TimescaleDB).

The models include (1) enterprise domain specific-models; (2) customized/finetuned open source models; and (3) third party models.

8.2.7.4 Agentic Workflow and Orchestration Layer

This module consists of the following:

- **Orchestration Layer**: This layer coordinates multi-agent workflows and task delegation; manages agent communication and result aggregation. Defines and executes complex, multi-step workflows.

  Frameworks/Tools: CrewAI, LangGraph Workflow Engine

- **Market Analysis Agents**: These consist of Sentiment Analyzer that is responsible for (1) multi-source sentiment analysis (news, social media, earnings calls); (2) sentiment trend tracking and correlation analysis; and (3) market mood indicators and sentiment-based signals.

  Frameworks/Tools/Models: LangChain + Transformers, FinBERT, RoBERTa-Financial.

- **Portfolio Risk Assessment Agent**: This Agent is responsible for (1) real-time portfolio risk assessment (VaR, CVaR, stress testing); (2) factor exposure analysis and risk attribution; and (3) correlation analysis and diversification metrics.

  Frameworks/Tools**:** LangChain + PyPortfolioOpt + Quantlib

- **Portfolio/Wealth management Agents**: These include (1) Product Recommendation Agent which uses collaborative filtering for suitability assessment based on risk profiles and goals and generates dynamic product recommendations; and (2) Portfolio Rebalancing and Optimizer Agent which implements multi-objective portfolio optimization (return, risk, ESG), provides dynamic rebalancing recommendations/implementation, and includes tax-efficient portfolio construction.

Frameworks/Tools**:** LangChain + PyPortfolioOpt + Quantlib

8.2.7.5 Client Services Agents

The client services agents consist of the following:

- **Personal Assistant Agent That Has the Following Responsibilities**: (1) Natural language client interaction and query resolution; (2) personalized market updates and investment insights; and (3) meeting scheduling and follow-up management. The implementation frameworks/tools include: LangChain + RAG + Conversational AI; OpenAI GPT-5, Anthropic Claude
- **Report Generator Agent That Has the Following Responsibilities**: (1) Automated generation of personalized client reports; (2) dynamic visualization creation and embedding; and (3) multi-format output generation (PDF, HTML, PowerPoint). The implementation frameworks/tools include: LangChain + Jinja2 + ReportLab

8.2.7.6 Compliance Agents

The compliance agents consist of the following:

- **Regulatory Monitor Agent That Has the Following Responsibilities**: (1) Monitor real-time regulatory changes, (2) interpret compliance rules, and (3) automate and validate regulatory filing.
- **Audit Trail Generator Agent That Has the Following Responsibilities**: (1) Generate comprehensive audit trails, (2) document rationale for decisions, and (3) automate regulatory reporting.

8.2.8 Business Benefits

The GenAI-powered market intelligence platform delivers substantial business value to GFG with the following outcomes:

- **Efficiency Gains**: Reduces advisor analysis time by 60%, freeing up 6–9 hours per week for client engagement and strategic planning.
- **Improved Forecast Accuracy**: Increases market forecast accuracy by 40% through advanced, real-time data synthesis and AI-driven modeling and multi-agent collaboration.
- **Enhanced Product Suitability**: Ensures that 80% of investment recommendations are dynamically tailored to current market conditions and client profiles, improving client outcomes and trust.
- **Advisor Empowerment**: Achieves a 70% adoption rate of AI-powered tools among advisors, driving digital transformation and upskilling the workforce.
- **Client Satisfaction**: Boosts client satisfaction scores related to investment advice and market insights by 25%, strengthening client loyalty and retention.
- **Scalability**: Enables GFG to handle increased data volumes and client growth without proportional increases in headcount or operational costs.
- **Regulatory Readiness**: Provides transparent, explainable recommendations and audit trails, supporting compliance with evolving regulatory requirements.

8.2.9 Summary

GFG's Agentic AI-powered Market Intelligence Platform represents the next evolution in financial services technology, moving beyond traditional AI to autonomous, collaborative agent systems. By leveraging frameworks such as CrewAI, LangChain, and AutoGen, the platform creates a dynamic ecosystem of specialized agents that work together to deliver comprehensive market intelligence and personalized investment recommendations.

The multi-agent architecture ensures robustness, scalability, and continuous improvement, while the integration of external tools and APIs provides access to real-time, comprehensive market data. This approach not only addresses current challenges in market analysis and forecasting but also positions GFG at the forefront of the Agentic AI revolution in financial services.

As the financial industry continues to evolve, Agentic AI systems like this platform will become essential for organizations seeking to deliver superior client outcomes while maintaining operational efficiency and regulatory compliance.

8.3 Use Case 2: Advanced Customer Insights and Hyper-Personalization

8.3.1 Problem Statement

At GFG, delivering truly personalized financial advice and generating deep customer insights remains a significant challenge despite having access to vast amounts of client data. The current approach to customer analysis relies heavily on static demographic segmentation and basic transactional history, failing to capture the nuanced behavioral patterns, life events, emotional drivers, and evolving preferences that influence financial decisions. This superficial understanding of clients results in generic recommendations that don't resonate with individual needs, missed cross-selling opportunities, and suboptimal client engagement. Furthermore, the inability to predict client behavior, anticipate life changes, or understand the emotional context behind financial decisions limit GFG's capacity to proactively serve clients and build lasting relationships. As clients increasingly expect Netflix-level personalization in their financial services, GFG's current capabilities fall short of delivering the sophisticated, contextual, and predictive insights necessary to remain competitive.

8.3.2 Current State, Challenges

- Advisors spend 12–15 hours per week manually analyzing client profiles and preparing personalized recommendations using outdated segmentation models based primarily on age, income, and basic risk tolerance.

- Only 25% of client interactions are informed by real-time behavioral insights, with the majority relying on static profiles that may be months or years out of date.
- Customer segmentation is limited to 8–10 broad categories, missing the granular insights needed for true personalization and failing to capture the complexity of individual client journeys.
- Opportunities to cross-sell and upsell are missed at a rate of 65% due to inadequate understanding of client needs, life stage transitions, and behavioral triggers.
- Client satisfaction surveys indicate that 45% of clients feel their advisor "*doesn't truly understand their unique situation*" or "*provides advice that feels too generic.*"
- The lack of predictive analytics means that GFG is reactive rather than proactive, often learning about major client life events (marriage, divorce, job changes, inheritance) after the fact rather than anticipating and preparing for them.
- Emotional and psychological factors influencing financial decisions are not captured or analyzed, leading to recommendations that may be technically sound but emotionally misaligned.
- Alternative data sources (social media sentiment, spending patterns, digital behavior) remain untapped, limiting the depth of customer insights.
- Advisors express frustration with the current client profiling tools, citing them as "too basic" and "not actionable" for delivering personalized advice.

8.3.3 Objective

Leverage advanced analytics, machine learning, and GenAI to develop comprehensive customer insights and deliver hyper-personalized financial experiences that anticipate client needs, understand behavioral drivers, and provide contextually relevant recommendations at every touchpoint.

8.3.4 Key Results

- **Enhance Customer Understanding**: Increase the depth of customer insights by implementing 360-degree client profiling that captures behavioral, emotional, and predictive dimensions, moving from 8–10 basic segments to 100+ micro-segments with dynamic, real-time updates.
- **Improve Personalization Accuracy**: Achieve 90% relevance in personalized recommendations as measured by client engagement rates and conversion metrics, up from the current 35% baseline.
- **Boost Proactive Service Delivery**: Identify and act on 80% of major life events and financial needs before clients explicitly request assistance, transforming GFG from reactive to predictive service delivery.
- **Increase Cross-Sell/Upsell Success**: Improve cross-sell and upsell conversion rates by 60% through better timing, targeting, and personalization of product recommendations.
- **Reduce Advisor Preparation Time**: Decrease advisor time spent on client research and preparation by 70%, freeing up 8–10 hours per week for high-value client interaction and relationship building.
- **Enhance Client Satisfaction**: Increase client satisfaction scores related to "advisor understanding" and "relevance of advice" by 40%, as measured by post-interaction surveys and Net Promoter Score (NPS).
- **Improve Client Retention**: Reduce client attrition by 30% through more engaging, relevant, and proactive service delivery that strengthens emotional connections and trust.
- **Enable Real-Time Personalization**: Achieve real-time personalization across all client touchpoints (meetings, communications, digital platforms) with contextually relevant content and recommendations updated continuously based on latest behavioral signals and market conditions.

8.3.5 Solution Overview: Agentic AI-Powered Customer Intelligence Platform

The challenges faced by GFG in delivering advanced customer insights and hyper-personalization present a transformative opportunity to leverage both GenAI and Agentic AI paradigms. This comprehensive solution proposes an *Intelligent Customer Experience Platform* powered by a sophisticated multi-agent ecosystem that continuously learns, adapts, and personalizes every client interaction.

The *Agentic AI-Powered Customer Intelligence Platform* employs a group of specialized autonomous agents that collaborate to create 360-degree customer profiles, predict behavioral patterns, anticipate life events, and deliver Netflix-level personalization in financial services. By leveraging advanced frameworks, including LangChain, CrewAI, AutoGen, LangGraph, and cutting-edge GenAI models, the platform creates a dynamic, self-improving ecosystem that transforms static client data into actionable, predictive insights and hyper-personalized experiences.

This solution addresses the core challenge of moving from reactive, generic advice to proactive, contextually aware financial guidance that resonates with each client's unique emotional, behavioral, and financial profile. The platform integrates behavioral analytics, emotional AI, predictive modeling, and real-time personalization to create an unprecedented level of customer understanding and service delivery.

8.3.6 Solution Architecture

Figure 8-2 depicts the solution architecture.

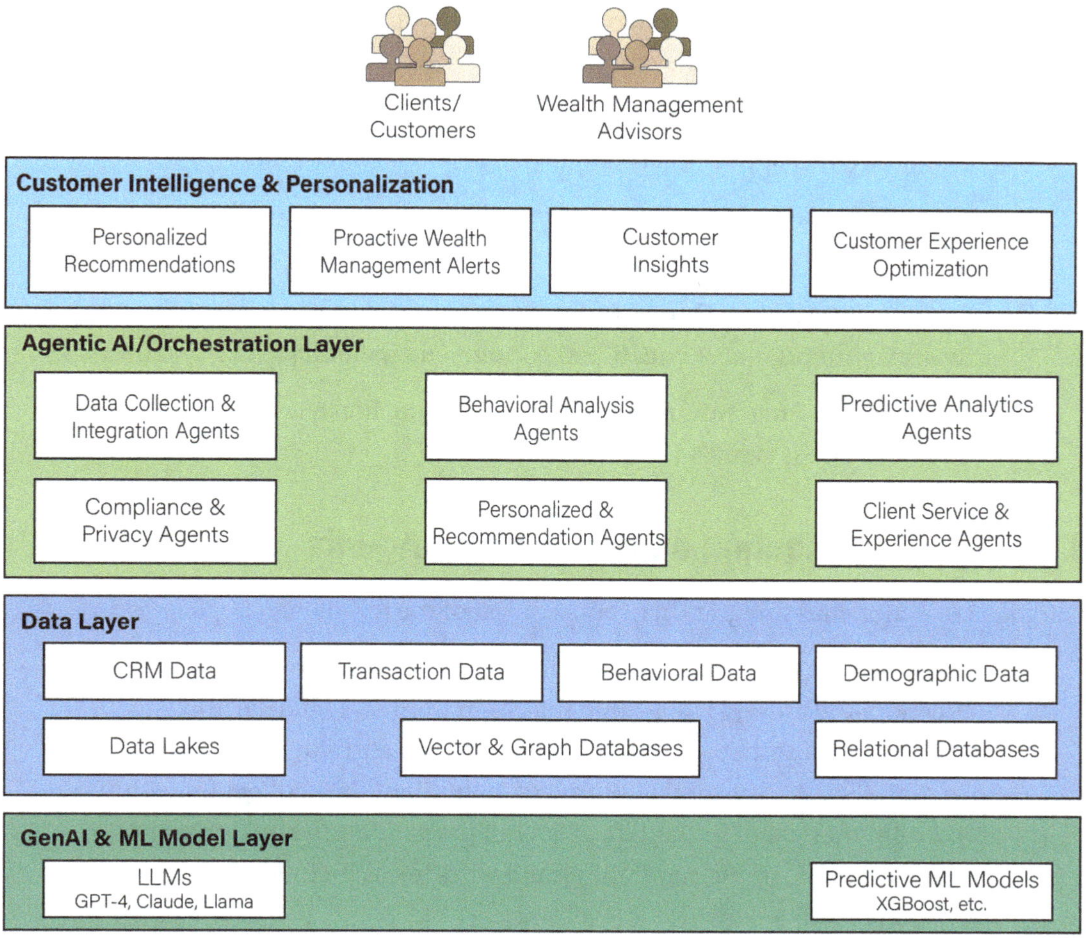

***Figure 8-2.** Solution Architecture*

8.3.7 Key Components of the Solution

8.3.7.1 Data Sources and Collection Infrastructure

The solution consists of a comprehensive data ecosystem that includes the following:

- **Transactional Data**: Account balances, transaction history, investment performance, payment patterns
- **Behavioral Data**: Digital engagement patterns, website/app usage, communication preferences, response rates

- **Demographic and Life Stage Data**: Age, income, family status, career progression, life events
- **Alternative Data Sources**: Social media sentiment, spending patterns (with consent), credit bureau data, public records
- **Communication Data**: Email interactions, call transcripts, meeting notes, survey responses
- **Market Interaction Data**: Product inquiries, research downloads, webinar attendance, educational content engagement
- **Third-party Enrichment**: Psychographic data, lifestyle indicators, financial stress signals

8.3.7.2 Data Collection and Integration Agents

The data collection and integration agents consist of the following:

- **Multisource Data Collector Agent That Has the Following Responsibilities**: (1) Real-time ingestion from 50+ internal and external data sources; (2) data harmonization and standardization across disparate systems; (3) privacy-compliant data collection with consent management; and (4) data quality validation and anomaly detection. The implementation framework/tools include: LangChain + Apache Kafka + Airbyte + Fivetran.

8.3.7.3 Behavioral Analysis Agents

The behavioral analysis agents include

- **Behavioral Pattern Analyzer Agent That Has the Following Responsibilities**: (1) Identify recurring behavioral patterns and preferences; (2) detect behavioral anomalies that may indicate life changes; (3) create behavioral fingerprints for each client; and (4) track behavioral evolution over time. This agent can be implemented using LangChain + TensorFlow + Behavioral Analytics Libraries.

- **Emotional AI Engine Agent That Has the Following Responsibilities**: (1) Analyze emotional context in client communications; (2) detect financial stress, anxiety, or excitement indicators; (3) map emotional states to financial decision-making patterns; and (4) provide emotional intelligence insights to advisors. This agent can be implemented using LangChain + Emotion Detection APIs + Sentiment Analysis + Voice Analytics.

- **Customer Journey Mapper Agent That Has the Following Responsibilities**: (1) Map complete customer journeys across all like touch points; (2) identify friction points and optimization opportunities; (3) predict the next likely actions in customer journey; and (4) personalize journey experiences based on behavioral patterns.

8.3.7.4 Predictive Analytics Agents

The predictive analytics agents include

- **Life Event Predictor Agent That Has the Following Responsibilities**: (1) Predict major life events (marriage, divorce, job change, retirement, inheritance, etc.); (2) analyze behavioral signals that precede life changes; (3) trigger proactive advisor outreach for anticipated needs; and (4) adjust financial recommendations based on predicted life changes. The Framework/Tools for implementation include: LangChain + XGBoost + Prophet + Life Event Detection Models.

- **Churn Risk Assessor Agent That Has the Following Responsibilities**: (1) Continuously assess client retention risk; (2) identify early warning signals of potential churn; (3) recommend intervention strategies; and (4) prioritize at-risk clients for proactive engagement. The Framework/Tools for implementation include: LangChain + Gradient Boosting.

- **Opportunity Identifier Agent That Has the Following Responsibilities**: (1) Identify cross-sell and upsell opportunities; (2) predict optimal timing for product recommendations; (3) assess product–client fit based on behavioral and financial profiles; and (4) generate personalized value propositions. The implementation Framework/Tools include: LangChain + Collaborative Filtering + Association Rules.

8.3.7.5 Personalization and Recommendation Agents

The personalization and recommendation agents include the following:

- **Dynamic Segmentation Agent That Has the Following Responsibilities**: (1) Create and maintain 100+ micro-segments based on behavioral, emotional, and financial characteristics; (2) continuously update segment membership based on evolving client profiles; (3) enable segment-of-one personalization for high-value clients; and (4) provide segment insights for marketing and product development. The implementation Framework/Tools include: LangChain + Advanced Clustering + Embedding Models.
- **Content Personalizer Agent That Has the Following Responsibilities**: (1) Generate personalized content for emails, reports, and communications; (2) adapt communication style to client preferences and emotional state; (3) create personalized educational content based on knowledge gaps; and (4) optimize content timing and channel selection. The implementation Framework/Tools include : LangChain + GPT-5 + Content Generation + A/B Testing.
- **Recommendation Engine Agent That Has the Following Responsibilities**: (1) Generate hyper-personalized product and service recommendations; (2) optimize recommendation timing based on behavioral signals; (3) continuously learn from recommendation outcomes; and (4) balance exploration vs. exploitation in recommendation strategies. The implementation Framework/Tools include: LangChain + Deep Learning Recommender Systems + Multi-Armed Bandits (MAB) algorithms.

8.3.7.6 Client Service and Experience Agents

The Client service and experience agents consist of the following:

- **Conversational AI Assistant Agent That Has the Following Responsibilities**: (1) Provide 24/7 personalized client support with full context awareness; (2) understand and respond to emotional context in conversations; (3) escalate complex issues to human advisors with full context; and (4) learn from each interaction to improve future responses. The implementation Framework/Tools include: LangChain + GPT-5 + RAG + Voice AI + Emotional Intelligence.
- **Experience Orchestrator Agent That Has the Following Responsibilities**: (1) Orchestrate personalized experiences across all touchpoints; (2) ensure consistent personalization across channels; (3) optimize experience flow based on real-time behavioral signals; and (4) coordinate between multiple agents for seamless client experience. The implementation Framework/Tools include: LangChain + Journey Orchestration + Real-time Decision Engine.
- **Proactive Outreach Agent That Has the Following Responsibilities**: (1) Identify optimal moments for proactive client outreach; (2) generate personalized outreach messages and recommendations; (3) schedule and coordinate advisor-client interactions; and (4) track outreach effectiveness and optimize strategies. The implementation Framework/Tools include: LangChain + Predictive Triggers + Communication Automation.

8.3.7.7 Compliance and Privacy Agents

The compliance and privacy agents consist of the following:

- **Privacy Guardian Agent That Has the Following Responsibilities**: (1) Ensure all personalization respects privacy preferences and regulations; (2) implement privacy-preserving analytics techniques; (3) manage consent and data usage permissions; and (4) provide transparency into data usage for clients. The implementation Framework/Tools include: LangChain + Privacy Engineering + Differential Privacy + Federated Learning.

- **Consent Manager Agent That Has the Following Responsibilities**: (1) Manage granular consent preferences for each client; (2) ensure personalization operates within consent boundaries; (3) provide easy consent modification interfaces; and (4) audit consent compliance across all personalization activities. The implementation Framework/Tools include: LangChain + Consent Management Platform + GDPR Compliance.

8.3.7.8 Enterprise Data and Models

Customer Data Lake

- **Contents**: Structured transaction data, unstructured communication data, behavioral event streams, external enrichment data
- **Technologies**: AWS S3, Apache Spark + Delta Lake + Apache Iceberg

Vector and Graph Databases

- **Vector DBs**: Pinecone, Chroma, Weaviate for semantic similarity and embedding storage
- **Graph DBs**: Neo4j for relationship mapping and network analysis
- **Purpose**: Enable semantic search, relationship analysis, and complex pattern detection

Real-Time Infrastructure

- **Streaming**: Apache Kafka, Apache Pulsar for real-time data processing
- **Caching**: Redis, Apache Ignite for low-latency personalization
- **APIs**: FastAPI, GraphQL for real-time data access

8.3.7.9 Agentic Workflow and Orchestration

CrewAI Multi-agent Orchestrator

- **Purpose**: Coordinate complex workflows involving multiple specialized agents
- **Capabilities**: Dynamic task assignment, agent collaboration, result synthesis

LangGraph Workflow Engine

- **Purpose**: Define and execute complex, multistep personalization workflows
- **Capabilities**: State management, conditional branching, real-time adaptation
- **Use Cases**: Customer journey orchestration, multitouch personalization campaigns

8.3.8 Business Benefits

The Agentic AI-powered Customer Intelligence Platform delivers transformative business value to GFG as detailed in this section.

8.3.8.1 Enhanced Customer Understanding

- **360-Degree Customer Profiles**: Move from 8–10 basic segments to 100+ dynamic micro-segments with real-time behavioral, emotional, and predictive insights.
- **Predictive Capabilities**: Achieve 80% accuracy in predicting major life events and financial needs before clients explicitly request assistance.

- **Behavioral Intelligence**: Capture and analyze emotional and psychological factors influencing financial decisions, leading to more empathetic and effective advice.

8.3.8.2 Operational Efficiency Gains

- **Advisor Productivity**: Reduce advisor preparation time by 70%, freeing up 8–10 hours per week for high-value client interactions and relationship building.
- **Automated Insights**: Generate comprehensive client insights automatically, eliminating manual research and analysis.
- **Proactive Service**: Transform from reactive to predictive service delivery, anticipating client needs before they arise.

8.3.8.3 Revenue Growth and Client Retention

- **Cross-Sell/Upsell Success**: Improve conversion rates by 60% through better timing, targeting, and personalization of product recommendations.
- **Client Retention**: Reduce client attrition by 30% through more engaging, relevant, and proactive service delivery.
- **Lifetime Value**: Increase average client lifetime value by 25% through deeper relationships and more relevant product offerings.

8.3.8.4 Client Experience Excellence

- **Personalization Accuracy**: Achieve 90% relevance in personalized recommendations, up from 35% baseline.
- **Client Satisfaction**: Increase satisfaction scores by 40% related to "advisor understanding" and "relevance of advice."
- **Real-Time Personalization**: Enable contextually relevant experiences across all touchpoints with continuous updates based on behavioral signals.

8.3.8.5 Competitive Advantage

- **Netflix-Level Personalization**: Deliver consumer-grade personalization experiences that differentiate GFG in the market.
- **Scalability**: Handle exponential growth in client data and interactions without proportional increases in operational costs.
- **Innovation Leadership**: Position GFG as a technology leader in the wealth management industry.

8.3.9 Summary

GFG's Agentic AI-powered customer intelligence platform represents a paradigm shift in wealth management, moving from static, demographic-based segmentation to dynamic, behavioral-driven hyper-personalization. By leveraging a sophisticated ecosystem of specialized AI agents working collaboratively through frameworks such as CrewAI, LangGraph, and AutoGen, the platform creates unprecedented customer understanding and delivers Netflix-level personalization in financial services.

The multi-agent architecture ensures comprehensive coverage of all aspects of customer intelligence, from data collection and behavioral analysis to predictive modeling and real-time personalization. The integration of GenAI enables natural, contextual interactions while maintaining privacy and compliance standards. This approach transforms every client touchpoint into an opportunity for deeper engagement and value creation.

The platform's ability to predict life events, understand emotional context, and deliver proactive, personalized experiences positions GFG to build stronger, more profitable client relationships while achieving operational excellence. As client expectations continue to evolve toward more personalized, digital-first experiences, this Agentic AI approach provides the foundation for sustained competitive advantage in the wealth management industry.

The solution's emphasis on privacy-preserving personalization and explainable AI ensures that enhanced customer insights and personalization capabilities are delivered responsibly, maintaining client trust while maximizing business value. This comprehensive approach to customer intelligence and hyper-personalization sets a new standard for client-centric financial services in the age of AI.

8.4 Use Case 3: Estate, Tax Planning, and Wealth Succession

8.4.1 Problem Statement

At GFG, estate planning, tax optimization, and wealth succession remain fragmented, reactive processes that fail to address the complex, interconnected nature of modern wealth transfer challenges. Currently, estate planning professionals rely on traditional, siloed approaches using outdated tools and manual processes to navigate an increasingly complex regulatory landscape, resulting in suboptimal tax strategies, missed succession opportunities, and inadequate preparation for the trillions of dollars of generational wealth transfer underway. The current approach struggles with the complexity of modern estates that include digital assets, international holdings, family businesses, and evolving tax regulations, while failing to provide the proactive, integrated planning required for successful multi-generational wealth preservation. Furthermore, GFG's clients face significant wealth erosion and family conflicts without comprehensive, technology-enabled estate and succession planning solutions. Additionally, a decisive 86% of professionals surveyed in the Bank of America Study[5] recommend updates to estate plans, citing gifting strategies (53%) and irrevocable trusts (40%) as top solutions.

8.4.2 Current State, Challenges

- Estate planning attorneys and wealth advisors spend 25–35 hours per week manually researching tax regulations, drafting documents, and coordinating between multiple service providers (attorneys, accountants, insurance specialists, trustees) for complex estate plans.
- Tax optimization strategies are developed reactively, often missing time-sensitive opportunities, and lacking efficient tools to implement changes quickly.

[5] https://images.go.informamail01.com/Web/PentonWRE/%7B0d1d4a75-2b87-4dca-9b23-2027dc689ed7%7D_WMIQ_2024_Trends_in_Trust_and_Estate_Planning_(1).pdf

- Family business succession planning consumes 40–50 hours per engagement due to complex valuation requirements, tax implications, and family dynamics coordination, while 54% of business owners prefer transferring to the next generation[6] but lack structured succession frameworks.
- Digital asset integration and management add 10–15 hours per estate plan as professionals struggle to incorporate cryptocurrencies, online accounts, and intellectual property into traditional estate structures.
- Cross-jurisdictional planning for international clients requires 20–30 additional hours per case due to complex regulatory research and coordination requirements. Document generation and compliance monitoring are predominantly manual processes, with estate plan reviews occurring annually at best, missing critical tax law changes and life event triggers that require immediate plan adjustments.

8.4.3 Objective

Leverage GenAI, predictive analytics, and automated workflow technologies to transform estate planning, tax optimization, and wealth succession. This will provide a system that is integrated and proactive to maximize wealth preservation, minimizes tax liabilities, and ensures seamless multi-generational wealth transfer while addressing the complexities of modern estates, including digital assets, international holdings, and family business succession.

8.4.4 Key Results

- **Enhance Planning Efficiency**: Reduce estate planning document preparation time by 70%, from 25–35 hours to 8–10 hours per comprehensive plan, through AI-powered document generation, automated regulatory compliance checking, and integrated workflow management systems.

[6] https://lifeinsurancetrustco.com/2024-trends-in-trust-and-estate-planning/

- **Optimize Tax Strategies**: Increase tax savings identification by 60% through real-time monitoring of tax law changes, predictive modeling of tax implications, and automated generation of tax-optimized strategies that adapt to changing regulations and client circumstances.
- **Accelerate Succession Planning**: Reduce family business succession planning time by 65%, from 40–50 hours to 15–18 hours per engagement, through automated business valuation integration, AI-generated succession scenarios, and streamlined family governance frameworks.
- **Improve Regulatory Compliance**: Achieve 95% real-time compliance monitoring across all jurisdictions, automatically flagging regulatory changes, deadline requirements, and required plan modifications to ensure continuous legal compliance and optimal tax positioning.
- **Enable Proactive Plan Management**: Implement continuous estate plan monitoring that automatically identifies 90% of life events, tax law changes, and optimization opportunities, triggering proactive plan updates and client communications rather than reactive annual reviews.
- **Integrate Digital Asset Management**: Successfully incorporate digital assets into 100% of estate plans through automated discovery, valuation, and succession planning for cryptocurrencies, online accounts, intellectual property, and other digital holdings.
- **Enhance Client Experience**: Increase client satisfaction scores by 45% through transparent, real-time plan monitoring, automated progress updates, and personalized succession planning recommendations that align with family values and long-term wealth preservation goals.
- **Scale International Capabilities**: Reduce cross-jurisdictional planning complexity by 50% through automated regulatory research, jurisdiction optimization recommendations, and integrated international tax planning that seamlessly coordinates multi-country estate structures.

This comprehensive approach addresses the critical challenges identified in current research, including the looming estate tax exemption reduction in 2026,[7] the need for proactive planning adjustments,[8] and the integration of technological advancements in estate planning while ensuring that GFG remains at the forefront of the evolving wealth management landscape.

8.4.5 Solution Overview – Agentic AI-Powered Estate Planning and Wealth Succession Platform

The estate planning, tax optimization, and wealth succession challenges faced by GFG represent a critical opportunity to revolutionize traditional wealth transfer processes through the strategic deployment of Agentic AI and GenAI technologies. This comprehensive solution introduces the Intelligent Estate Planning and Succession Platform (IEPSP), a sophisticated multi-agent ecosystem that transforms fragmented, reactive estate planning into a proactive, integrated, and continuously adaptive wealth preservation system.

- The IEPSP employs a constellation of specialized autonomous agents that collaborate seamlessly to navigate the complex intersection of tax law, family dynamics, regulatory compliance, and multi-generational wealth transfer strategies. By leveraging advanced frameworks, including LangChain, CrewAI, AutoGen, LangGraph, and state-of-the-art GenAI models, the platform creates a dynamic, self-optimizing ecosystem that transforms static estate plans into living, breathing wealth preservation strategies that adapt in real-time to changing circumstances.
- This solution addresses the fundamental challenge of moving from siloed, manual estate planning processes to an integrated, AI-driven approach that proactively identifies opportunities, mitigates risks, and ensures optimal wealth transfer outcomes. The platform integrates regulatory intelligence, tax optimization modeling, family governance frameworks, and digital asset management to create an unprecedented level of estate planning sophistication and efficiency.

[7] https://www.privatewealthinsights.com/2024/01/estate-planning-in-2024-opportunities-and-challenges-ahead/

[8] https://lifeinsurancetrustco.com/2024-trends-in-trust-and-estate-planning/

- The IEPSP represents a paradigm shift from traditional estate planning methodologies to a predictive, personalized, and continuously optimized approach that anticipates regulatory changes, identifies tax-saving opportunities, and orchestrates complex multi-jurisdictional wealth transfer strategies with precision and efficiency.

8.4.6 Detailed Solution Architecture

The Agentic AI-powered estate planning and wealth succession platform is built on a sophisticated multi-layer architecture that seamlessly integrates data intelligence, regulatory monitoring, tax optimization, and automated workflow orchestration. The architecture employs a hub-and-spoke model with specialized agent clusters working collaboratively to deliver comprehensive estate planning solutions. This section describes each of the core architecture components.

8.4.6.1 Data Intelligence Layer

- Comprehensive client data aggregation from financial institutions, legal documents, and family records
- Real-time regulatory and tax law monitoring across multiple jurisdictions
- Digital asset discovery and valuation systems
- Family business intelligence and succession planning data

8.4.6.2 Agentic Processing Layer

- Specialized AI agents for tax optimization, regulatory compliance, document generation, and succession planning
- Multi-agent orchestration through CrewAI and LangGraph frameworks
- Collaborative decision-making and workflow coordination
- Continuous learning and adaptation mechanisms

8.4.6.3 GenAI Services Layer

- Advanced document generation for wills, trusts, and succession plans
- Personalized tax strategy recommendations
- Automated regulatory compliance documentation
- Family governance framework creation

8.4.6.4 Integration and Orchestration Layer

- Seamless integration with existing wealth management systems with APIs implemented using API gateways
- Real-time data synchronization and workflow management using tools such as Apache Airflow or Camunda
- Cross-jurisdictional coordination and compliance monitoring
- Client communication and advisor collaboration tools

8.4.7 Key Components of the Solution

8.4.7.1 Regulatory Intelligence and Monitoring Agents

The regulatory intelligence and monitoring agents consist of the following:

- **Tax Law Intelligence Agent That Has the Following Responsibilities**: (1) Monitor tax law changes across federal, state, and international jurisdictions; (2) analyze impact of regulatory changes on existing estate plans; (3) generate proactive recommendations for plan modifications; and (4) maintain a comprehensive tax code knowledge base with real-time updates. The implementation Framework/Tools include: LangChain + Regulatory APIs + Legal Document Processing + Tax Code Analysis.
- **Compliance Monitoring Agent That Has the Following Responsibilities**: (1) Ensure continuous compliance across all jurisdictions; (2) track filing deadlines and regulatory requirements; (3) generate compliance reports and audit trails; and (4) flag

potential compliance risks and violations. The implementation Framework/Tools include: LangChain + Compliance Management Systems + Regulatory Databases + Alert Systems.

- **International Coordination Agent That Has the Following Responsibilities**: (1) Navigate cross-border estate planning requirements; (2) optimize international tax treaty benefits; (3) coordinate multi-jurisdictional compliance; and (4) manage foreign asset reporting requirements. The implementation Framework/Tools include: LangChain + International Tax Databases + Treaty Analysis + Cross-Bord.

8.4.7.2 Tax Optimization and Strategy Agents

The tax optimization and strategy agents consist of the following:

- **Tax Strategy Optimizer Agent That Has the Following Responsibilities**: (1) Develop comprehensive tax minimization strategies; (2) model various estate planning scenarios and outcomes; (3) optimize gift and estate tax exemption utilization; and (4) generate dynamic tax-efficient wealth transfer plans. The implementation Framework/Tools include: LangChain + Tax Modeling Software + Monte Carlo Simulations + Optimization Algorithms. The models used include: Tax optimization models, scenario analysis, and predictive tax liability modeling.
- **Gift and Estate Tax Planner Agent That Has the Following Responsibilities**: (1) Optimize annual exclusion and lifetime exemption strategies; (2) plan strategic gifting programs and timing; (3) model estate tax implications under various scenarios; and (4) generate tax-efficient wealth transfer recommendations. The implementation Framework/Tools include: LangChain + Estate Tax Calculators + Actuarial Models + Gift Planning Software.
- **Generation-Skipping Transfer Tax Agent That Has the Following Responsibilities**: (1) Optimize GST tax exemption allocation; (2) plan multi-generational wealth transfer strategies; (3) model dynasty trust

structures and benefits; and (4) generate GST-efficient succession plans. The implementation Framework/Tools include: LangChain + GST Tax Modeling + Dynasty Trust Analysis + Multi-Generational Planning.

8.4.7.3 Document Generation and Management Agents

The document generation and management agents consist of the following:

- **Estate Document Generator Agent That Has the Following Responsibilities**: (1) Generate comprehensive wills, trusts, and estate planning documents; (2) customize documents based on client circumstances and objectives; (3) ensure legal compliance and best practice adherence and (4) maintain document version control and audit trails. The implementation Framework/Tools include: LangChain + GPT-5 + Legal Document Templates + Document Assembly Systems. The models used include: Legal document generation models, clause optimization, and compliance checking.
- **Trust Structure Designer Agent That Has the Following Responsibilities**: (1) Design optimal trust structures for specific objectives; (2) generate trust documents with appropriate provisions; (3) model trust performance and tax implications; and (4) recommend trust modifications based on changing circumstances. The implementation Framework/Tools include: LangChain + Trust Design Software + Tax Modeling + Legal Compliance Systems.
- **Digital Asset Integration Agent That Has the Following Responsibilities**: (1) Identify and catalog digital assets across platforms; (2) generate digital asset succession plans; (3) integrate cryptocurrency and online account management; and (4) ensure secure digital asset transfer protocols. The implementation Framework/Tools include: LangChain + Digital Asset Discovery + Blockchain Analysis.

8.4.7.4 Family Business Succession Agents

The family business succession agents consist of the following:

- **Business Valuation Agent That has the Following Responsibilities**: (1) Perform automated business valuations using multiple methodologies; (2) monitor valuation changes and optimization opportunities; (3) generate valuation discounts for estate planning purposes; and (4) integrate with external valuation services and databases. The implementation Framework/Tools include: LangChain + Valuation Models + Financial Analysis + Market Data Integration. The models used include: DCF models, comparable company analysis, asset-based valuation, and discount modeling.
- **Succession Planning Orchestrator Agent That Has the Following Responsibilities**: (1) Design comprehensive family business succession strategies; (2) coordinate between family members, advisors, and stakeholders; (3) generate succession timelines and milestone tracking; and (4) facilitate family governance and decision-making processes. The implementation Framework/Tools include: LangChain + Succession Planning Software + Family Governance Tools + Stakeholder Management.
- **Buy-Sell Agreement Generator Agent That Has the Following Responsibilities**: (1) Generate customized buy-sell agreements; (2) model various trigger events and valuation mechanisms; (3) ensure tax-efficient ownership transfer structures; and (4) integrate with business succession and estate plans. The implementation Framework/Tools include: LangChain + Legal Document Generation + Valuation Integration + Tax Optimization.

8.4.7.5 Client Communication and Advisory Agents

The client communication and advisory agents consist of the following:

- **Client Communication Agent That Has the Following Responsibilities:** (1) Generate personalized client communications and updates; (2) explain complex estate planning concepts in accessible language; (3) provide regular plan performance and optimization reports; and (4) facilitate family meetings and succession discussions. The implementation Framework/Tools include: LangChain + GPT-5 + Communication Templates + Client Portal Integration.

- **Advisory Coordination Agent That Has the Following Responsibilities**: (1) Coordinate between attorneys, accountants, and wealth advisors; (2) manage multidisciplinary project timelines and deliverables; (3) facilitate expert consultations and decision-making; and (4) ensure seamless advisor collaboration and communication. The implementation Framework/Tools include: LangChain + Project Management + Collaboration Tools + Expert Networks.
- **Family Governance Facilitator Agent That Has the Following Responsibilities**: (1) Design family governance structures and processes; (2) facilitate family meetings and decision-making; (3) generate family mission statements and wealth transfer philosophies; and (4) coordinate next-generation education and preparation. The implementation Framework/Tools include: LangChain + Family Governance Frameworks + Meeting Facilitation + Educational Content.

8.4.7.6 Predictive Analytics and Monitoring Agents

The predictive analytics and monitoring agents consist of the following:

- **Life Event Predictor Agent That Has the Following Responsibilities**: (1) Predict major life events affecting estate plans; (2) monitor behavioral and financial signals indicating life changes; (3) trigger proactive plan reviews and modifications; and (4) generate personalized life event planning recommendations. The implementation Framework/Tools include: LangChain + Predictive Analytics + Life Event Models + Behavioral Analysis.

- **Plan Performance Monitor Agent That Has the Following Responsibilities**: (1) Continuously monitor estate plan performance and effectiveness; (2) track tax savings and wealth preservation metrics; (3) identify optimization opportunities and plan modifications; and (4) generate performance reports and recommendations. The implementation Framework/Tools include: LangChain + Performance Analytics + Tax Tracking + Optimization Algorithms.
- **Risk Assessment Agent That Has the Following Responsibilities**: (1) Assess estate planning risks and vulnerabilities; (2) monitor regulatory and tax law changes affecting plans; (3) generate risk mitigation strategies and recommendations; and (4) provide early warning systems for potential issues. The implementation Framework/Tools include: LangChain + Risk Models + Regulatory Monitoring + Alert Systems.

8.4.7.7 Enterprise Data and Infrastructure

The enterprise data and infrastructure consist of the following:

- **Estate planning data lake** contains client financial data, legal documents, family information, business records, digital assets, and regulatory data. The technologies used include: AWS S3 + Apache Spark + Delta Lake + Apache Iceberg. The purpose is to provide a centralized repository for all estate planning data with version control and audit trails.
- **Legal and regulatory knowledge base** uses vector databases such as Pinecone and Chroma for legal document similarity and precedent analysis, and graph databases such as Neo4j for family relationship mapping and asset ownership structures. The purpose is to enable semantic search of legal precedents, regulatory requirements, and best practices.
- **Real-time processing infrastructure** includes Apache Kafka for real-time regulatory updates and client data changes, Redis for low-latency access to frequently used calculations and documents, and APIs such as FastAPI and GraphQL for seamless integration with existing systems.

8.4.7.8 Agentic Workflow and Orchestration

The Agentic workflow and orchestration consist of the following:

- **CrewAI estate planning orchestrator**, whose purpose is to coordinate complex estate planning workflows involving multiple specialized agents. Its capabilities include dynamic task assignment, multi-agent collaboration, result synthesis, and quality assurance.
- **LangGraph succession workflow engine**, whose purpose is to define and execute complex, multi-step succession planning workflows. Its capabilities include state management, conditional branching, real-time adaptation, and stakeholder coordination. Use cases include family business succession, multigenerational planning, and cross-border estate coordination.

8.4.8 Business Benefits

The Agentic AI-Powered Estate Planning and Wealth Succession Platform delivers transformative business value to GFG.

8.4.8.1 Operational Efficiency Revolution

- **Document Preparation Acceleration**: Reduce estate planning document preparation time by 70%, from 25–35 hours to 8–10 hours per comprehensive plan through AI-powered document generation and automated compliance checking.
- **Succession Planning Efficiency**: Decrease family business succession planning time by 65%, from 40–50 hours to 15–18 hours per engagement through automated valuation integration and streamlined governance frameworks.
- **Advisor Productivity**: Free up 15–20 hours per week per advisor for high-value client relationship building and strategic planning activities.

8.4.8.2 Tax Optimization Excellence

- **Enhanced Tax Savings**: Increase tax savings identification by 60% through real-time monitoring of tax law changes and predictive modeling of tax implications.
- **Proactive Strategy Adaptation**: Automatically identify 90% of tax optimization opportunities triggered by regulatory changes or life events.
- **Multi-jurisdictional Efficiency**: Reduce cross-jurisdictional planning complexity by 50% through automated regulatory research and optimization recommendations.

8.4.8.3 Compliance and Risk Management

- **Real-Time Compliance Monitoring**: Achieve 95% real-time compliance monitoring across all jurisdictions with automated flagging of regulatory changes and required modifications.
- **Regulatory Adaptation**: Automatically update estate plans within 24–48 hours of relevant regulatory changes.
- **Risk Mitigation**: Reduce compliance-related risks by 80% through continuous monitoring and proactive plan adjustments.

8.4.8.4 Client Experience and Satisfaction

- **Enhanced Client Satisfaction**: Increase client satisfaction scores by 45% through transparent, real-time plan monitoring and personalized recommendations.
- **Proactive Service Delivery**: Transform from reactive annual reviews to continuous, proactive plan optimization and client communication.
- **Digital Asset Integration**: Successfully incorporate digital assets into 100% of estate plans through automated discovery and succession planning.

8.4.8.5 Revenue Growth and Scalability

- **Service Capacity Expansion**: Handle three times more estate planning engagements with existing staff through automation and efficiency gains.
- **Premium Service Offerings**: Introduce high-value, technology-enabled services commanding 25–30% premium pricing.
- **Cross-Selling Opportunities**: Increase related service adoption by 40% through integrated wealth management and estate planning recommendations.

8.4.8.6 Competitive Differentiation

- **Technology Leadership**: Position GFG as the premier technology-enabled estate planning provider in the market.
- **Scalable Excellence**: Deliver consistent, high-quality estate planning services regardless of engagement complexity or advisor experience level.
- **Innovation Advantage**: Maintain competitive mode through continuous AI-driven service enhancement and optimization.

8.4.9 Summary

GFG's Agentic AI-powered estate planning and wealth succession platform represents a revolutionary transformation of traditional estate planning methodologies, moving from fragmented, reactive processes to an integrated, proactive, and continuously adaptive wealth preservation ecosystem. By leveraging a sophisticated constellation of specialized AI agents working collaboratively through frameworks such as CrewAI, LangGraph, and AutoGen, the platform creates unprecedented efficiency, accuracy, and client value in estate planning and wealth succession.

The multi-agent architecture ensures comprehensive coverage of all aspects of estate planning, from regulatory monitoring and tax optimization to document generation and family governance. The integration of GenAI enables natural, contextual document creation and client communication while maintaining the highest standards of legal compliance and professional excellence. This approach transforms every aspect of the estate planning process into an opportunity for enhanced efficiency, improved outcomes, and deeper client relationships.

The platform's ability to predict regulatory changes, optimize tax strategies in real-time, and orchestrate complex multi-generational wealth transfer plans positions GFG to deliver superior outcomes while achieving operational excellence. As estate planning complexity continues to increase with evolving regulations, digital assets, and international wealth structures, this Agentic AI approach provides the foundation for sustained competitive advantage and client value creation.

The solution's emphasis on continuous learning, regulatory compliance, and family-centered planning ensures that enhanced estate planning capabilities are delivered responsibly and effectively, maintaining client trust while maximizing wealth preservation outcomes. This comprehensive approach to estate planning and wealth succession sets a new standard for professional excellence in the age of AI, enabling GFG to serve as the premier destination for sophisticated, technology-enabled estate planning services.

The platform's integration of predictive analytics, automated compliance monitoring, and intelligent workflow orchestration creates a self-improving system that becomes more effective and efficient over time, ensuring that GFG remains at the forefront of estate planning innovation while delivering exceptional value to clients navigating the complexities of modern wealth transfer and succession planning.

8.5 Other Use Cases

In this section, we outline other use cases in the wealth and asset management domain. Note that these use cases are for illustration purposes and to provide direction for your own solution development.

8.5.1 Client Segmentation and Lead Generation, Marketing, and Onboarding

GFG faces mounting pressure to grow its client base and deliver seamless onboarding experiences in an increasingly digital and competitive marketplace. Traditional client segmentation methods, often based on static demographic data fail to capture the nuanced behaviors, preferences, and life events that drive client needs. As a result, marketing campaigns are less targeted, conversion rates are suboptimal, and high-potential prospects are frequently overlooked.

The onboarding process itself is often fragmented, involving multiple manual steps, redundant data entry, and compliance checks that slow down the client journey. This leads to frustration, higher abandonment rates, and lost revenue opportunities. According to a 2024 Deloitte survey, 60% of wealth management firms report that inefficient onboarding processes are a top reason for client attrition, while 55% cite poor segmentation as a barrier to effective marketing and lead generation.[9]

In a market where digital-first competitors and robo-advisors are setting new standards for speed and personalization, GFG's leadership recognizes the urgent need to modernize its approach. The challenge is to leverage advanced analytics and GenAI to dynamically segment clients, identify high-value leads, and deliver frictionless, personalized onboarding and marketing experiences, all while maintaining compliance and data security.

8.6 Future Innovation

In the future, we expect the following innovations in this Wealth and Asset Management:

- **Pervasive AI Integration**: We anticipate that within the next 3–5 years, Agentic AI and GenAI will be deeply embedded across all facets of wealth and asset management, moving beyond siloed applications to form interconnected, self-optimizing ecosystems. Gartner predicts at least 15% of day-to-day work decisions will be made autonomously through Agentic AI by 2028, up from 0% in 2024. In addition, 33% of enterprise software applications will include Agentic AI by 2028, up from less than 1% in 2024.
- **Hyper-Personalization As the New Standard**: Client expectations for personalized financial advice and services will continue to escalate, making Netflix-level hyper-personalization a non-negotiable differentiator. Firms that fail to adopt advanced AI for customer insights will struggle with client acquisition and retention.

[9] https://www2.deloitte.com/global/en/pages/financial-services/articles/global-asset-management-industry-outlook.html

- **Predictive and Proactive Service Models**: The industry will fully transition from reactive advisory models to predictive and proactive service delivery, where AI anticipates client needs, life events, and market shifts, enabling advisors to offer timely and relevant guidance before clients even ask.
- **Increased Advisor Augmentation**: AI will not replace human advisors but will profoundly augment their capabilities, freeing them from routine, time-consuming tasks and empowering them to focus on high-value activities such as complex problem-solving, emotional support, and deep relationship building.
- **New Revenue Streams and Business Models**: The efficiencies and enhanced capabilities enabled by AI will pave the way for innovative service offerings and business models, including subscription-based advisory services, micro-personalization at scale, and AI-driven wealth transfer consulting, commanding premium pricing.
- **Emphasis on Explainable AI and Ethical Governance**: As AI becomes more integral to financial decision-making, there will be an increased focus on developing explainable AI models to ensure transparency, build client trust, and comply with evolving ethical and regulatory guidelines. Robust governance frameworks for AI will become standard.
- **Enhanced Cybersecurity and Data Privacy**: The increased reliance on vast datasets and AI models will necessitate even more sophisticated cybersecurity measures and stringent data privacy protocols, ensuring the secure and compliant handling of sensitive client information.
- **Talent Transformation**: The demand for AI-literate professionals in wealth management will skyrocket, leading to significant investment in upskilling existing workforces and attracting new talent with expertise in AI, data science, and behavioral economics.

8.7 Chapter Summary

The adoption of GenAI, particularly the Agentic AI framework, is no longer a luxury but a strategic imperative for wealth and asset management firms and FSOs. The detailed use cases presented in this chapter demonstrate how these technologies can fundamentally transform operations, client engagement, and revenue generation. By moving from reactive, manual processes to proactive, AI-driven solutions, firms can overcome current challenges, meet evolving client expectations, and gain a significant competitive advantage. The multi-agent architectures outlined offer a robust, scalable, and continuously improving ecosystem, ensuring that firms can adapt to market shifts and regulatory changes in real time.

The future of wealth and asset management is undeniably AI-driven, promising a more efficient, personalized, and proactive financial landscape for both firms and their clients.

In the next chapter, we discuss putting all the concepts we covered so far into action – this includes the methodology for deploying the applications into production and the best practices for operations and maintenance of GenAI applications.

CHAPTER 9

Implementation, Operations, and Maintenance of GenAI Applications

In the previous chapters, we discussed how GenAI can help transform the Financial Services Sector (FSS) by illustrating the strategy, architecture, relevant use cases, objectives, and key results. In this chapter, we outline how you can put the concepts we learned so far into action with a focus on implementation, operations, and maintenance of GenAI applications.

The FSS stands at the forefront of a transformative revolution driven by GenAI. While traditional machine learning has been a cornerstone of financial operations for decades, the emergence of GenAI and Agentic AI systems represents a paradigm shift that demands entirely new operational frameworks. This chapter explores a set of comprehensive considerations for operating and maintaining these advanced AI systems in financial services, from the evolution of traditional MLOps to FMOps/LLMOps, through the complexities of managing autonomous AI agents that can make independent decisions.

The stakes could not be higher. As Bloomberg Intelligence analysis[1] indicates, Agentic AI's impact on bank productivity will likely exceed expectations, yet full autonomy may take more than five years due to data governance challenges and legacy

[1] https://www.bloomberg.com/professional/insights/artificial-intelligence/banks-enter-agentic-ai-era-as-tech-race-heats-up-roi-in-focus/

S. Godavarthi, R. Nagvekar, *Transforming Financial Services with Generative AI*,
https://doi.org/10.1007/979-8-8688-2053-3_9

system constraints. Financial institutions must navigate this transformation while maintaining regulatory compliance, managing unprecedented risks, and ensuring operational resilience in an increasingly complex technological landscape.

Our goal in this chapter is to equip readers with specific technical considerations and nuances for GenAI implementation. We will dive deep into the following topics:

- **Anatomy of a GenAI Application**: We review this from a technical perspective. This includes tools and technologies across six components: security, application, orchestration, model, data, and infrastructure.
- **Foundation Model/Large Language Model Operations (FMOps/LLMOps)**: This is a methodology that focuses on the processes, techniques, and best practices applied for managing the model and data components of a GenAI application.
- **Security and Privacy Considerations**: These are some of the most important aspects for any application in the FSS, especially for GenAI-based applications. We therefore cover security and privacy aspects separately in detail.
- **Performance, Reliability, and Scalability Management**: These are aspects that can address increasing demands and workloads while delivering consistent and reliable results. We discuss this for all components except security.
- **Cost Optimization**: Costs are an important consideration for FSOs operating within constrained budgets. We review various costs incurred throughout the GenAI life cycle and examine approaches to optimizing the costs and maximizing the value of GenAI investments.

9.1 Anatomy of a GenAI Application

To understand the key aspects of operations and maintenance, let's start by reviewing a typical GenAI application from a technical point of view. Figure 9-1 illustrates the anatomy of a GenAI application with multiple components. Each component represents a set of technologies fulfilling certain key functionalities.

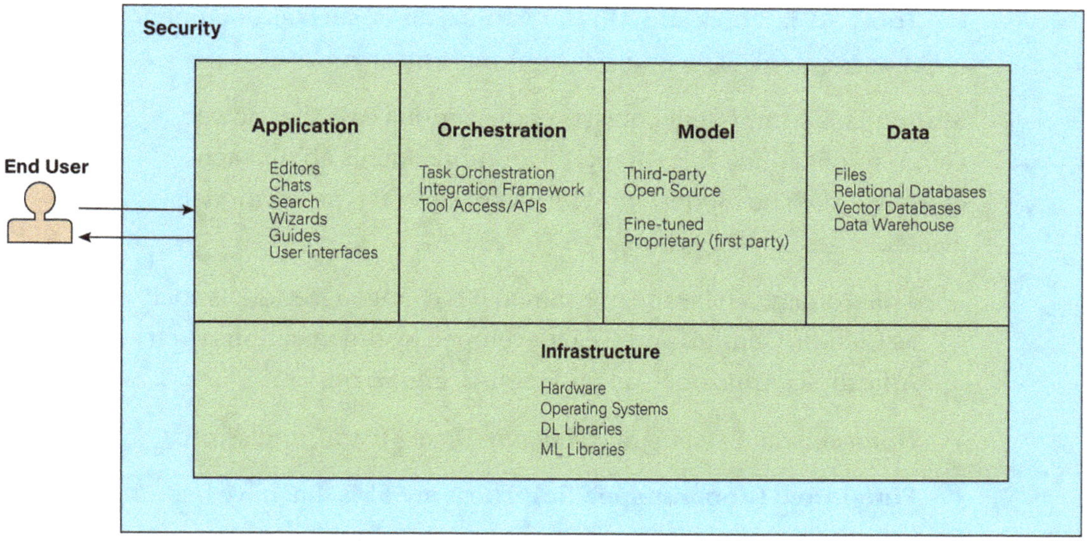

Figure 9-1. *Anatomy of a GenAI Application*

Let's review each of the above components starting with the Security layer and then working our way from Application to Infrastructure layers.

- **Security**: This component represents the security measures and controls that are implemented across the entire GenAI application stack to ensure data privacy, security, and guardrails for content safety and compliance.
- **Application**: This component represents the front end applications that end users use to leverage GenAI capabilities. This includes web and mobile applications and user interfaces. This component includes technology and software for various use cases we discussed throughout this book.
- **Orchestration:** This component includes the Integration Framework, Task Orchestration, and Tools/APIs, as follows:
    - **Integration Framework**: This includes out-of-the-box libraries and packages used to interact with third party and open source FMs.
    - **Task Orchestration**: Task orchestration manages the interaction across components within the GenAI anatomy.

- **Tools/APIs**: Tools and APIs for various tasks, such as document management, SQL, image formatting, and so on.

- **Model:** This component consists of the various FMs that power GenAI applications. See Chapter 3 for more details about each of these FMs. The model could be one of several types of models available:
    - **Third-party**: These are pretrained large language models such as Claude, Gemini, and GPT, developed by organizations such as Anthropic, Amazon, Google, OpenAI, and so on.
    - **Open source FMs**: Llama, Hugging Face, Mistral, and so on.
    - **Fine-tuned (domain-specific)**: These are FMs that have been further fine-tuned for specific use cases or domains.
    - **Proprietary (first party)**: These FMs are proprietary models developed and trained by the organization itself. Developing an FM is a complex activity which needs a lot of expertise and specialized resources. We expect that most FSOs will not need to develop these models. Therefore, we don't discuss considerations for these models in this chapter.
- **Data:** These are all the technologies associated with data and metadata storage such as vector databases, graph databases, files, relational databases, object databases, data warehouses, etc.
- **Infrastructure:** This component involves the hardware for running all the other components. The infrastructure includes operating systems such as Linux or Windows, Deep Learning libraries such as TensorFlow and PyTorch that are necessary to run FMs, end-to-end ML platforms such as Amazon SageMaker, and Azure Machine Learning Service, and Google Vertex AI.

This approach allows us to clearly view the technical aspects of GenAI applications by separating concerns across different application layers.

9.2 Operations Framework: From MLOps to FMOps to LLMOps

The transition from traditional MLOps to FMOps/LLMOps represents one of the most significant operational shifts for GenAI applications. Unlike traditional ML models that are trained for specific tasks with structured datasets, foundation models are pretrained on vast amounts of diverse data and can be adapted for multiple use cases through fine-tuning or prompt engineering. The key differences between MLOPs and FMOps/LLMOps are highlighted in Table 9-1.

Table 9-1. *Key Architectural Differences Between MLOps and FMOps/LLMOps*

Feature	MLOps	FM/LLMOps
Input	Structured data pipelines (e.g., for credit scoring models)	Multimodal data inputs (text, images, audio, video)
Training	Specific model training (e.g., for fraud detection)	Models with billions or trillions of parameters
Output	Deterministic outputs for regulatory compliance	Non-deterministic outputs requiring extensive validation
Model size and scale	Small to Medium (MB to GBs)	Large to Massive (GB to TBs)
Training and inference	Standard CPU/GPU clusters	Massive GPU clusters
Data pipelines	ETL pipelines/feature stores	High – massive data ingestion, preprocessing pipelines
Fine-tuning	Transfer learning, domain adaptation	Parameter efficient fine-tuning, LoRA, QloRA
Observability	Standard – quantitative metrics (accuracy, latency, infrastructure costs)	Need additional guardrails for hallucinations, quality assessment (human evaluation, safety, alignment)

LLMOps represents a specialized subset of FMOps focused specifically on text-to-text applications, which constitute the majority of current generative AI use cases in financial services.

Figure 9-2 illustrates the types of activities associated with FMs. Note, that we are not including the pre-training activities of FMs. As mentioned earlier, pre-training is a complex activity and a discussion of that subject is out of scope for this book.

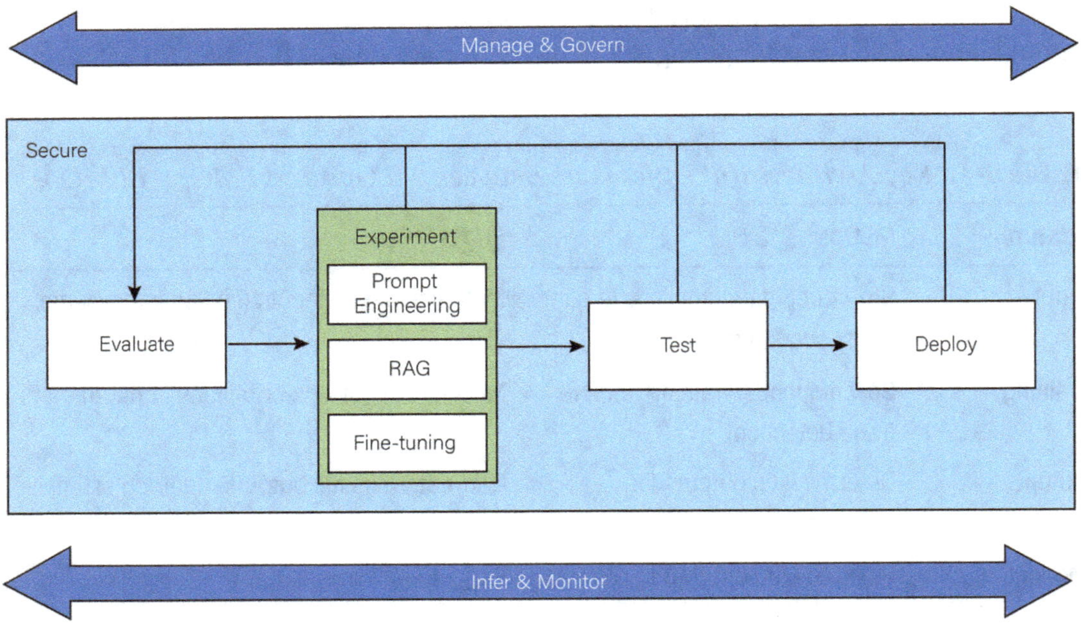

Figure 9-2. *Foundation Model Operations*

So, one might ask, what's the difference between the FMOps and the GenAI life cycle introduced in Chapter 3? The main difference lies in scope and focus. The GenAI life cycle is the broader framework encompassing the entire development and management process of developing a GenAI application. It includes project and product management, management of users, strategies, business cases, and so on. FMOps, on the other hand, focuses on tools and best practices to manage and streamline FM-specific activities in a production environment. Let's go through each of the activities mentioned in Figure 9-2 to understand them in more detail. Note that some tools and best practices apply to multiple activities.

9.2.1 Manage and Govern

This includes tools and best practices to manage the entire life cycle of FMs, from model pre-training, fine-tuning, and versioning to deployment. FMOps provides tools to set up a model repository with automated processes and APIs for updating, saving, and versioning models. The model repository provides a model catalog with detailed metadata about each model to allow downstream users to pick the model of choice. It also allows users to switch between different models and model providers via a unified interface.

9.2.2 Evaluate

In Chapter 4, we discussed evaluation techniques for measuring the effectiveness of FMs as well as for techniques such as Retrieval Augmented Generation (RAG). FMOps recommends tools and best practices to automate the evaluation process. This includes workflows for evaluation when selecting a model for a use case. It also includes evaluation when a model is moved into testing and production.

9.2.3 Experiment

Effective utilization of FMs relies heavily on crafting appropriate prompts and guiding the model's generation process. FMOps advocates prompt libraries, catalogs, and use of automated tools for prompt management, version control, testing, and optimization to improve model outputs and align them with desired behaviors. These tools allow users to track and visualize prompting and fine-tuning experiments in real time. They also work hand-in-hand with model management tools to enable development, testing, and rollout of optimal prompts, parameters, models, and model providers for a given use case. FMOps also recommends using automation and tools for RAG and fine-tuning. For RAG, the tools would assist with evaluation using some of the metrics described in Chapter 4. Fine-tuning tools include the capability to train, version models, and use the same evaluation techniques mentioned for measuring effectiveness above to determine the best models.

9.2.4 Test

We discussed model evaluations as well as measuring effectiveness of RAG and fine-tuning approaches in the Experiment phase. However, in a production environment, having a separate end-to-end activity for testing the application that leverages the FM is essential. To some extent, this may also be covered under the DevOps methodology. Testing should ideally be carried out using a series of standardized test cases and scenarios and should cover FM performance, latency, accuracy, robustness, toxicity, security, integration with other tools, and compliance with regulations. The tools used here could be standardized testing platforms such as Jenkins or cloud-based tools such as AWS CodePipeline and Azure DevOps.

9.2.5 Deploy

FSOs have three broad choices for GenAI application deployment:

1. Use comprehensive cloud-based services such as Amazon Bedrock, Azure OpenAI Service, and Google's Vertex AI that provide access to a number of open source and proprietary FMs. In this case, the cloud services provide APIs for model deployment.
2. Use model hubs such as Amazon Sagemaker Jumpstart, Azure Model Catalog, or Google Model Garden to deploy open source or proprietary FMs to cloud-based infrastructure. In this case, the FSO has to manage deployments, although the infrastructure itself is provided by the cloud service provider. However, the cloud provider may offer libraries, packages, and necessary guidance to reduce complexity of deployments.
3. Directly deploy open source models. In this case, FSOs can deploy open-source models available on Hugging Face, either on infrastructure in the cloud or on premises. These deployments in particular can be highly complex and challenging due to the size, computational requirements, and potential impact. FMs often require specialized hardware infrastructure, such as GPU clusters or TPU pods, due to their massive computational requirements. To reduce the computational footprint and deployment

complexity, techniques such as knowledge distillation or model compression can be employed.

These methods create smaller, more efficient models that approximate the behavior of the larger FM, making deployment easier. In scenarios where data privacy or regulatory constraints are a concern, federated learning[2] or decentralized deployment strategies can be used for activities such as fine-tuning. In these approaches, the FM is deployed across multiple distributed locations without centralizing the data.

FMOps activities for deployment also include consideration and tools for different types of rollout options. Let's review these.

- **Approvals**: Before rollout, a workflow needs to be established for model approvals. This is especially necessary for FSOs for compliance and regulatory reasons.
- **Incremental Rollout**: Instead of deploying the FM (pretrained or fine-tuned) all at once, this strategy involves rolling it out gradually to a subset of users or use cases. This is important because providers keep releasing updates and versions of models. This allows for monitoring, feedback collection, and adjustments before a broader release. Techniques such as canary deployments, where a small percentage of traffic is routed to the new model, can be employed.
- **Staged Deployment**: This is similar to incremental rollout but with distinct stages or phases. For example, the FM might first be deployed internally for testing, then to a limited set of beta users, and finally to the broader customers or production environment.
- **Blue-green Deployment**: In blue-green deployment you create two separate, but identical environments. For deployments, you deploy to the one environment, complete testing, and then deploy the model to the second environment.

[2] `https://research.google/blog/federated-learning-collaborative-machine-learning-without-centralized-training-data/`

The specific deployment and rollout strategy chosen will depend on factors such as the intended use case, computational resources available, data privacy and regulatory requirements, and the organization's risk tolerance and governance processes.

9.2.6 Infer and Monitor

This phase consists of inference using deployed FMs as well as monitoring of the inferences. As explained in Chapter 1, inference is using the FMs to generate outputs. In other words, this is where end user applications, such as chatbots, invoke the deployed FM for various tasks, including search, content generation, and summarization.

Monitoring the outputs from the FM is an important activity given the nature of FMs. FMOps recommends tools and processes to continuously monitor outputs of FMs to measure effectiveness using the metrics described in Chapter 4. The automation could also include raising alerts when discrepancies are found, or thresholds exceeded.

FMOps also recommends tools to continuously examine responsible and ethical use of models, aligning with organizational policies and regulatory requirements.[3] For example, use guardrails to ensure automatic flagging and correction of prompts and outputs to remove undesirable and toxic content. In addition to these tools, you also need tools for real-time logging, and error tracking of FM invocations to evaluate latency, time-outs, and metrics such as queries per second and tokens per second.

9.2.7 Secure

Given the potential sensitivity of data used by FMs and the risk of privacy violations or misuse, FMOps emphasizes implementing robust security measures, such as access controls, data encryption, and secure communication protocols to protect sensitive information and maintain user privacy. We go into more detail on security later in the "Cost Optimization" section.

[3] https://www.whitehouse.gov/briefing-room/presidential-actions/2023/10/30/executive-order-on-the-safe-secure-and-trustworthy-development-and-use-of-artificial-intelligence/

9.2.8 Industry Examples

The following implementation examples from the financial services sector highlight some of the concepts we introduced earlier on MLOps/LLMOps/FMOps.

1. **Bank of America's Erica Enhancement:**[4] Bank of America has evolved their virtual assistant Erica to incorporate LLM capabilities, requiring sophisticated LLMOps practices.
2. **JPMorgan Chase's LLM Deployment:**[5] JPMorgan Chase has implemented a comprehensive FMOps framework for their internal LLM deployment, which they've named "IndexGPT."
3. **Goldman Sachs (GS) AI platform:**[6] GS is implementing an AI platform to aggressively scale AI for increased productivity and efficiency. They are partnering with tech companies and focusing on security.

9.3 Security and Privacy

In previous chapters, we discussed how GenAI can be used for a wide range of applications in the FSS. However, without adequate security- and privacy-related controls, FSOs face an increased level of risk of privacy-related attacks and risks. FSOs can leverage resources such as MITRE ATLAS knowledge base,[7] OWASP AI Security and Privacy Guide,[8] and NIST's Artificial Intelligence Risk Management Framework (AI RMF 1.0)[9] for details on how to handle the various security- and privacy-related risks associated with AI in general. Note that these may apply to AI in general and are not necessarily specific to GenAI. Given this is a relatively new field, a lot of organizations are still in the process of establishing standards for mitigation of GenAI-specific risks.

[4] https://info.bankofamerica.com/en/digital-banking/erica

[5] https://www.jpmorgan.com/insights/markets/indices/indexgpt

[6] https://www.pymnts.com/artificial-intelligence-2/2025/inside-goldman-sachs-big-bet-on-ai-at-scale/

[7] https://atlas.mitre.org/

[8] https://owasp.org/www-project-ai-security-and-privacy-guide/

[9] https://nvlpubs.nist.gov/nistpubs/ai/nist.ai.100-1.pdf

In this section, we distill the most critical risks and mitigation strategies for each component of the GenAI application anatomy represented in Figure 9-1. As in previous sections, considerations vary between self-hosting and cloud-based hosting strategies. Cloud-based providers offer features to ensure security and privacy out of the box. However, they do adopt a Shared Responsibility model for security, and there may be some aspects of security for which the FSO needs to be responsible.

Figure 9-3 provides a high-level security framework for GenAI applications.

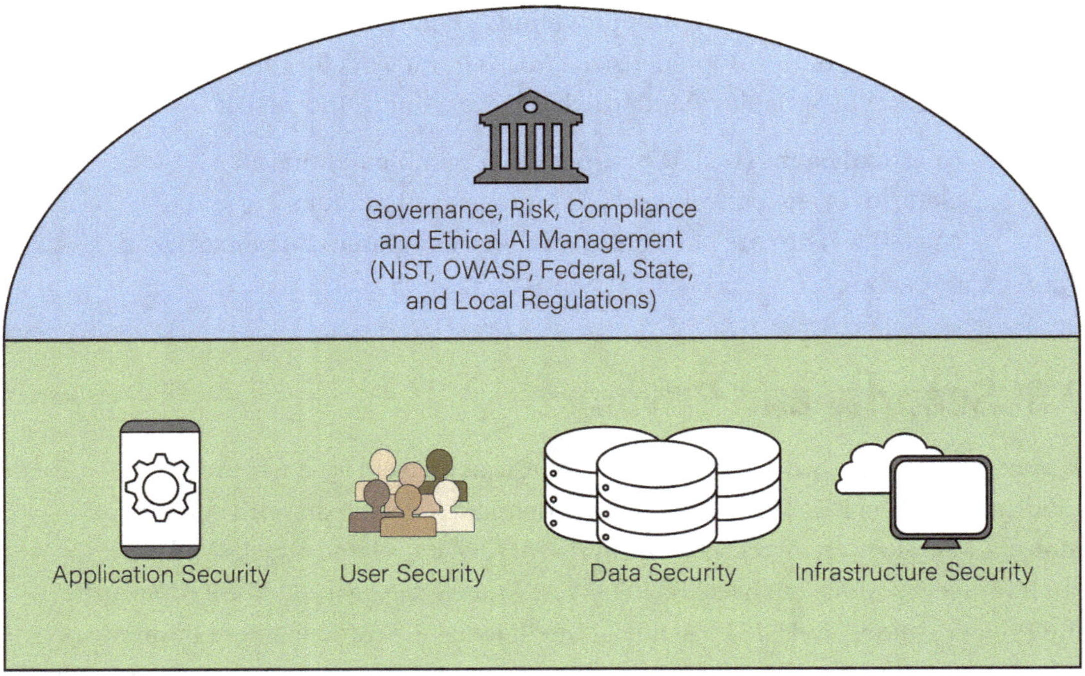

Figure 9-3. *Security Framework for Generative AI applications*

9.3.1 Governance, Risk, Compliance, and Ethical AI Management Frameworks

For GenAI applications, robust Governance, Risk, Compliance (GRC), and ethical AI management frameworks are not merely optional but absolutely critical for ensuring responsible and sustainable deployment. These frameworks provide the necessary structure to navigate the complex landscape of AI, addressing inherent risks such as bias, data privacy violations, intellectual property infringement, and the generation of harmful or misleading content. By establishing clear policies, processes, and accountability mechanisms, GRC frameworks enable organizations to proactively identify, assess, and mitigate risks throughout the entire AI life cycle, from design and development to deployment and ongoing operation. Furthermore, ethical AI management ensures that applications align with societal values, promoting fairness, transparency, and human-centric outcomes, which in turn builds trust with users and stakeholders. Without these comprehensive frameworks, GenAI applications risk legal penalties, reputational damage, and a significant erosion of public confidence, ultimately hindering their potential for positive impact. Some of these frameworks are summarized in Table 9-2. Note that these include federal, state, and local government regulations as well.

Table 9-2. *GenAI Frameworks*

Framework	Origin/context	Key features
NIST AI Risk Management Framework (AIRMF)	US framework for AI risk management	Risk-based approach, trustworthiness, mapping risks, voluntary framework
EU AI Act	European Union regulation for AI	Risk-based (unacceptable, high, limited), legal compliance, enforcement
OWASP GenAI Security Project	Community-driven security guide	Threats and mitigations for prompt injection, data poisoning, model leaks
CSA AI Controls Matrix (AICM)	Cloud Security Alliance framework	AI security controls mapped to NIST/ISO, focus on cloud and SaaS
ISO/IEC AI Standards	International standards body	ISO/IEC 23894 (AI risk management), 42001 (AI management system)
OECD AI Principles	Global intergovernmental principles	Fairness, transparency, accountability, human-centric AI
MITRE ATLAS	Threat modeling framework for AI	Catalog of adversarial tactics and techniques for AI systems
National Initiatives	US, UK, Singapore, etc.	Sector-specific AI guidelines (e.g., finance)
COSAIS (Common Secure AI Systems)	Emerging international initiative	Baseline controls, harmonized assurance and security standards for AI/GenAI
SEC/OCC/FINRA regulations	US Government	Model Risk Management, Model Transparency

9.3.2 Application

In securing GenAI systems, the application layer plays a critical role as it serves as the primary interface between users and foundation models. This layer requires targeted safeguards to prevent misuse, protect sensitive data, and enforce organizational and regulatory policies. The following are some of the best practices for application security:

- **Content Filtering**: Use content filters to evaluate prompts. Ideally, ensure that any Personally Identifiable Information (PII) is not presented to the FM. Censure prompts that violate industry, regulatory, and organizational standards.
- **Implement Data Upload Controls**:[10] Control the data that is uploaded to your application. For example, implement Data Loss and Prevention (DLP) solutions to detect and prevent the upload of data that violates organization policies.
- **Prompt Injection and Jailbreak**: Implement mechanisms to analyze prompts for attempts to discover or override system instructions, which could lead to the model behaving maliciously. This could involve techniques such as prompt filtering, watermarking, or other defensive measures.
- **Sensitive Data Phishing:** Analyze prompts for attempts to gain access to sensitive information, such as trade secrets, financial data, or personal information. Implement appropriate access controls and monitoring mechanisms to detect and prevent such attempts.

9.3.3 User and Access Controls

Effective user authentication and access controls are foundational to securing GenAI applications, as they govern how internal users, external clients, and integrated systems interact with models and APIs. Robust identity, credential, and access management practices help minimize unauthorized use, reduce exposure of sensitive data, and ensure

[10] https://aws.amazon.com/blogs/security/securing-generative-ai-applying-relevant-security-controls/

compliance with security and privacy standards. The following are some of the best practices for user security:

- **User Authentication and Authorization**: Robust user authentication and access controls are paramount to safeguarding sensitive data, preventing unauthorized model access, and maintaining the integrity of AI-driven processes. These controls ensure that only authorized individuals and systems can interact with foundation models and their associated data, mitigating risks such as prompt injection, data exfiltration, and model misuse. Implementing strong authentication mechanisms, such as multi-factor authentication, alongside granular access control policies such as Role-Based Access Control (RBAC) or Attribute-Based Access Control (ABAC), allows organizations to define and enforce precise permissions based on user roles and specific operational needs. APIs should have robust access control mechanisms in place.
- **API Keys**: Orchestrators access models using API endpoints. Most APIs use API keys to authenticate users and authorize access to specific functionalities. Proper storage and management of API keys are essential. Avoid hardcoding API keys in code or scripts, as this can lead to unauthorized access if the code is compromised. Instead, store API keys securely in a centralized key management system or use environment variables.
- **Provider Security**: When integrating with third-party FM providers, it is crucial to assess their security practices and reputation. Look for adherence to relevant compliance standards (such as ISO 27001 or SOC 2) and secure coding practices. Verify their security measures and stay updated on any vulnerabilities reported in their APIs.
- **Data Sharing**: Be mindful of the data you share with third-party FM providers and understand their data privacy practices. Avoid sharing sensitive information or PII unless absolutely necessary and ensure that proper data protection measures are in place.
- **Integration**: Orchestrators use agents to connect to a number of tools within your organization. Ensure that the identity of the application user is propagated correctly to the systems so that the source systems are not compromised in any manner.

9.3.4 Data and Model Security

Ensuring data and model security is essential for protecting the integrity and confidentiality of GenAI systems. Strong safeguards around model endpoints, training data, and fine-tuned artifacts help prevent unauthorized access, malicious manipulation, and safeguard sensitive data throughout the AI life cycle. Note that the data and model security should align with the principles Confidentiality, Integrity, and Availability (CIA) triad. The following are some of the best practices for data and model security:

- **Data Encryption**: Implement encryption for data used for techniques such as RAG and fine-tuning. Also, ensure encryption is in place in transit to protect the confidentiality and integrity of sensitive data. Use strong encryption algorithms (such as AES-256) and secure key management practices. Encrypt model artifacts, whether pretrained or fine-tuned and ensure that data poisoning and leakage are prevented.
- **Data Access Controls**: Apply granular access controls to restrict access to sensitive data based on user roles and permissions. Regularly review and revoke unnecessary data access privileges.
- **Data Masking**: Use data masking techniques to obfuscate sensitive information in non-production environments, such as development or testing environments, where full data access may not be necessary.
- **Model Access**: Limit direct access to the FM's API endpoints, whether you self-host the FM or consume the FM from a cloud provider. Access should be controlled based on users' needs and profiles. For self-hosting, consider setting up access through centralized platforms as opposed to allowing users to directly query from endpoints. Control access to the fine-tuned model artifacts and endpoints according to the classification of the data used in the fine-tuning.
- **Content Filtering**: Analyze outputs of the FMs for inappropriate content. Develop a set of rules and benchmarks to continuously test and evaluate the quality of the output. This includes minimizing hallucinations and ensuring that toxicity, bias, and discrimination are controlled.

- **Denial of Service (DOS)**: Prevent behavior that may lead to stalling the model for legitimate uses. This could involve rate-limiting, resource monitoring, and other techniques to ensure fair and equitable access to the model.
- **Anomalous Behavior**: Scan for general anomalous access or prompt content that warrants additional inspection. This could involve machine learning-based anomaly detection, user behavior analytics, or other techniques to identify and investigate suspicious activity.
- **Model Source Verification**: Verify that the model artifacts are from a trusted source with digital signature verification and implement scanning the model artifacts for vulnerabilities. If you're consuming the FM from a cloud provider, verify that the cloud provider implements these controls.
- **Red-Teaming**:[11] Conduct regular red team exercises to identify potential vulnerabilities and weaknesses in your GenAI system. This can help uncover blind spots and inform continuous improvement of your security posture.

9.3.5 Infrastructure

A secure and resilient infrastructure layer is the backbone of GenAI applications, providing the foundational controls needed to safeguard networks, systems, and operational environments. By hardening hosting platforms, segmenting networks, and implementing continuous monitoring and incident response, organizations can reduce attack surfaces and ensure reliable, secure operations for AI workloads. The following are some of the best practices for infrastructure security:

- **Network Security**: Implement firewalls, intrusion detection/prevention systems (IDS/IPS) to monitor network traffic for suspicious activity. Configure these tools to alert on and block unauthorized or malicious traffic patterns. Consider using private connections to cloud providers instead of routing traffic through the Internet.

[11] https://hbr.org/2024/01/how-to-red-team-a-gen-ai-model

- **Network Segmentation**: Segment your network to isolate workflow orchestration systems and GenAI components from other critical resources, minimizing the potential impact of a breach. Use virtual private networks (VPNs) or software-defined perimeters to secure communication between different network segments.
- **System Hardening**: Keep operating systems and software on your infrastructure patched and updated to address known vulnerabilities. Implement a robust patch management process to ensure timely and consistent application of security updates.
- **Operating System Authentication and Authorization**: Enforce strong authentication and authorization mechanisms for accessing operating systems and infrastructure components. Use multifactor authentication (MFA), strong password policies, and principle of least privilege for user accounts and service accounts.
- **Security Monitoring and Logging**: Implement comprehensive security monitoring and logging capabilities to detect and investigate potential security incidents. Leverage security information and event management (SIEM) solutions to collect and analyze logs from various sources, including network devices, servers, applications, and security tools.
- **Incident Response and Disaster Recovery**: Develop and regularly test incident response and disaster recovery plans to ensure resilience and business continuity in the event of a security breach or other disruptive events.
- **Regular Security Assessments**: Conduct regular security assessments, such as penetration testing, vulnerability assessments, and code reviews, to identify and remediate potential vulnerabilities proactively.

By implementing these security and privacy measures across the different components of your GenAI application, FSOs can mitigate risks and build trust in their solutions, enabling the safe and responsible use of GenAI.

9.4 Performance, Reliability, and Scalability of GenAI Applications

Building an application for a proof-of-concept is vastly different from building a production-ready application. For example, a user interacting with a GenAI chatbot may not want to wait 30 seconds for a response to simple questions. The difference comes down to factors such as performance, scalability, and reliability.

In this section, we discuss important considerations for these factors for all the components in the GenAI anatomy, shown in Figure 9-1, except security, which we discuss separately in the "Cost Optimization" section. We discuss considerations for FSOs looking to self-host open source FMs on premise or in the cloud, as well as FSOs looking to use third-party models in the cloud. Note that our intent is to focus more on the specific nuances relevant to GenAI for each component.

9.4.1 Application

From an application standpoint, enhancing performance, scalability, and reliability is no different from any other web or mobile application. For the front end itself, consider techniques that include code minification, image optimization, asynchronous processing, and Content Delivery Networks (CDNs). The front end should be complemented by a scalable microservices and event-driven architecture. Techniques such as load balancing, use of in-memory data stores, and caching further help optimize performance. Additionally, redundancy in critical components, robust error handling, and monitoring with alerts all enhance reliability. Again, these approaches are the same as for any other web or mobile application in production.

9.4.2 Orchestration

Open-source orchestration frameworks, such as Langchain and LLamaIndex, are valuable for testing and proof-of-concept. However, a key challenge lies in scaling the embedding generation process for large datasets, which requires significant memory and processing power. Frameworks, such as Ray, can address this by parallelizing the process, significantly reducing processing time. Additionally, utilizing cloud-based platforms and services can further aid in scaling your GenAI application.

Major cloud providers are increasingly offering orchestration capabilities. For example, AWS provides knowledge bases for Amazon Bedrock and Google offers Vertex AI Search and Conversation.

So how can we measure the performance of the Orchestrator Layer? Depending on the type of use case, a number of metrics can be used. For example, if the orchestrator is executing a RAG pipeline, the following metrics are used:

- **Indexing Metrics**: These measure recall, indicating the number of relevant results returned by the vector search algorithm.
- **Retrieval Metrics**: This includes Normalized Discounted Cumulative Gain (nDCG), a metric to assess ranking quality based on how much relevant content is captured (recall), and how many retrieved results are truly relevant (precision).
- **Generation Metrics**: These evaluate the faithfulness, answer relevance, and overall quality of generated responses using metrics similar to Sensibleness and Specificity Average (SSA).

Tools offer readily available libraries to simplify the evaluation process. Ragas, for example, is a powerful library that analyzes performance by collecting the input, output, and context to derive metrics for both the retriever and generator components. It measures context precision and recall for retrieval, faithfulness, and answer relevancy for generation.

9.4.3 Model

The deployment approach described earlier in the section under FMOps has a large say in the performance implications of FMs. Cloud-based services such as Amazon Bedrock, Azure OpenAI Service, and Google's Vertex AI handle all the engineering needed to optimize the performance of models. However, FSOs evaluating self-hosting of open-source models can consider the following strategies:

- **Knowledge Distillation**: Train a smaller model to mimic the predictions of the larger foundation model. The smaller model becomes faster for inference while retaining good accuracy.
- **Batching**: When possible, group multiple inference requests into batches for the model to process simultaneously. This can improve efficiency on some hardware architectures.

- **Asynchronous Inference**: Offload model inference to background threads to avoid blocking the main application thread. This keeps the UI responsive while waiting for model results.
- **Model Caching**: Cache frequently used model outputs to avoid redundant inference calls. This can significantly improve performance for repetitive tasks.

9.4.4 Data

Performance at the data level is crucial for any application. Regardless of how well optimized the rest of your architecture is, storage, processing, and retrieval of data from databases can severely impact the performance, scalability, and reliability of your application. Data storage and retrieval is especially critical for techniques such as RAG and fine-tuning. A thorough examination of advanced retrieval strategies is outlined in the paper "Retrieval-Augmented Generation for Large Language Models: A Survey."[12] Let's review some of the most important considerations and techniques for optimizing performance of data storage, processing, and retrieval, including some techniques outlined in this paper:

- **Distributed File and Processing Systems**: Explore distributed file systems such as Hadoop Distributed File System (HDFS), large-scale data processing systems for large datasets such as Apache Spark and distributed search and analytics platforms such as OpenSearch. These systems distribute data across multiple machines, enabling parallel access and improved performance for GenAI applications that process massive datasets.
- **Data Lifecycle Management (DLM)**: Implement DLM strategies to optimize data storage utilization. DLM involves automatically archiving or deleting less frequently accessed data, freeing up space on high-performance storage for active training data. This keeps storage costs under control while maintaining performance for critical tasks.

[12] http://arxiv.org/pdf/2312.10997

- **Data Compression**: Explore data compression techniques suitable for your GenAI application's data format. Compression reduces storage requirements and can improve access times, especially for frequently accessed datasets.
- **Data Cleaning and Preprocessing**: Ensure data is clean and free of errors, including inconsistencies and irrelevant information. Techniques such as text normalization, entity recognition, and duplicate removal can be used.
- **Data Filtering and Selection**: Focus on high-quality data relevant to the specific task or domain. This improves the effectiveness of RAG retrieval and fine-tuning by providing the model with the most pertinent information.
- **Indexing Optimization**: In RAG, the indexing phase involves processing documents, segmenting them, and converting them into embeddings for storage in a vector database. In the indexing phase, chunking strategies that determine the granularity of retrieved data (e.g., tokens, sentences, documents) is very important. This involves finding the right balance between context length and the ability to capture meaning. Metadata attachments such as timestamps or author information can be used to filter retrieval results. Building a hierarchical structure for documents can improve retrieval efficiency.
- **Embedding Models**: As discussed in the RAG section in Chapter 4, embeddings are used to calculate similarity between the query (prompt) and document chunks for retrieval. Popular choices include sparse encoders (BM25) and dense retrievers (BERT-based models). Recent advancements include embedding models such as AngIE, Voyage, and BGE, which benefit from multitask training. Cloud providers may provide proprietary embedding models such as Amazon Titan and Cohere Embed.

The best embedding model depends on the specific use case. Hybrid approaches combining sparse and dense retrieval can leverage the strengths of both methods. Fine-tuning embedding models on domain-specific datasets can improve performance, especially for specialized fields with unique jargon.

9.4.5 Infrastructure

Just as a high-performance car needs a strong engine and smooth roads, GenAI applications rely heavily on the infrastructure components of the GenAI application anatomy. The infrastructure provides immense processing power to

1. Train and run complex models
2. Store and manage massive datasets
3. Scale to adapt to growth
4. Optimize performance for faster results

Ensure reliability and security for sensitive data.

All of these are crucial factors for GenAI to function effectively and reach its full potential.

FSOs using comprehensive cloud-based services such as Amazon Bedrock, Azure OpenAI Service, and Google's Vertex AI do not need to concern themselves with this aspect as the service takes care of all the heavy lifting required behind the scenes. However, FSOs that don't use these services need to review the following considerations for a high performing, reliable, and scalable GenAI application.

- **Graphics Processing Units (GPUs) or Similar Accelerators**: GenAI models are computationally intensive and using machines that offer GPUs significantly speeds up inference. However, with the advent of GenAI, GPUs are becoming increasingly difficult to obtain. FSOs can also explore other options such as AWS Inferentia, a high performing chip designed by AWS for high-performance inference predictions.
- **Memory (RAM)**: Ensure sufficient RAM to handle the model and data being processed. Insufficient RAM can lead to bottlenecks.
- **Storage**: Use a combination of Solid-State Drives (SSDs) for fast data access during training and inference, and Hard Disk Drives (HDDs) for larger datasets that aren't constantly accessed. Plan for future growth: GenAI models and datasets can be large, so ensure there is enough storage to accommodate them.

- **Distributed Storage**: Explore distributed storage systems across multiple machines for larger datasets and redundancy.
- **Deep Learning Frameworks**: Leverage frameworks such as TensorFlow and PyTorch that support distributed training across multiple GPUs or machines for faster training of complex models. Explore framework-specific optimizations such as model pruning or quantization to reduce computational requirements.
- **Containers**: Explore containerization technologies such as Docker to package model dependencies and to ensure consistent performance across environments.
- **Open-Source Frameworks**: For open-source models, consider tools for optimized model serving and efficient inference.
- **Cloud-Based ML Platforms**: FSOs leveraging cloud platforms can explore end-to-end ML platforms such as SageMaker, Azure Machine Learning, or Vertex AI. These platforms provide most of the capabilities listed above, such as automatic model optimization, resource management, and scaling. They also provide capabilities to automatically adjust resources based on workload, optimizing cost and performance. This includes features such as auto-scaling or managed versions of container orchestration tools such as Kubernetes to automatically scale compute resources up or down based on demand.

As we conclude this section, it is important to note that achieving optimal performance, scalability, and reliability for GenAI applications is a multifaceted endeavor that requires careful consideration of various components within the GenAI application anatomy. From optimizing front-end and back-end architectures to leveraging advanced data management techniques, orchestration frameworks, and efficient model deployment strategies, a holistic approach is necessary to ensure a seamless user experience. Because of the complexity involved, harnessing the power of cloud-based services can particularly help FSOs accelerate their journey into GenAI.

9.4.6 Representative Metrics for Performance, Scalability, and Availability

Table 9-3 represents potential metrics that you can consider for tracking performance, scalability, and availability of your GenAI applications.

Table 9-3. *Representative Metrics*

Layer	Category	Metrics tracked
Application	User experience	Response Time (p95/p99), error rate, availability SLA
Application	Scalability	Throughput (req/sec), concurrency
Application	Resilience/disaster recovery	Failover success rate, session continuity, RTO/RPO
Application	Retrieval	Recall, precision, query latency
Application	Generation	Faithfulness, answer relevance, user feedback score
Model	Performance	Inference latency, tokens/sec throughput, GPU/TPU utilization
Model	Optimization	Batch efficiency, cache hit ratio
Model	Quality	Hallucination rate, toxicity/bias incidents, accuracy benchmarks
Data	Data life cycle	Retention vs. access ratio, compression ratio, cleaning coverage
Infrastructure	Compute	GPU utilization, queue latency, RAM utilization, SSD IOPS and latency, distributed storage efficiency
Infrastructure	Scalability and reliability	Autoscaling latency, cost per request, container restarts, MTTR/MTTF
Cross-cutting	End-to-end	End-to-end latency, SLO violations, error attribution, cost efficiency, sustainability (energy per inference)

9.5 Cost Optimization

GenAI applications offer tremendous opportunities for innovation and automation. However, these applications can incur significant costs over time if they are not well architected, built, managed, and optimized.

In this section, we analyze infrastructure, hardware, and tooling costs, as well as personnel and human expertise costs related to implementing a GenAI application. We divide the costs into two types: up-front, and ongoing. Up-front costs primarily occur during the development stages of a GenAI application. Ongoing costs are generated continuously while the application is in operation. We wrap up the discussion by reviewing various strategies to optimize expenses, using relevant examples from the FSS.

9.5.1 Infrastructure, Hardware, and Tooling Costs

These are costs associated with the platform and tools used throughout the GenAI life cycle, illustrated in Chapter 3. Table 9-4 illustrates the costs for each phase of the life cycle and defines whether each cost is up-front or ongoing.

Table 9-4. *GenAI Life Cycle Costs*

Life cycle stage	Cost categories	Up-front or ongoing cost
Business problem definition and planning	Data acquisition for analysis (external data sources, internal data retrieval)	Up-front
Data collection and processing	Data acquisition (purchase/license data)	Up-front
	Data storage (cloud storage)	Ongoing
	Data processing (cleaning, preparation, transformation)	Up-front
FM evaluation and selection	Cloud services (model evaluation and testing)	Up-front
FM fine-tuning	Hardware (computing resources: GPUs, servers)	Up-front
	Software tools (model training frameworks)	Up-front
	Cloud services (model fine-tuning)	Up-front

(*continued*)

Table 9-4. *(continued)*

Life cycle stage	Cost categories	Up-front or ongoing cost
Application and orchestration layer development	Software Development (APIs, connectors, user interfaces)	Up-front
	Cloud services (application and orchestration layer development)	Up-front
	Third-party tools (orchestration and integration)	Up-front
Testing, validation, monitoring, and auditing	Cloud services (testing and performance monitoring)	Ongoing
	Auditing tools (bias detection, model output analysis)	Up-front
Production deployment	Infrastructure (servers, network resources)	Up-front
	Cloud services	Ongoing
	Scalability (infrastructure scaling for user load and data volume)	Ongoing
	Disaster recovery (infrastructure redundancy)	Up-front
Hardware licensing fees	Licensing fees for different kinds of hardware if self-hosted	Ongoing
Software licensing fees	Licensing fees for different kinds of software if self-hosted	Ongoing
Continuous monitoring, auditing, and fine-tuning	Cloud services (monitoring and data processing)	Ongoing
	Application updates	Ongoing
	Model updates (retraining, updates from FM provider)	Ongoing
	Costs associated with bias mitigation, fairness audits	Ongoing
	Costs associated with data privacy and security compliance	Ongoing

Let's review these costs using the development of a chatbot as an example.

9.5.1.1 Up-Front Costs

Up-front costs primarily occur during the development stages of a GenAI application. However, this may also be a function of the type of deployment. For example, for FSOs that use self-hosting models, there may be up-front costs to acquire the infrastructure and software.

After defining the chatbot's scope and functionality, the FSO may leverage a RAG solution, which requires collecting and preparing data to build a vector database.

Acquiring and curating domain-specific data, such as customer inquiries or policy documents, into the GenAI application repository can be expensive, depending on the complexity and level of processing required. In addition, ingesting the processed data into the vector database incurs a data embedding and ingestion cost.

Various pretrained language models need to be tested to find the best fit for performance expectations, which involves configuring parameters, designing prompts, and iterative experimentation - all generating costs in compute resources such as GPUs.

If none of the pretrained models meet the needs, fine-tuning may be necessary. This process involves additional data collection, processing, and iterative experiments to find the optimal fine-tuning strategies and hyperparameters, further increasing up-front costs.

After selecting the language model, the orchestrator and front-end interface need to be developed, incurring tooling costs. Finally, deploying the end-to-end application in production requires infrastructure costs for testing, ensuring workload handling, error management, and concurrency.

9.5.1.2 Ongoing Costs

Ongoing costs are generated continuously while the application is in operation. Again, the timing of the costs may depend on the deployment model. For example, infrastructure costs for cloud-based providers could be classified as ongoing.

The primary ongoing cost from an FM perspective is inference expenses. These are the costs incurred each time a user query (prompt) hits the FM. If the deployment is cloud-based, this could be based on the number of tokens processed by the FM or based on a fixed throughput capacity. As the user base grows and demand increases, these costs will escalate.

In a RAG solution, the vector database also generates ongoing costs for vector storage, search, and query operations. Maintaining the application requires continuous monitoring and periodic performance analysis, incurring costs for tooling and hardware.

If the application's performance degrades, the agency must investigate the root cause and determine whether prompt engineering techniques or a better model is required, generating additional experimentation costs.

Furthermore, updating the vector database to keep information current will incur recurring costs associated with data collection, preparation, embedding, and ingestion.

Last but not least, costs are incurred with implementation of security and privacy tools for bias mitigation, fairness audits, and security compliance.

9.5.2 Human Expertise Costs

Building a GenAI application requires a team of skilled professionals with expertise in data engineering, machine learning, software development, project management, and more, as described in Chapter 3. Attracting and retaining such talent can be expensive and challenging for FSOs. Ongoing training and professional development may also be necessary to keep the team up-to-date with the latest GenAI advancements. Table 9-5 shows the costs incurred across the different phases of the GenAI life cycle.

Table 9-5. *GenAI Staffing Costs*

Life cycle stage	Human resource costs	Up-front or ongoing
Business problem definition and planning	Stakeholder engagement and requirements gathering (project managers, domain experts)	Ongoing
Data collection and processing	Data acquisition (data engineers)	Up-front
FM evaluation and selection	Research and evaluation of foundation models (Data Scientists)	Up-front
FM training and fine-tuning	Data scientists and ML engineers for model fine-tuning	Up-front

(*continued*)

Table 9-5. *(continued)*

Life cycle stage	Human resource costs	Up-front or ongoing
Application and orchestration layer development	Software developers for building APIs, connectors, and user interfaces	Up-front
Testing, validation, monitoring, and auditing	ML Engineers for testing, validation, and ongoing monitoring	Ongoing
Production deployment	System administrators and IT personnel for infrastructure management	Ongoing
Continuous monitoring, Auditing, and fine-tuning	Data scientists and ML engineers for ongoing monitoring, performance analysis, and potential model adjustments	Ongoing
Responsible AI practices	Personnel with expertise in bias mitigation, fairness audits, and ethical considerations	Ongoing
Legal and regulatory compliance	Legal counsel and compliance specialists to ensure data privacy and security adherence	Ongoing

Let's take a look at these costs using the same example of developing a chatbot.

9.5.2.1 Up-Front Costs

These are costs of the personnel involved in activities such as gathering requirements, pre-processing relevant data from internal or external sources, researching and evaluating different FMs, fine-tuning the model if required, building APIs and user interfaces, and prompt engineering.

9.5.2.2 Ongoing Costs

These are costs associated with continuously testing and validating the chatbot's performance and outputs, ongoing monitoring to identify potential biases or issues requiring adjustments, managing the infrastructure, potentially fine-tuning or adjusting the model based on user interactions and feedback, requiring data scientists and machine learning engineers, and ongoing efforts by legal counsel and compliance specialists to ensure the chatbot adheres to data privacy regulations and security standards within the FSS.

9.5.3 Considerations to Optimize the Cost

As we see above, there are a number of different costs that are incurred with a GenAI implementation. Optimizing these costs is crucial to the success of these projects. Here we discuss some considerations to optimize the cost. By making the right choices at the onset of your GenAI effort, you can better control the up-front and ongoing costs for your GenAI application.

9.5.3.1 Project Planning

- **Focus on High-Impact Use Cases**: Prioritize projects with clear ROI potential, such as automating repetitive tasks, personalizing customer services, or optimizing resource allocation. This ensures GenAI delivers significant benefits and cost savings.
- **Phased Implementation**: Break down the project into manageable phases. This allows for better cost control, resource allocation, and adaptation based on learnings from each phase.

9.5.3.2 Cost-Effective Solutions

- **Leverage Open-Source Models**: Use pretrained, open-source models whenever possible to significantly reduce up-front development and training costs. However, consider the trade-off with functionality because proprietary models may offer better options.
- **Data Sharing and Collaboration**: Explore partnerships with other FSOs to share data resources and potentially collaborate on building and maintaining GenAI models.

- **Hybrid Team Structure**: Combine in-house talent with external expertise. Build a core team with essential skills and outsource-specific tasks such as data labeling or model training to specialized vendors when cost-effective.
- **Upskilling and Reskilling**: Invest in training existing staff on relevant GenAI concepts and tools. This leverages existing talent and reduces reliance on expensive external consultants.

9.5.3.3 Infrastructure and Pricing Models

- **Cloud-Based Infrastructure**: Use cloud platforms for training and deploying GenAI models. Cloud services offer scalability, cost optimization features, and pay-as-you-go models, reducing up-front infrastructure investments.
- **Evaluate Pricing Models**: Choose pricing models based on usage. For high usage, consider time-based or fixed pricing instead of token-based pricing. While token-based pricing might be suitable for proof-of-concepts, it can rapidly expand with increased usage, especially for summarization of large documents.
- **Resource Optimization Techniques**: For self-hosting FSOs, implement strategies such as model compression and efficient resource allocation within the cloud environment to minimize unnecessary compute costs without sacrificing performance.

9.5.3.4 Model and Infrastructure Selection

- **Right-Sizing Your FM**: Choose the appropriate model size based on your use case. Larger models handle complex tasks better but you may not always need the biggest one. Different FMs have strengths in different tasks; selecting the optimal size and type is crucial for cost optimization.

- **Choosing the Optimal Infrastructure**: Explore a broad range of GPUs and accelerators to balance performance and cost. Use dynamic resource provisioning for UI, API gateways, orchestrators, and language models. If using cloud services, leverage auto-scaling features or serverless options for usage-based cost reflection.

9.5.3.5 Additional Considerations

- **Optimizing Prompts**: Prompt engineers should optimize prompts to reduce the number of round trips between the orchestrator and the language model, minimizing processing costs.
- **Reduce Development Time with Better Tools**: Use fully managed cloud services to accelerate the development cycle and reduce overhead associated with infrastructure management.
- **Continuous Monitoring and Optimization**: Continuously monitor the GenAI application's performance to identify further cost optimization opportunities, such as adjusting resource allocation, fine-tuning models, or exploring alternative solutions.

By implementing the above strategies, FSOs can optimize the cost of GenAI implementation while maximizing its potential benefits. While GenAI costs might seem significant, it is essential to consider the potential long-term cost savings through increased efficiency, reduced manual labor, and improved service delivery. Therefore, conducting thorough ROI analyses to quantify the expected cost savings and benefits associated with each GenAI project provides a path forward. Using this approach, FSOs can prioritize the right initiatives, enabling improved service delivery and customer engagement.

9.6 Chapter Summary

The implementation, operation, and maintenance of GenAI applications in financial services represents a fundamental transformation that extends far beyond traditional technology deployments. As we have explored throughout this chapter, the journey from proof-of-concept to production-ready GenAI systems requires a comprehensive understanding of operational frameworks, security imperatives, performance optimization, and cost management strategies. The evolution from MLOps to FMOps/LLMOps reflects not merely a technological upgrade but a paradigm shift that demands new methodologies, specialized expertise, and unprecedented attention to governance and compliance.

FSOs stand at a critical juncture where the successful operationalization of GenAI applications will determine competitive advantage and regulatory compliance for years to come. The security and privacy considerations we have examined are not merely technical requirements but fundamental pillars that will determine consumer trust and regulatory acceptance of GenAI in financial services. Similarly, the performance, reliability, and scalability challenges associated with GenAI applications demand careful architectural planning and continuous optimization across all system components.

Perhaps most critically, the cost optimization strategies outlined in this chapter highlight the economic realities of GenAI implementation. While the up-front investments in infrastructure, tooling, and human expertise are substantial, the ongoing operational costs, from inference expenses to continuous monitoring and compliance require careful management to ensure sustainable ROI. The successful FSOs will be those that can balance innovation with fiscal responsibility, leveraging cloud-based services, optimizing model selection, and implementing efficient resource management practices to maximize the value of their GenAI investments.

As we prepare to explore the emerging trends that will shape the future of GenAI in financial services, it becomes clear that the operational foundations established today will determine an organization's ability to adapt and thrive in an increasingly AI-driven financial landscape. The next chapter will examine the cutting-edge developments and future trajectories that promise to further revolutionize how financial institutions leverage GenAI to serve their customers and stakeholders.

CHAPTER 10

Summary, Emerging Industry Trends, and Next Steps

In this book, we provided an overview of GenAI, how it can transform the financial services sector (FSS), and enhance the quality of services provided to customers and stakeholders. From intelligent trading systems to personalized financial advisory and advanced risk management, GenAI has tremendous potential to drive efficiencies and enhance service delivery across diverse financial domains. In this chapter, we provide a recap of the topics we discussed so far, provide emerging industry trends that you should be aware of and, and discuss the next steps.

As we discussed earlier in the book, GenAI is a groundbreaking technology that builds upon AI/ML concepts such as neural networks and transformers. The unique generative abilities unlocked by Foundation Models (FMs), including GPT, Claude, Gemini, and specialized financial models such as BloombergGPT, represent a significant technological leap. The FSS, with its data-intensive operations, complex regulatory requirements, and customer-centric mission, stands to reap substantial benefits from GenAI adoption.

10.1 Recap and Summary

Let's recap a few of the key takeaways and considerations from throughout the book:

- **GenAI Is a Transformative Opportunity for Financial Institutions**: FMs such as GPT, Claude, Gemini, Llama, and domain-specific models offer financial services organizations (FSOs) the opportunity to enhance customer services, improve operational efficiency, and drive innovation in product development.

S. Godavarthi, R. Nagvekar, *Transforming Financial Services with Generative AI*,
https://doi.org/10.1007/979-8-8688-2053-3_10

- **Strategy Is Key for Successful GenAI Adoption**: GenAI represents a transformative change that necessitates strategic commitment from leadership, workforce reskilling, agile processes, securing adequate funding, and fostering a data- and AI-driven culture. We provided a blueprint for developing GenAI strategy and the key factors for successful implementation, including people, processes, technology, and data governance.
- **Architecting, Building, and Delivering GenAI Applications**: GenAI brings unique considerations for architecting, building, and delivering financial applications. We discussed key concepts such as prompts, prompt engineering, model parameters, Retrieval Augmented Generation (RAG), fine-tuning, agents, and Agentic AI concepts specifically for financial use cases.
- **Deep Dive into Financial Services Use Cases**: GenAI can be applied across a broad spectrum of financial services use cases. We reviewed specific examples, including automated report generation, intelligent document processing, conversational banking interfaces, risk assessment automation, regulatory compliance monitoring, and personalized investment advisory services.
- **Responsible AI and Regulatory Alignment**: With growing oversight from regulators such as the SEC, OCC, CFPB, and international bodies (EU AI Act, UK FCA guidance), FSOs must frame GenAI adoption within robust governance, risk management, compliance, and ethical AI frameworks to ensure transparency, fairness, and accountability.
- **Implementation and Operations**: We highlighted the challenges and considerations for deploying GenAI solutions at scale in financial services. We outlined best practices for performance optimization, scalability, security, and regulatory compliance for safe and effective implementations.

Looking ahead, the GenAI journey for financial services is accelerating rapidly. As the technology matures and regulatory frameworks evolve, new frontiers will open up, further enhancing productivity through intelligent automation while maintaining the trust and security that financial services demand.

10.2 Emerging GenAI Industry Trends

The GenAI landscape in financial services is rapidly evolving, with several key trends emerging that will significantly impact the industry in 2025 and beyond. According to NVIDIA's State of AI in Financial Services Report,[1] 91% of financial services companies are either assessing AI or already using it in production, with GenAI emerging as a particularly promising tool used by 43% of organizations.

10.2.1 Multimodal AI: The Next Frontier in Financial Intelligence

Traditional GenAI models have primarily focused on text-based applications, but the capabilities of FMs now extend far beyond this. Multimodal AI systems in finance[2] can comprehend, synthesize, and transform data across various modalities, including text, images, audio, video, and numerical data simultaneously. According to a McKinsey report,[3] by 2025, 40% of financial decision-making tools will rely on multimodal AI, up from just 15% in 2023.

Imagine a scenario where a financial analyst needs to assess market sentiment around a particular stock. Here's how an advanced multimodal GenAI system could assist:

- **Market Intelligence**: The system analyzes earnings call transcripts (text), interprets the CEO's tone and sentiment during the call (audio), examines technical chart patterns (images), and processes real-time news feeds and social media sentiment (text and images).
- **Real-Time Risk Assessment**: The AI cross-references regulatory filings, news sentiment, and economic indicators to provide comprehensive risk analysis that considers multiple data sources simultaneously.
- **Customer Interaction**: A customer service system that can read email inquiries, interpret voice calls, analyze account statements, and even process uploaded documents to provide comprehensive support.

[1] https://blogs.nvidia.com/blog/ai-in-financial-services-survey-2024/
[2] https://finaigenius.com/multimodal-ai-in-finance-2025/
[3] https://www.mckinsey.com/business-functions/mckinsey-digital/our-insights

- **Fraud Detection:** Systems that combine transaction data analysis with voice pattern recognition, behavioral biometrics, and visual document verification to identify sophisticated fraud attempts.

In the FSS, multimodal AI systems enhance fraud detection compliance and risk management capabilities by compiling user activity, historical records, and transaction logs. Integrating and analyzing diverse data sets enables detailed analysis, which helps FSOs identify suspicious patterns and leads to more enhanced risk assessment and fraud detection.

As an example, JPMorgan's DocLLM[4] utilizes multimodal AI capabilities. It combines textual and contextual data from financial documents with metadata to improve the accuracy of document analysis. It offers better risk evaluation, compliance, automated document processing, and a deeper insight into financial risks.

10.2.2 The Rise of Agentic AI: Autonomous Financial Decision-Making

While GenAI responds to specific prompts, Agentic AI represents a significant evolution toward autonomous systems[5] that can independently perceive, reason, act, and learn without constant human guidance.

- **Autonomous Trading Agents**: AI agents that can analyze market data, monitor trends, adjust strategies, and execute trades in real time while continuously learning from market patterns and outcomes
- **Compliance Monitoring Agents**: Systems that autonomously track regulatory changes across multiple jurisdictions, assess their impact on business operations, and recommend compliance actions
- **Customer Advisory Agents**: Personalized AI advisors that can analyze individual financial situations, market conditions, and life goals to provide ongoing financial guidance and portfolio adjustments

[4] https://www.jpmorgan.com/technology/artificial-intelligence/initiatives/datasets

[5] https://www.weforum.org/stories/2024/12/agentic-ai-financial-services-autonomy-efficiency-and-inclusion/

- **Risk Management Agents**: Autonomous systems that continuously monitor portfolio risk, market volatility, and economic indicators to proactively adjust risk exposure and alert human managers to potential issues

According to Bank of America Global Research analysis,[6] spending on Agentic AI could reach $155 billion by 2030, with the FSS being a major driver of this growth. Table 10-1 summarizes the levels of autonomy for Agentic AI systems.

Table 10-1. *Agentic AI Levels of Autonomy and Required Governance*

Autonomy level	AI role	Required governance structures
Level 0 – No autonomy	Assistive analytics; humans retain full control	Standard model risk management (MRM), explainability, auditability
Level 1 – Assisted autonomy	AI provides recommendations only; human-in-the-loop approvals	Access controls, bias and privacy testing, decision provenance
Level 2 – Conditional autonomy	Executes actions under predefined constraints; human override available	Policies and guardrails, continuous monitoring, stress testing
Level 3 – High autonomy	Acts independently within defined domains, escalates anomalies or complex cases	Board-level oversight, independent validation, fail-safe mechanisms
Level 4 – Full autonomy (future-state)	Cross-domain autonomous decision-making and continuous learning	AI Ethics Board, mandatory red-teaming, continuous regulatory reporting

10.2.3 Domain-Specific Financial AI Models

The trend toward building domain-specific GenAI models and applications is gaining significant traction in financial services. Models such as BloombergGPT demonstrate the power of training AI systems specifically on financial data and terminology.

[6] https://www.msn.com/en-us/technology/artificial-intelligence/agentic-ai-spending-could-reach-155-billion-by-2030-say-bofa-analysts/ar-AA1HsZ88

The following provides a few examples of domain-specific models – for a comprehensive curated list of these models, refer to the compilation[7] on GitHub.

- **Specialized Financial Language Models**: AI models trained specifically on financial documents, regulations, market data, and industry-specific terminology to provide more accurate and relevant outputs for financial use cases. Specific examples of this include
- **Bloomberg GPT**: Trained on a massive corpus of financial data, including news, filings, and proprietary Bloomberg data. It is designed to understand financial terminology, generate financial reports, summarize news, and answer finance-specific queries with high accuracy.
- **Bitext Mistral-7b-Banking**: A fine-tuned version of Mistral-7B-Instruct-v0.2, specifically tailored for the banking domain. It is optimized to answer questions and assist users with various banking transactions, leveraging a dataset of banking-related documents and Q&A pairs.
- **FinBloom 7B**: Built on Bloom 7B, this model is trained on 14 million financial news articles and 12 million SEC filings, then fine-tuned with 50,000 financial queries for enhanced real-time data retrieval and contextual understanding for financial decision-making.
- **Regulatory-Aware AI Systems**: Models that understand complex regulatory frameworks such as Basel III, MiFID II, or Dodd-Frank and can assist with compliance monitoring and reporting. Specific examples of these include
    - **BNY Mellon Eliza**:[8] An AI chatbot leveraging multiple LLMs (OpenAI GPT-5, Google Gemini, LLaMA) to assist employees with complex queries, including compliance and regulatory documentation, by retrieving information from internal databases.

[7] https://github.com/kennethleungty/Finance-LLMs?tab=readme-ov-file

[8] https://github.com/kennethleungty/Finance-LLMs

- **Market-Specific Models**: AI systems trained on specific market data (equities, fixed income, derivatives, etc.) that can provide specialized insights and analysis for different asset classes. Specific example of these include
    - **Rogo** (Fine-tuned OpenAI models): Rogo's platform uses fine-tuned OpenAI models and integrates financial datasets (S&P Global, Crunchbase, FactSet) to deliver real-time financial intelligence and analysis for professionals, focusing on equities, credit, and other asset classes.
    - **Fin-E5**: A finance-adapted embedding model built on the E5 model, trained using persona-based data synthesis to enhance performance across financial embedding tasks, such as market analysis and asset class-specific insights.
- **Regional Financial Models**: AI systems adapted for specific geographic markets, understanding local regulations, market dynamics, and cultural factors that impact financial services. An example of this includes
    - **BBT-FinT5**: A financial pretraining language model (1B parameters) based on T5, pretrained on a 300GB financial corpus (FinCorpus) to support Chinese-language financial analysis and reporting.

10.2.4 Small Language Models (SLMs) for Specialized Financial Tasks

While Large Language Models (LLMs) dominate discussions, Small Language Models (SLMs) may offer distinct advantages for specific financial applications, requiring less computational power and offering faster deployment.

- **Specialized Applications:** SLMs may excel in focused tasks such as
    - Credit scoring and risk classification
    - Regulatory document analysis
    - Customer sentiment analysis

- Fraud pattern recognition
- Automated compliance checking

- **Edge Deployment:** SLMs can run on local devices or edge computing infrastructure, enabling real-time processing without cloud dependencies, crucial for high-frequency trading or mobile banking applications.
- **Cost-Efficiency:** Lower computational requirements make SLMs more cost-effective for routine financial tasks, allowing institutions to deploy AI more broadly across their operations.

10.2.5 Multi-agent Ecosystems in Financial Services

The evolution toward multi-agent systems represents a significant advancement in how financial institutions can leverage AI for complex, coordinated tasks. As an example, in Chapter 8, we reviewed a comprehensive wealth management system powered by multiple specialized AI agents:

- **Portfolio Analysis Agent:** Continuously monitors market conditions, analyzes portfolio performance, and identifies optimization opportunities based on client risk profiles and market trends.
- **Research Agent:** Scans financial news, analyst reports, earnings calls, and market data to identify investment opportunities and risks across different asset classes.
- **Compliance Agent:** Ensures all investment recommendations and transactions comply with regulatory requirements, client mandates, and internal risk policies.
- **Client Communication Agent:** Generates personalized reports, explanations, and recommendations tailored to each client's communication preferences and financial literacy level.
- **Risk Management Agent:** Monitors overall portfolio risk, stress-tests scenarios, and coordinates with other agents to maintain appropriate risk levels across all client portfolios.

This multi-agent approach enables more sophisticated, coordinated financial services that can adapt to changing market conditions while maintaining regulatory compliance and client satisfaction.

Specific examples of multi-agent systems in the industry include

- **Hebbia Matrix Platform** (with OpenAI Multi-Agent System): Integrates multiple OpenAI models (GPT-5o, o1, o3-mini) as specialized agents, each handling a different part of the financial research workflow. The system consists of multiple agents to draft investment committee memos, extract key terms from credit agreements, and flag red flags in legal documents. These agents pass outputs and context to each other, automating what used to be hours of manual research.
- **Endex AI Platform** (Autonomous Financial Agents): Endex uses a multi-agent system powered by OpenAI's GPT-5o, o1-mini, and o3-mini models to automate complex financial data workflows. The Agents autonomously retrieve, synthesize, and analyze financial data. They also automate tasks such as earnings summaries, investment memos, and due diligence. Each agent specializes in a subtask and collaborates with others for end-to-end automation. Using this approach, FSOs can automate research and reporting with greater speed and accuracy, freeing analysts for higher-value work.
- **MUFG Bank** (RAG + Multi-Agent for Financial Analysis): MUFG Bank uses a retrieval-augmented generation (RAG) system with multiple agents for data extraction and summarization from corporate reports. The system includes multiple agents to retrieve relevant data, summarize and structure the information, and prepare client-ready presentations. This system helps reduce preparation time from hours to minutes.

10.2.6 Embedded GenAI Capabilities for Enhanced Productivity

The integration of GenAI capabilities directly into existing financial software and platforms is becoming increasingly prevalent, similar to Microsoft Office Copilot but specifically designed for financial workflows.

- **Trading Platform Integration:** GenAI embedded in trading systems to provide real-time market analysis, trade suggestions, and risk assessments directly within the trader's workflow.
- **Banking System Enhancement:** Core banking platforms enhanced with GenAI for automated document processing, customer inquiry handling, and regulatory reporting.
- **Financial Planning Tools:** Investment advisory platforms with embedded AI that can generate personalized financial plans, investment recommendations, and scenario analyses.
- **Regulatory Compliance Systems:** Compliance platforms enhanced with GenAI for automated policy interpretation, risk assessment, and regulatory filing preparation.

10.2.7 GenAI at the Edge: Real-Time Financial Decision-Making

The convergence of GenAI and edge computing is enabling real-time financial processing and decision-making at unprecedented scales.

- **High-Frequency Trading:** Edge-deployed GenAI systems that can analyze market data and execute trades with minimal latency, crucial for algorithmic trading strategies
- **Branch Banking:** Local AI systems in bank branches that can provide immediate customer service, loan pre-approvals, and financial advisory without requiring cloud connectivity

- **Mobile Banking:** Smartphone-based AI that can provide personalized financial insights, spending analysis, and investment recommendations using on-device processing
- **ATM and Kiosk Enhancement:** Self-service banking terminals enhanced with GenAI for natural language interaction, document processing, and personalized service recommendations
- **Fraud Detection:** Real-time transaction monitoring at point-of-sale terminals and payment processors using edge-deployed AI to identify and prevent fraudulent transactions instantly

10.3 Next Steps: Accelerating Your GenAI Journey in Financial Services

The future of finance is being written today through the thoughtful integration of GenAI. Your organization's success in this transformation depends on strategic planning, responsible implementation, and continuous adaptation to this rapidly evolving technological landscape. We discuss the next steps you need to take to accelerate your journey.

10.3.1 Expand Your Knowledge

To successfully navigate the transformative impact of GenAI in financial services, it is essential to build a strong foundation of knowledge and strategic awareness. Begin by deepening your understanding of the GenAI ecosystem, operating models, and industry benchmarks to ensure your organization remains competitive and well-prepared for ongoing advancements. You can achieve these objectives with the following activities:

- **Stay Informed on the Evolving GenAI Ecosystem**: The GenAI landscape is rapidly changing, with new models, tools, and regulatory frameworks emerging every quarter. Regularly review updates from major technology providers, regulatory bodies, and industry consortia. Review studies from credible industry analysts, including McKinsey, Gartner, and participate in industry forums to keep your knowledge current.

- **Understand Operating Models**: Recent research shows that a centrally led GenAI operating model is currently the most effective for scaling and risk management in financial services. Centralization enables better talent allocation, risk oversight, and faster scaling of successful use cases. As your organization matures, consider evolving toward a more federated approach for greater agility.
- **Benchmark Against Peers**: Compare your GenAI maturity and adoption roadmap with industry benchmarks and case studies. Leverage resources from consulting firms, industry groups, and academic research to identify gaps and opportunities.

10.3.2 Prepare Your Workforce

Empowering your workforce is a critical step in realizing the full potential of GenAI within financial services. By investing in targeted training, cultivating cross-functional expertise, and promoting a culture of responsible AI, organizations can ensure their teams are equipped to drive innovation while maintaining trust and compliance. You can achieve this objective with the following activities:

- **Invest in Cross-Disciplinary Training**: The most successful financial institutions are upskilling both technical and business staff. Prioritize programs that blend AI/ML fundamentals, financial domain expertise, and regulatory compliance. Identify the current gaps for AI and GenAI adoption within the organization based on business imperatives, and upskill to meet the needs. Encourage certifications from cloud providers, fintech associations, and AI ethics organizations.
- **Develop AI Architects:** Identify and train AI Architects, the professionals who can bridge the gap between business needs and technical implementation. These roles are critical for aligning GenAI solutions with real-world financial objectives.
- **Foster a Culture of Responsible AI**: Embed responsible AI principles into your workforce training, emphasizing fairness, transparency, and ethical use of AI in regulated environments.

10.3.3 Identify and Prioritize Use Cases

Selecting the right use cases is essential for maximizing the value and minimizing the risks of GenAI adoption in financial services. A thoughtful, phased approach grounded in strategic alignment, measurable value, and careful piloting will set the stage for successful and scalable implementation. You can achieve these objectives with the following activities:

- **Strategic Use Case Selection**: Focus on high-impact, high-feasibility use cases that align with your business strategy and regulatory requirements. Examples include personalized customer experiences, enhanced risk management (fraud, AML, credit), and operational automation.
- **Establish a Value Framework**: Create a system for business users to experiment with, measure, and benchmark GenAI applications. Quantify the value and risk of each use case before scaling.
- **Pilot, Then Scale**: Start with controlled pilots in internal-facing functions (e.g., compliance, reporting, knowledge management) before expanding to customer-facing applications.

10.3.4 Experiment and Learn

A culture of experimentation and continuous learning is vital for safely and effectively integrating GenAI into financial services. By establishing secure testing environments, refining models and data practices, and prioritizing production readiness, organizations can innovate confidently while maintaining compliance and control. You can achieve these objectives with the following activities:

- **Regulatory Sandboxes**: Set up compliant, secure environments for GenAI experimentation. Engage with regulators early and often to ensure alignment with evolving standards.
- **Model Selection and Customization**: Choose models that are explainable, auditable, and tailored to your specific financial use cases. Consider domain-specific LLMs and fine-tune them for your needs.

- **Prompt Engineering and RAG**: Develop expertise in prompt engineering and advanced RAG to maximize model accuracy and relevance for financial documents and data.
- **Data Quality and Governance**: Invest in data cleansing, labeling, and governance frameworks. High quality, well-governed data is foundational for GenAI success.
- **Production Readiness**: Plan for robust risk management, monitoring, and governance. Implement continuous model validation, bias detection, and explainability tools.

10.3.5 Stay Ahead of the Curve

Remaining proactive and adaptable is essential as the GenAI landscape continues to evolve at a rapid pace. Ongoing learning, collaboration, and a steadfast commitment to trust, security, and regulatory alignment will position your organization to lead and thrive in the future of financial services. You can achieve these objectives with the following activities:

- **Continuous Learning and Collaboration**: Attend financial technology conferences, AI summits, and regulatory briefings. Collaborate with fintechs, technology partners, and academic institutions to stay at the forefront of innovation.
- **Monitor Regulatory Developments**: Track updates from global and regional regulators. Proactively adapt your AI governance and compliance frameworks to new requirements.
- **Adopt Agile Change Management**: Implement agile, cross-functional teams to drive GenAI adoption. Regularly review and adapt your operating model, funding mechanisms, and talent strategies as the technology and regulatory landscape evolve.
- **Prioritize Trust and Security**: Ensure robust data privacy, cybersecurity, and ethical safeguards are in place. Transparent, explainable AI builds trust with customers, regulators, and stakeholders.

The future of finance will be shaped by those who combine strategic vision, responsible implementation, and continuous adaptation. By following these next steps and staying grounded in the latest industry research and best practices, you can position your organization to lead in the era of GenAI, delivering innovation, efficiency, and trust in every aspect of financial services.

Index

A

S. Godavarthi, R. Nagvekar, *Transforming Financial Services with Generative AI*,
https://doi.org/10.1007/979-8-8688-2053-3

B

C

D

E

F

N

O

P, Q

R

S

T

U

V

W, X, Y

Z

GPSR Compliance
The European Union's (EU) General Product Safety Regulation (GPSR) is a set of rules that requires consumer products to be safe and our obligations to ensure this.

If you have any concerns about our products, you can contact us on

ProductSafety@springernature.com

In case Publisher is established outside the EU, the EU authorized representative is:

Springer Nature Customer Service Center GmbH
Europaplatz 3
69115 Heidelberg, Germany

www.ingramcontent.com/pod-product-compliance
Lightning Source LLC
LaVergne TN
LVHW080020210926
848481LV00011B/3071

* 9 7 9 8 8 6 8 8 2 0 5 2 6 *